Child Psychotherapy
(PGPS-152)

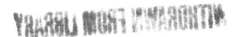

Pergamon Titles of Related Interest

Gelfand/Hartmann CHILD BEHAVIOR ANALYSIS AND THERAPY,
Second Edition
Johnson/Rasbury/Siegel APPROACHES TO CHILD TREATMENT:
Introduction to Theory, Research and Practice
Morris/Kratochwill THE PRACTICE OF CHILD THERAPY
Pope/McHale/Craighead SELF-ESTEEM ENHANCEMENT WITH
CHILDREN AND ADOLESCENTS
Santostefano COGNITIVE CONTROL THERAPY WITH CHILDREN
AND ADOLESCENTS
Schwartz/Johnson PSYCHOPATHOLOGY OF CHILDHOOD:
A Clinical-Experimental Approach, Second Edition

Related Journals*

CHILD ABUSE AND NEGLECT
CLINICAL PSYCHOLOGY REVIEW
JOURNAL OF CHILD PSYCHOLOGY AND PSYCHIATRY
AND ALLIED DISCIPLINES
*Free sample copies available upon request

PERGAMON GENERAL PSYCHOLOGY SERIES

EDITORS
Arnold P. Goldstein, Syracuse University
Leonard Krasner, Stanford University & SUNY at Stony Brook

Child Psychotherapy
Developing and Identifying Effective Treatments

by

ALAN E. KAZDIN
University of Pittsburgh School of Medicine

PERGAMON PRESS
New York · Oxford · Beijing · Frankfurt
São Paulo · Sydney · Tokyo · Toronto

U.S.A.	Pergamon Press, Maxwell House, Fairview Park, Elmsford, New York 10523, U.S.A.
U.K.	Pergamon Press, Headington Hill Hall, Oxford OX3 0BW, England
PEOPLE'S REPUBLIC OF CHINA	Pergamon Press, Room 4037, Qianmen Hotel, Beijing, People's Republic of China
FEDERAL REPUBLIC OF GERMANY	Pergamon Press, Hammerweg 6, D-6242 Kronberg, Federal Republic of Germany
BRAZIL	Pergamon Editora, Rua Eça de Queiros, 346, CEP 04011, Paraiso, São Paulo, Brazil
AUSTRALIA	Pergamon Press Australia, P.O. Box 544, Potts Point, N.S.W. 2011, Australia
JAPAN	Pergamon Press, 8th Floor, Matsuoka Central Building, 1-7-1 Nishishinjuku, Shinjuku-ku, Tokyo 160, Japan
CANADA	Pergamon Press Canada, Suite No. 271, 253 College Street, Toronto, Ontario, Canada M5T 1R5

Copyright © 1988 Pergamon Books Inc.

First edition 1988

Library of Congress Cataloging-in-Publication Data
Kazdin, Alan E.
Child psychotherapy.
(Pergamon general psychology series; 152)
Bibliography: p.
Includes indexes.
1. Child psychotherapy. I. Title. II. Series.
RJ504.K37 1987 618.92'8914 87-21032

British Library Cataloguing in Publication Data
Kazdin, Alan E.
Child psychotherapy: developing and
identifying effective treatments.-
(Pergamon general psychology series).
1. Child psychotherapy
I. Title
618.92'8914 RJ504

ISBN 0-08-034961-7 (Hardcover)
ISBN 0-08-034960-9 (Flexicover)

*Reproduced, printed and bound in Great Britain by
Hazell Watson & Viney Limited
Member of BPCC plc
Aylesbury Bucks*

To Bundle and Vugie

Contents

PREFACE   x

ACKNOWLEDGMENTS   xii

1 EVALUATING PSYCHOTHERAPY   1

   The Nature of the Task   1
   The "Ultimate" Question   3
   Need for Effective Treatments   5
   Purpose of this Book   8
   Overview of Remaining Chapters   10

2 ISSUES AND OBSTACLES IN EVALUATING CHILD
   TREATMENT   12

   Diagnosis of Childhood Disorders   12
   Developmental Considerations   19
   Referral of Children for Treatment   23
   Diversity of Clinical Problems   24
   Focus of Treatment   25
   General Comments   26
   Conclusions   27

3 THE EFFECTIVENESS OF CHILD PSYCHOTHERAPY   29

   Historical Overview: A Review of the Reviews   30
     Narrative Reviews   30
     General Comments   31

Contemporary Evaluations   32
  Meta-analysis   32
  Limitations of the Analyses   37
  Focused Narrative Reviews   38
Conclusions   41

4 PROMISING APPROACHES TO TREATMENT   45

Individual Studies   45
  School-based Treatments of Neurotic and Antisocial
  Behavior   46
  Community-based Treatment for Antisocial Youths   49
  General Comments   52
Illustrations of Research Programs   52
  Parent Management Training   53
  Functional Family Therapy   56
  Cognitive Problem-solving Skills Training   59
  General Comments   62
Conclusions   62

5 METHODOLOGICAL AND SUBSTANTIVE ISSUES
   IN CHILD THERAPY RESEARCH   64

Patient Issues   64
  Identification of Clinical Dysfunction   64
  Potential Moderating Variables   65
Treatment Issues   68
  Representativeness of Treatment   68
  Specification and Integrity of Treatment   69
Therapist Issues   72
  Training   72
  Therapist Characteristics   73
Assessment Issues   75
  Selection of Outcome Measures   75
  Reducing Symptoms and Increasing Prosocial Functioning   75
  Other Types of Measures   77
  Timing of Follow-up Assessment   78
Other Design Issues   80
  Power to Detect Group Differences   80
  Clinical versus Statistical Significance   83
Conclusions   85

6 MODELS OF TREATMENT OUTCOME RESEARCH 88

Alternative Models 88
    Conventional Treatment Model 88
    High-strength Intervention Model 92
    Amenability-to-treatment Model 96
    Broad-based Intervention Model 98
    A Chronic Disease Model 103
Conclusions 105

7 RECOMMENDATIONS AND FUTURE DIRECTIONS 107

Recommendations and Issues 107
    Basic Theory and Research on Child Dysfunction 107
    Problem Identification 110
    Treatments 111
    Replication of Research 114
Planning, Implementing, and Evaluating an Outcome Study 115
    Sample Characteristics 116
    Therapists/Trainers 118
    Treatment 119
    Assessment 120
    General Comments 121
Professional Issues 122
    Myths, Half-truths, and Therapy Clichés 122
    "Set" Toward Evaluation 127
    Training Issues 127
Conclusions 128

REFERENCES 131

AUTHOR INDEX 145

SUBJECT INDEX 151

ABOUT THE AUTHOR 156

PERGAMON GENERAL PSYCHOLOGY SERIES 157

Preface

Children and adolescents are treated in clinics, hospitals, and other mental health facilities for a number of psychological problems including anxiety, hyperactivity, antisocial behavior, depression, eating disorders, and other sources of dysfunction. Many psychological treatment techniques are available for these problems and are routinely applied. Unfortunately, relatively little evidence is available attesting to the efficacy of alternative techniques for childhood disorders. This book focuses on the effectiveness of psychotherapeutic treatments for children and adolescents. These treatments refer broadly to the full gamut of psychological and psychosocial techniques (e.g., individual and group psychotherapies, behavioral and cognitive therapies, family therapies, and others).

There is a clear need to accelerate progress on identifying effective treatments for children and adolescents. The overriding purpose of this book is to address this need. The purpose is accomplished by evaluating the current status of psychotherapies for children, by identifying issues and problems that have impeded progress, and by outlining the methodological requirements to increase the yield from research. Yet, the purpose goes beyond merely describing and evaluating the limited progress of research on child therapies. Rather, the book identifies substantive, methodological, and practical issues and outlines models for future research to help accelerate the development of effective treatments.

Several features make the book unique. First, the book evaluates the current status of child psychotherapy. Evaluations of therapy have frequently been published for adult treatments. The differences between adult and child treatment go beyond the different ages of the clientele. Unique issues emerge in the treatment of children because of the nature of their problems, changes over the course of their development, and the ways in which child problems are identified and manifest at home and at school. This book evaluates child therapy in the context of developmental issues and considerations.

Second, the book does not review alternative therapy techniques and individual investigations in great detail. Although many different techniques and investigations are discussed to illustrate key points throughout the text, the purpose of the book goes beyond the usual literature review of individual treatment techniques. The book makes no attempt to be encyclopedic nor to promulgate a particular theoretical approach or treatment technique. Rather, the book identifies issues, problems, and strategies for the field as a whole.

Third, the book draws upon research in diverse areas within clinical child psychology, child development, and child psychiatry. Major areas include epidemiology, psychodiagnosis, and assessment. Each of these areas raises important considerations for the identification and evaluation of effective psychotherapies.

Finally, the book provides a critical evaluation of the field but, more importantly, outlines positive and concrete steps that need to be taken to make further progress. The serious problems that currently exist in research on treatments for childhood disorders make the field an easy target for criticism. Yet, such criticism alone is not likely to have impact. The issue for the field is how to alter research and how to proceed next. This book provides alternative models for such progress.

The brevity of this book is designed to facilitate wide circulation to professionals as well as students in graduate or advanced undergraduate courses. Among the professional audiences, the book will hopefully appeal to researchers, practitioners, and those who have been able to combine these roles. The book should be of interest to professionals and students in the fields of clinical child psychology, child and adolescent psychiatry, counseling, education, social work, and related mental health professions.

There are many other books on the topic of child psychotherapy. In the main, these books present individual techniques or alternative approaches to various clinical problems. Impetus for this text can be traced to such sources that focus narrowly on specific techniques and their alleged or demonstrated efficacy. A broader view is needed to evaluate the current status of treatments and to provide a resource, overview, and plan for action to improve existing work. This book outlines the current status of treatment, identifies important issues related to children that need to be considered in treatment evaluation, describes methodological requirements for child treatment research, and develops and proposes alternative models for treatment evaluation. Important impediments and practical and professional issues that affect research on child treatments, and utilization of research findings in clinical practice are also covered.

Acknowledgments

With completion of this book, I am pleased to express my gratitude for several sources of support. The focus on psychosocial treatments for children and the opportunity to undertake their evaluation have been greatly facilitated by support of a Research Scientist Development Award (MH00353) from the National Institute of Mental Health (NIMH) and related projects devoted to childhood dysfunction (MH35408, MH39642, MH39976, and MH40021). These projects are by no means mine alone. They involve several collaborators including David J. Kolko, Larry Michelson, Karen Marchione, Cynthia G. Last, and Michel Hersen whose works and contacts have been enlightening. I am also grateful to the Rivendell Foundation, which provided support to evaluate child treatment among hospitalized children during the period in which this book was prepared. Many persons were involved in completion of this project as well. Informal discussions with several people, including Drs. Sigmund Dragastin, Michael Fishman and Jon Shaw at NIMH, were quite helpful in shaping the thrust of the present focus. Mary Dulgeroff typed and examined many drafts as efforts were made to "translate" my writing into English. Both Mary and Claudia Wolfson endlessly checked and corrected the manuscript to reach the point you now have before you. (You can imagine what the manuscript looked like before their efforts!)

June 1987

Alan E. Kazdin

Chapter 1

Evaluating Psychotherapy

THE NATURE OF THE TASK

The effectiveness of psychotherapy has been a topic of keen interest in the last 30–40 years. There are many intriguing questions about the effects of therapy that immediately come to mind. What does psychotherapy accomplish? Can psychotherapy ameliorate the many personal, family, and social problems to which the human condition is heir, and if so, which ones? Among the many different treatment techniques, which ones work and with whom? These are only some of the initial questions that arise in considering the effectiveness of psychotherapy, yet the very phrase itself is problematic.

The definition and characteristics of psychotherapy pose obstacles in providing clear answers to questions about the effectiveness of psychotherapy. For our purposes, we can be content to begin with a general definition. Psychotherapy consists of a special interaction between two (or more) individuals where one person (the patient, or client) has sought help for a particular problem, and where another person (the therapist) provides conditions to alleviate that person's distress and to improve functioning in everyday life (Garfield, 1980). The interaction is designed to alter the feelings, thoughts, attitudes, or actions of the person who has sought or has been brought to treatment. Typically, very special conditions define the interactions of therapist and client.[1] The client usually describes his or her difficulties and life circumstances, and the reasons for seeking help. The therapist provides conditions (e.g., support, acceptance, encouragement) to foster the interpersonal relationship and structures the sessions in such a way as to help the client.

It is, of course, useful to distinguish the goals of therapy from the means

[1]The terms *client* and *patient* are often distinguished in discussions of psychotherapy. The differences reflect varying approaches and views of the entire enterprise of therapy, the nature of the problems that participants experience, and the manner in which they should be conceptualized and treated. For present purposes, the terms are used interchangeably to refer to the person who comes or is brought to treatment and/or is the focus of the intervention.

1

used to obtain them. The *goals* can only be stated generally if they are to encompass the full range of interventions that fall under the rubric of psychotherapy. These goals consist of improving adjustment and functioning in both intrapersonal and interpersonal spheres and reducing maladaptive behaviors and various psychological (and often physical) complaints. Intrapersonal adjustment reflects such areas as how one views or feels about oneself. Interpersonal functioning refers to how one adjusts in interactions with others.

The *means* by which the goals are sought are primarily interpersonal contact; for most treatments this consists of verbal interaction. In child therapy, the means can include talking, playing, rewarding new behaviors, or rehearsing activities with the child. Also, the persons who carry out these actions may include therapists, parents, teachers, or peers. A variety of therapeutic aids such as puppets, games, and stories may be used as the means through which goals of treatment are sought.

For summary purposes then, let us consider psychotherapy as an interaction in which the goals and means roughly follow the characteristics noted here. The definition of psychotherapy is restricted to *psychosocial interventions,* in which the means rely primarily on various interpersonal sources of influence such as learning, persuasion, discussion, and similar processes. The focus is on some facet regarding how clients feel (affect), think (cognition), and act (behavior). The definition is necessarily general because of the range of approaches that need to be accommodated. Thus the definition includes a variety of treatments subsumed under many general rubrics such as individual, group, family, insight-oriented, behavioral, and cognitive therapies.

The definition can be sharpened a bit by delineating the boundaries. Excluded from the definition are interventions that focus on biological and biomedical methods such as medication, diet, megavitamins, and psychosurgery. Although such interventions are often directed toward improved psychological functioning (e.g., medication to control hyperactivity, exercise to reduce depression), the methods, theoretical rationales, and clinical–research issues differ from those of psychosocial procedures. Also excluded are interventions directed toward educational objectives. Thus, various tutorial and counseling procedures singularly directed to enhance achievement and academic performance of children and adolescents are excluded here. The exclusion of biological/biomedical procedures and interventions with exclusively educational objectives is not intended in any way to slight the significance or utility of these approaches and goals. The definition is restricted to focus on the special problems in the development, identification, and evaluation of alternative psychotherapy techniques.

The hazy definition of psychotherapy is not too comforting as a way of beginning because it can encompass so many different procedures. This is not the only problem. The notion of "effectiveness" is rather slippery as well. Deciding whether treatment is effective is not straightforward. The effects of treatment can be measured in several ways including the reduction of symptoms, improvements in adjustment at home or in the community, increases in self-reported happiness, evaluations of relatives and friends that progress is evident, and so on. Which of these or other indices should define effectiveness? Perhaps one should look for changes in several of these measures to really be sure that the treatment has worked. Yet, improvements in one measure or set of measures are not always associated with improvements on other measures. So, whether treatment is considered to be effective may depend on the specific measure one examines. Also, how much change on a measure is needed to consider the treatment as "effective"? Symptoms, adjustment, and happiness are a matter of degree. Suppose the client's depression or fears decrease a little by the end of treatment. At what point would an improvement be regarded as a sign that therapy is effective or successful? There are no widely agreed-upon answers to such questions.

THE "ULTIMATE" QUESTION

Ambiguities of what psychotherapy is and how to define effectiveness have naturally helped fuel debates about treatments and their effects. There is reasonable consensus on the nature of the task of evaluating the effects of psychotherapy. To begin with, the effectiveness of psychotherapy has been phrased as a question: "Does psychotherapy work?" In the adult psychotherapy literature, that question has long been rejected as much too general to warrant serious attention (Bergin & Lambert, 1978; Edwards & Cronbach, 1952). If psychotherapy is a general term that encompasses many different treatments, it is not particularly meaningful to lump all procedures together and to provide a single and simple yes or no answer to the question. In place of such a global question, a more specific question has been substituted: "*What* treatment, by *whom*, is most effective for *this* individual with *that* specific problem, under *which* set of circumstances?" (Paul, 1967, p. 111). This is often regarded as the "ultimate" question toward which psychotherapy outcome research should be directed. The question highlights the importance of examining the specific effects of alternative treatments for a particular clinical problem and acknowledges that the effects of treatments may depend on characteristics of the patients, therapists, and conditions under which treatment is provided.

There are problems evident within the adult psychotherapy literature that make this question difficult to address. The sheer number of available treatment techniques alone makes the task monumental. Although at any given time it is difficult to pinpoint the precise number of techniques in use, surveys have revealed a continued proliferation. In the early 1960s, approximately 60 different types of psychotherapy were identified (Garfield, 1982). By the mid 1970s, over 130 techniques were delineated (National Institute of Mental Health, 1975). Growth continued so that by the late 1970s over 250 techniques were identified (Herink, 1980). A more recent count has placed the number of existing techniques over 400 (Karasu, 1985). Determining the effectiveness of these different therapies is a task of considerable proportions.

The many different techniques need to be evaluated in relation to specific clinical problems. The symptoms, maladaptive behaviors, target complaints, and dysfunctions now recognized as clinical problems have also proliferated. Consider, for example, the classification of psychiatric disorders over the last 35 years. In the United States, the list of recognized disorders is provided by the *Diagnostic and Statistical Manual of Mental Disorders* (referred to as the DSM). This document is updated periodically and serves to delineate alternative disorders and criteria that are invoked for their diagnosis. Changes in the DSM illustrate the proliferation of recognized disorders. In the first edition (American Psychiatric Association [APA], 1952), slightly over 100 diagnostic categories were recognized; in the second edition (APA, 1968), this increased to over 180. In the third edition (APA, 1980), over 260 diagnostic categories were included. Even if the number of disorders did not continue to increase with further revisions of the DSM, evaluation of treatment in relation to disorders currently recognized is an obviously formidable task.

Also, the different measures that have emerged to evaluate the effects of treatment have expanded over time (e.g., Lambert, Christensen, & DeJulio, 1983). The further development and proliferation of assessment techniques increases the potential diversity of answers that can be reached about alternative treatments. Effectiveness can be defined in an indefinite number of ways based on the area of functioning that is measured (e.g., symptoms, social behavior), the source of information that evaluates treatment (e.g., patient, relative, or therapist), and the type of measure that is applied (e.g., direct observation of the patient's behavior, ratings completed by others).

For example, the conclusions reached about the effectiveness of treatment or the relative effectiveness of two different treatments may be quite different depending on whether one examines the ratings of symptoms completed by the patients or by their therapists. Results from these measures may differ from those obtained by directly observing the patients in situations in which their problems (e.g., compulsive acts, anxiety in leaving their homes) are evident. The large number of relevant measures makes answering the question of therapy effectiveness a Herculean task. The fact that different measures may lead to different conclusions in a given study may make this a Sisyphean task, as well.

In general, the growth and complexity of the field have made the ultimate question to psychotherapy virtually impossible to answer. To convey the task more concretely, Parloff (1982) noted that 4.7 million separate comparisons would require investigation if there were 250 different psychosocial therapy techniques and 150 classes of different clinical disorders. There are of course many more techniques and disorders than this illustration suggests. Clearly the number of available techniques, the range of diagnosable clinical disorders, and the alternative measures and perspectives by which treatment can be evaluated operate to make the ultimate question about the effects of psychotherapies beyond the scope of any reasonable set of studies (Kazdin, 1986a).

Obviously, there can be no simple verdict regarding whether psychotherapy is effective. The task is to discuss the impact of specific treatments on various clinical problems. Because of the importance and complexity of the task of evaluating psychotherapy, it is no surprise that the topic has occupied a prominent place in clinical psychology, psychiatry, and related mental health professions. Indeed, the topic is so often written about that the titles of many books are unusually similar because of effort to capture the central idea of the effectiveness of psychotherapy.[2] Yet, the focus within the field has been almost exclusively on the effects of psychotherapy with adults.

NEED FOR EFFECTIVE TREATMENTS

There are obvious reasons to focus on psychotherapy for children and adolescents.[3] To begin, the mental-health needs of children are relatively great (United States Congress, Office of Technology Assessment [U.S. Congress, OTA], 1986). The need for psychotherapy services might be inferred from the scope and type of problems that children suffer. Yet data on the extent to which children suffer specific types of dysfunctions are difficult to obtain. Standardized and agreed-upon diagnostic criteria for various childhood disorders have only been developed and invoked fairly recently (APA, 1980). Consequently, studies have utilized a variety of nonstandardized criteria and labels such as *emotionally disturbed* or *clinically maladjusted* (Gould, Wunsch-Hitzig, & Dohrenwend, 1980). This

---

[2]A sample of available writings illustrates similar titles: *The effects of psychotherapy* (Eysenck, 1966); *Effective psychotherapy* (Gurman & Razin, 1977); *The effects of psychotherapy* (Lambert, 1979); *The effects of psychological therapy* (Rachman & Wilson, 1980); *The benefits of psychotherapy* (Smith, Glass, & Miller, 1980).

[3]Although the primary focus of this book is on children, most of the comments refer to adolescents as well. The term *children* is used generically and includes children and adolescents. There are specific points in the text where age is discussed; separate age ranges or terms will be used.

level of dysfunction usually requires that there is some impairment in daily life, as defined by not functioning well in social interactions or showing signs of distress or disturbance in the family or community (Graham, 1977).

Without an agreed-upon system to define, diagnose, and assess childhood dysfunction, one would expect little agreement among different studies. Actually, there has been surprising consistency in studies of the extent of dysfunction among children. Independent efforts to evaluate child mental health problems and clinical services have drawn similar conclusions. In 1969, the Joint Commission on Mental Health of Children concluded that 13.6% of children were "emotionally disturbed." This included approximately 2–4% of the children with severe disorders (including psychoses) and 8–10% with other disturbances also requiring treatment. The overall percentage of 13.6% translates to approximately 9 million children in the United States (U.S. Congress, OTA, 1986). A subsequent evaluation by the President's Commission on Mental Health (1978) identified between 5–15% of all children and adolescents as in need of some form of mental health services. This would translate approximately to between 3 and 10 million children in the United States. A review of several epidemiological studies in the United States and Great Britain estimated clinical dysfunction among approximately 12% of children, although the range varied considerably among the different studies (approximately 6–37%) (Gould et al., 1980). The studies do not convey precisely the scope of the problem because they refer nebulously to terms that do not have consistent meanings. The terms *severe disorders, emotional disturbance,* and *need for services* refer to children with specific symptoms or target problems such as excessive anxiety, hyperactivity, aggressive behavior, and other problems that parents, teachers, or mental health professionals consider to impair daily functioning.

The rates of childhood dysfunction vary as a function of several factors that include age, sex, type of disorder, ethnic background and geographical region, to mention a few. For example, prevalence of disturbance is greater for boys than for girls, and for youths in urban rather than rural settings (Graham, 1977; Rutter, Cox, Tupling, Berger, & Yule, 1975). Black and Hispanic youths evince more dysfunction than white youths (Langner, Gersten, & Eisenberg, 1974). Other factors such as lower socioeconomic status, single versus two-parent families, and age also influence prevalence rates (Gould et al., 1980). Thus, a single set of percentages cannot represent the full complexity of the problem. Nevertheless, it is critical to acknowledge that several million youths in the United States alone are in need of, and might profit from, psychological intervention. Consequently, the identification of effective treatments is an important priority.

An issue related to the need for treatment is the extent to which children actually receive care. Apparently, most of the children who need mental health services do not receive them. Estimates have shown that only 20-33% of children with clinically significant dysfunction actually receive treatment (Knitzer, 1982; Rutter, Tizard, & Whitmore, 1970). Children with more serious dysfunctions are slightly less likely to receive treatment than those with less serious dysfunctions (Sowder, 1975). This information conveys a problem seemingly unrelated to the identification of effective treatments. However, some of the complexities of evaluating treatments for children have implications for dissemination and utilization of psychotherapy. There has been considerable ambiguity regarding what treatments are available and effective for children, and whether certain types of problems are amenable to treatment, or whether they should be focused on at all. Evaluation of alternative treatments may help to clarify approaches that can be effectively implemented, and for which problems. This information would provide clearer guidelines for disseminating currently available treatments.

The preceding overview suggests that there is a good market for effective forms of treatment for children. Even so, the actual needs for psychotherapy are not entirely clear. The incidence of different behavioral problems does not necessarily mean that these should be treated. Studies of children who are not referred for treatment have often shown that maladaptive behaviors (e.g., fighting, stuttering, enuresis) that are disturbing to parents and teachers commonly emerge over the course of normal development (Lapouse & Monk, 1958; MacFarlane, Allen, & Honzik, 1954; Werry & Quay, 1971). Most of these behaviors disappear over the course of development without consequence. Thus, for many, if not most disturbing behaviors, no intervention may be the best intervention. Among clinical cases that are brought for treatment, a significant percentage of patients may improve without receiving alternative forms of psychotherapy (Kolvin et al., 1981; Levitt, 1957). It is difficult to specify the rates of improvement because they vary for alternative disorders, ages, sex of the child, and other factors. Although some clinically referred children improve without treatment, this does not mean that psychotherapy is not a needed service. Yet ambiguities regarding the incidence rates for particular types of dysfunction or behavioral problems and the changes in these behaviors over the course of development make the need of such services difficult to pinpoint.

Another ambiguity in identifying the need for psychotherapeutic services is the fact that psychotherapy is only one of the many alternatives to address the specific problems that children present. School, community, and health-care programs for parents and teachers can be directed toward many of the personal and interpersonal problems that child psychotherapy is designed to address. Yet, outpatient treatment for children appears to reach more children than any other type of mental health service (Sowder & Burt, 1980). The children who receive outpatient therapy are likely to receive individual therapy (54%), family therapy (34%), group therapy (8%), or other forms of treatment including medication (7%) (Sowder, 1975). Given services that are provided, there is a need to ensure that the treatments approach or attain the goals toward which they are directed.

Apart from the specific problems that children present, effective interventions are important to identify for preventive purposes. Leaving aside the misery that children may experience, identification of alternative forms of psychotherapy or related services would be a worthwhile goal in its own right as a means of minimizing or averting adult dysfunction. Many early signs of dysfunction evident in childhood are likely to be precursors of adult disorders. For example, children who show early signs of dysfunction such as unmanageability, aggression, social withdrawal, speech and language problems, are at risk for subsequent psychiatric disorders (Lerner, Inui, Trupin, & Douglas, 1985). For such youths, there is a need for interventions aimed at secondary prevention, that is, intervening in response to early signs of dysfunction to prevent them from becoming worse.[4] Psychotherapy or the procedures that are developed and evaluated in the context of treatment may play an important role in such preventive efforts, albeit prevention strategies often are administered as school or community-based programs.

PURPOSE OF THIS BOOK

Progress in the development and evaluation of psychotherapies for children has been slow relative to research that has been completed with adults. The neglect and limited progress of child psychotherapy research are attested to in several ways. For example, within the last 5 years, major books, special journal issues, and conferences devoted exclusively to psychotherapy have almost completely neglected treatments for children.

The neglect of child psychotherapy can be illustrated more concretely in different ways. For example, the *Handbook of psychotherapy and behavior change* (3rd edition, Garfield & Bergin, 1986) is one of the foremost texts on psychotherapy research. The most recent edition excluded a chapter on child psychotherapy because the editors felt that there was so little research and progress since the previous edition (1978) that a chapter was not warranted. Psychotherapy research has also been a special topic where entire journal issues or conferences review the current status and issues of the field (*American Psychologist*, 1986; *Journal of Consulting and Clinical Psychology*, 1986; Williams & Spitzer, 1983). Almost no mention is made of child psychotherapy among the constituent articles. Finally, the Society of

---

[4]There are different types of preventive efforts that can be distinguished. *Primary* prevention refers to efforts to reduce the development of a particular dysfunction or disorder or to reduce the number of new cases; *secondary* prevention refers to efforts to reduce the duration, severity, and consequences of dysfunction among those who show early signs of dysfunction.

Psychotherapy Research is an organization involving mental health professionals (e.g., psychologists, psychiatrists) who are engaged in psychotherapy research. The annual meetings reflect the foremost work in the field and major process and outcome studies. Perusal of the convention programs from recent years (e.g., 1985-1987) reveals that the contemporary research is almost exclusively devoted to the treatment of adult disorders.

It is not that little is written on the topic of child therapy; there are many sources available (e.g., Gumaer, 1984; Harrison, 1979; Schaefer, Briesmeister, & Fitton, 1984; Schaefer, Johnson, & Wherry, 1982; Schaefer & Millman, 1977). With few exceptions, the focus is on clinical practice, interpretive and anecdotal accounts of treatment, and recommendations for clinical care. The activity in the field is represented by the constant appearance of new books on child treatment (e.g., Dodds, 1985; Johnson, Rasbury, & Siegel, 1986; Lord, 1985; Prout & Brown, 1985; Schaefer, Millman, Sichel, & Zwilling, 1986). Yet there is relatively little available devoted to empirical work on child therapies.

With many texts currently available, it is legitimate to ask why another book is needed and why it is specifically on the question of effectiveness. The answer reflects a judgment about the field. The author believes the progress in the area of child treatment has been slow. There are many different treatments — indeed over 230 for children and adolescents (see chapter 3). The great majority of these have not been shown to be effective. Even more regrettably, most of these techniques have never been carefully evaluated.

Yet, the absence of data on the effectiveness of alternative treatments is not the basis for a book, or at least not this book. The absence of the pertinent data is resolved by an investigation or set of investigations designed specifically to evaluate alternative treatments. The impetus for this book has to do with the slow pace at which such data are emerging and hence the limited progress within the field. There is some urgency to the task of stimulating further work. The urgency does not drive from an imminent crisis or new psychological problem of childhood or adolescence that requires immediate attention before reaching epidemic proportions. To be sure, there are enough crises because of the tragedy of many childhood and adolescent problems that occur on any scale (e.g., suicide, depression, antisocial behavior). The urgency for further work derives from greater dangers in the field, namely inertia and tacit acceptance of the status quo, and limited avenues to progress. There is an unfelt problem vis-à-vis child treatment research. Unfelt problems are dangerous because they are likely to be neglected and ignored.

Research on child psychotherapy is floundering. No doubt progress will be made, but the pace of such progress is difficult to detect. An overall goal of this book is to accelerate progress. Such a goal will be achieved by examining the current status of the field, pointing to special issues that have thwarted progress, identifying promising leads and findings, and outlining new directions. The purpose is not to review all of the currently available interventions for children and to comment on their effects. Apart from the nihilism to which such a review might lead, the likely impact of such a focus is predictably, if not deservedly, nugatory. The familiar refrain, "more research is needed," can be played here as part of the overture rather than as part of the finale. Much more is needed than simply more research. This book is designed to provoke thought about what is needed and to promote action in the use of alternative research strategies.

OVERVIEW OF REMAINING CHAPTERS

Chapter 2, *Issues and Obstacles in Evaluating Child Treatment,* discusses issues of special characteristics of children that make research difficult, and characteristics of the field that have delayed progress in evaluating alternative treatments. The course of normal development and the delineation of dysfunction have been poorly understood. These and related issues need to be considered in designing individual treatment investigations and in evaluating the therapy outcome literature.

Chapter 3, *The Effectiveness of Child Psychotherapy,* highlights historically important reviews in the field, their conclusions, and limitations. Contemporary reviews including meta-analyses of child psychotherapy are examined in greater detail to provide summary statements regarding treatment efficacy. The reviews, whether qualitative or quantitative, are limited in the information they provide. The paucity of studies and their checkered quality limit the conclusions that large-scale reviews can produce.

The efficacy of treatment can be examined in other ways than through reviews. In chapter 4, *Promising Approaches to Treatment,* child therapy is evaluated differently. Individual studies are selected for close scrutiny to convey high-quality research in the field and to show the difficulties that emerge in conducting treatment research as well. In addition, selected techniques evaluated in various programs of research are illustrated to show the progress that has been achieved for selected treatment techniques. A more molecular evaluation of child therapies illustrates the type of excellent work underway.

In chapter 5, *Methodological and Substantive Issues in Child Therapy Research,* attention is directed to a variety of patient, therapist, assessment and treatment issues. The goal is not to criticize the extant literature, but rather to suggest positive tactics that can be incorporated into research to maximize the yield. The points incorporate special issues that emerge in research with children in particular, many of which have clear implications for the design of treatment trials.

In chapter 6, *Models of Treatment Outcome Research,* different ways of evaluating treatments are discussed. In the conventional approach to treatment, some predetermined number of treatment sessions are provided and patient functioning is assessed to see if there are gains, and if these gains are sustained over time. The way this is carried out is reasonable and certainly has become *de rigueur.* Yet, there are many alternatives to the usual way of implementing and evaluating treatment. This chapter considers alternative models that are designed to accelerate progress in identifying effective treatments.

In chapter 7, *Recommendations and Future Directions,* comments are made to integrate the previous chapters. Included in this final chapter are abbreviated (and opinionated) statements of the current status of the outcome research on child therapies, and a statement of obstacles that may impede progress. Research methods that can improve treatment outcome studies are discussed at the level of the individual investigation. Professional beliefs, myths, and half-truths that may cloud treatment evaluation are commented upon as well.

Chapter 2

Issues and Obstacles in Evaluating Child Treatment

Conducting psychotherapy research, whether with children or adults, raises difficulties and is plagued by "slippery methodological problems" (Levitt, 1971, p. 477). These problems include recruiting homogeneous patient populations, securing therapists to administer treatments, selecting control conditions (e.g., no treatment) to address the specific treatment question, and keeping patients in the study over the course of treatment and follow-up assessment periods. The individual issues are weighty and have been the subject of considerable attention (e.g., Howard, Krause, & Orlinsky, 1986; Kazdin, 1986b; Parloff, 1986). Yet, there are additional obstacles and issues that emerge in the treatment of children. These issues have impeded progress in conducting child psychotherapy research. This chapter discusses the many issues that emerge in the evaluation of child psychotherapy. Consideration of these problems helps to understand the basis for the slow development of child psychotherapy research, and previews both substantive and methodological issues that need to be addressed in the evaluation of child treatment.

DIAGNOSIS OF CHILDHOOD DISORDERS

The diagnosis of psychiatric disorders or psychological problems among adults has advanced considerably. Perhaps one of the most significant advances emerged with efforts to develop specific criteria for a number of disorders (Feighner et al., 1972; Spitzer, Endicott, & Robins, 1975). The advances have fostered and greatly enhanced research on the incidence, prevalence, causes, treatment, and clinical course of various disorders.

Until recently, childhood disorders have been relatively neglected in

12

nosology and taxonomy. The neglect may be due in part to some of the special complexities of childhood. In adults, psychiatric dysfunction is generally viewed in the context of relatively stable development in social, cognitive, affective, and biological spheres. Although stages and changes are increasingly recognized in adult development, such changes are probably less marked or at least more gradual than those evident in childhood and adolescence. The changing picture of childhood makes diagnosis of dysfunction problematic. Indeed, the diagnosis of many childhood dysfunctions very much depends more upon age and developmental considerations. For example, some behaviors (e.g., enuresis, fighting) are viewed quite differently as a function of the child's age (e.g., a 2 year-old vs. a 10 year-old child). Many emotional and behavioral characteristics such as fears and depression are likely to vary markedly across different ages in childhood and adolescence. The great deal that remains to be learned about developmental stages and normal child development makes the delineation or diagnosis of disorders among children and adolescents especially difficult (Gelfand & Peterson, 1985).

The neglect of childhood disorders has, so to speak, a respectable history beginning with Kraepelin's (1883) pioneering work on classification. Kraepelin developed a taxonomy of psychiatric disorders by observing many different cases of adult patients. Specific childhood disorders were not systematically studied. Over time, severe disorders were recognized in clinical work as evident, for example, in the identification of childhood autism in the 1940s. Isolated efforts to identify and classify childhood disorders more generally have been evident for the last 50 years (Dreger, 1981). Yet, few efforts have resulted in a systematic and widely adopted nosology for children.

In the United States, the *Diagnostic and Statistical Manual of Mental Disorders* (DSM) is the document that enumerates and codifies the range of psychological dysfunction (disorders) that are currently recognized.[1] The system was developed by the American Psychiatric Association (APA) and has been revised periodically. In the first edition, which emerged in 1952 (DSM I), the disorders of children and adolescents were accorded little attention. The disorders considered to arise in childhood were restricted to two categories, namely Adjustment Reactions (habit disturbances, conduct disturbances, and psychoneurotic traits) and Schizophrenia (Childhood Type). Even the few categories available for children, leaving aside the complement of those designed for adults but applicable to children, were rarely used. Approximately two-thirds of the children referred for treatment

---

[1]Although the DSM is the system in use in the United States, it is developed from and consistent with the ninth edition of the International Classification of Diseases (ICD-9; World Health Organization, 1978) which is used world-wide as a basis of identifying medical diseases and psychiatric disorders.

received either no diagnosis or a nonspecific diagnosis of adjustment reaction (Rosen, Bahn, & Kramer, 1964). Thus, there seemed to be no clear pressure to delineate various disorders based on careful clinical evaluation of the problems that children experienced.

In 1966, the Group for the Advancement of Psychiatry (GAP) responded to rectify the neglect of childhood psychopathology in the classification scheme of the DSM. The GAP provided a classification system that permitted greater differentiation of childhood disorders. Several different categories were recognized including Psychoneurotic, Personality, and Psychophysiological Disorders, each having several subtypes. Deviations from normal development and positive assets ("healthy responses") were also included which added unique features beyond the exclusive focus on psychopathology. The GAP system greatly elaborated childhood disorders, but did not enjoy widespread use. The DSM had taken a firm and dominant place in psychiatry and mental health services, at least in the United States.

By 1968, the second edition of the DSM appeared. DSM II improved upon DSM I with regard to children and adolescents by including Behavior Disorders of Childhood and Adolescence (e.g., hyperkinetic reactions, withdrawing reactions, overanxious reactions, group delinquent reactions, undersocialized aggressive reaction, running away reaction), Adjustment Reactions of Infancy, Childhood and Adolescence, and Schizophrenia (Childhood Type). The category of Behavior Disorders began greater differentiation of the dysfunctions that youth might suffer. However, children and adolescents were considered, especially in retrospect, to have received short shrift.

In 1980, the third edition of the DSM appeared. DSM III reflected a quantum leap from DSM II in the attention accorded disorders of infancy, childhood, and adolescence. In DSM III, five major groups of disorders were distinguished including intellectual (Mental Retardation), behavioral (e.g., Conduct Disorder), emotional (e.g., Anxiety Disorder), physical (e.g., Eating Disorder), and developmental disorders (e.g., Pervasive Developmental Delay). Within the separate categories different disorders and subtypes of disorders were delineated.

DSM III had other distinguishing characteristics than the expansion of recognizable disorders. A significant departure from previous editions was the use of different axes or dimensions to evaluate dysfunction. The five axes were: Clinical Syndromes (Axis I), Personality and Devlopmental Disorders (Axis II), Physical Disorders and Conditions (Axis III), Severity of Stressors (Axis IV), and the Highest Level of Adaptive Functioning (Axis V). The multiple axes not only permit diagnosis of psychiatric dysfunctions (Axes I and II), but also other conditions and circumstances relevant to managing and treating the case.

Beginning in 1983, the diagnostic categories of the DSM have been reevaluated to incorporate research findings on alternative disorders and experience in applying the specific diagnostic categories. Revised criteria have emerged and are referred to as DSM III-R (APA, 1987). These are now the current DSM criteria. The major groups of disorders have remained quite similar in DSM III and III-R.

Table 2.1 lists the range of disorders that are currently recognized within DSM III-R as arising in infancy, childhood and adolescence. Identification of a large number of disorders in childhood evident in DSM III and III-R has been a mixed blessing. For present purposes, the major point is the significance of the greater attention accorded children and adolescents. However, concerns have been voiced that there is not strong evidence to support the existence of many of the problems, or that some of the problems may not warrant diagnosis (Achenbach, 1985; Kazdin, 1983).

Table 2.1
Disorders First Evident in Infancy, Childhood or Adolescence

Mental Retardation: (a) Significantly subaverage general intellectual functioning, (b) resulting in, or associated with, deficits or impairments in adaptive behavior, (c) with onset before the age of 18.

Autistic Disorder: Profound disturbance in social interactions, communication, language, and symbolic (imaginative development) and a restricted repertoire of activities (e.g., stereotyped body movements).

Conduct Disorder: Repetitive and persistent pattern of conduct in which either the basic rights of others or major age-appropriate societal norms or rules are violated. The conduct is more serious than ordinary mischief and pranks of children and adolescents.

Attention Deficit–Hyperactivity Disorder: Signs of developmentally inappropriate inattention, impulsivity, and hyperactivity. In the classroom, attentional difficulties and impulsivity are evidenced by the child's not staying with tasks and having difficulty organizing and completing work.

Oppositional–Defiant Disorder: A pattern of disobedient, negativistic, and provocative opposition to authority figures.

Separation Anxiety Disorder: Clinical picture in which the predominant disturbance is persistent and excessive anxiety on separation from major attachment figures or from home or other familiar surroundings. When separation occurs, the child may experience anxiety to the point of panic.

Overanxious Disorder: Clinical picture in which the predominant disturbance is excessive worrying about future or past events and fearful behavior that is not focused on a specific situation or object (such as separation from a parent or entering new social interaction) and that is not due to a recent psychosocial stressor.

Pica: The persistent eating of a nonnutritive substance. Infants with the disorder typically eat paint, plaster, string, hair, or cloth. Older children may eat animal droppings, sand, bugs, leaves, or pebbles. There is no aversion to food.

Rumination Disorder of Infancy: Repeated regurgitation without nausea or associated gastrointestinal illness and associated with weight loss or a failure to make expected weight gain.

Transsexualism: Persistent discomfort and sense of inappropriateness about one's assigned gender and preoccupation with acquiring sex characteristics of the other sex.

Nontranssexual Cross Gender Disorder: Persistent discomfort and sense of inappropriateness about one's assigned gender and recurrent cross-dressing in the role of the other sex (but no preoccupation of changing one's sex characteristics).

Gender Identity Disorder of Childhood: Persistent and intense distress of being a girl (for females) or boy (for males). Manifested in a marked aversion to normative sex-typed clothing and insistence on wearing clothing of the opposite sex and repudiation of one's own sex anatomical structures.

Tourette's Disorder: Recurrent, involuntary, repetitive, rapid movements (tics), including multiple vocal tics. The movements can be voluntarily suppressed for minutes to hours; and the intensity, frequency, and location of the symptoms vary over weeks or months.

Chronic Motor or Vocal Tic Disorder: Recurrent, involuntary, repetitive, rapid movements (motor tics) usually involving no more than three muscle groups at any one time or repetition of words, hissing, throat clearing (vocal tics). The tics occur many times a day nearly everyday for more than one year.

Transient Tic Disorder: Recurrent, involuntary, repetitive, motor or vocal tics. The duration is at least two weeks but no longer than 12 consecutive months.

Functional Enuresis: Repeated involuntary voiding of urine during the day or at night, after an age at which continence is expected, that is not due to any physical disorder.

Functional Encopresis: Repeated voluntary or involuntary passage of feces of normal or near-normal consistency into places not appropriate for that purpose in the individual's own sociocultural setting, not due to any physical disorder.

Reactive Attachment Disorder of Infancy and Early Childhood: Signs of poor emotional development (lack of age-appropriate signs of social responsiveness), apathetic mood and physical development (failure to thrive), with onset before the age of 5, because of lack of adequate caretaking including psychological and physical abuse or neglect. The disturbance is not due to a physical disorder or to Autistic Disorder.

Stereotypy/Habit Disorder: Presence of intentional, repetitive, and nonfunctional behaviors such as handshaking or waving, body rocking, headbanging, and mouthing of objects.

Elective Mutism: Continuous refusal to speak in one or more social situations, including at school, despite ability to comprehend spoken language and to speak. These children may communicate via gestures, by nodding or shaking the head, or in some cases, by monosyllabic or short, monotone utterances.

Anorexia Nervosa: Intense fear of becoming obese, disturbance of body image, significant weight loss, refusal to maintain a minimal normal body weight, and amenorrhea (in females). This disorder is likely to emerge in adolescence or adulthood.

Bulimia Nervosa: Episodic binge eating, accompanied by an awareness that the eating pattern is abnormal, and fear of not being able to stop eating voluntarily.

Articulation Disorder: Consistent failure to use developmentally expected speech sounds.

Stuttering: Frequent repetitions or prolongations of sounds, syllables, or words, or frequent, unusual hesitations and pauses that disrupt the rhythmic flow of speech.

Cluttering: A disorder of speech involving both the rate and rhythm of speech resulting in impaired speech and intelligibility. Speech is erratic and dysrhythmic consisting of rapid and jerky spurts that may also involve faulty phrasing.

Expressive Language Disorder: Use of language that is markedly below what would be expected given the child's nonverbal intellectual capacity.

Receptive Language Disorder: Comprehension of language is markedly below what would be expected given the child's nonverbal intellectual capacity.

Reading Disorder: Performance in daily activities requiring reading is markedly below the child's intellectual capacity.

Expressive Writing Disorder: Performance in daily activities requiring the composition of written text (spelling words, expressing thoughts, organizing paragraphs) is markedly below the child's intellectual capacity.

Arithmetic Disorder: Performance in daily activities requiring arithmetic skills is markedly below the child's intellectual capacity.

Coordination Disorder: Performance in daily activities requiring motor coordination is markedly below the expected level, given the child's chronological age and intellectual capacity. Marked delays in achieving developmental milestones in motor behavior (walking, crawling) or poor performance in sports may be manifestations.

---

*These disorders are likely to *arise* in infancy, childhood or adolescence as identified in the *Diagnostic and Statistical Manual of Mental Disorders* (DSM III-R; APA, 1987). There are a number of other disorders in which the essential features are considered to be the same in children and adults. Mood disorders and schizophrenia are primary examples. No special categories are provided for children because the criteria utilized with adults are considered to be applicable across the age spectrum.

More than recognition of a number of different types of dysfunction, DSM III and III-R provide improved opportunities to investigate various disorders. The criteria for invoking diagnoses have been clarified so that the symptoms, their duration, and other characteristics are better-described for adults as well as children than in previous editions. Greater emphasis has been placed on being able to measure alternative symptoms and to assign diagnoses to cases in a reliable (consistent) fashion. Identification and assessment of various disorders obviously need to be resolved to study the disorders in depth. For years, several measures have been available to assess psychiatric dysfunction among adults (e.g., Endicott & Spitzer, 1978; Wing, Cooper, & Sartorius, 1974). More recently, diagnostic interviews have emerged for the diagnosis of disorders among children and adolescents as well (e.g., Chambers et al., 1985; Herjanic & Reich, 1982).

DSM III-R and its antecedents reflect clinically derived diagnostic systems. The systems have relied upon clinical observations and abstractions from these observations to identify diagnostic entities. Advances have been evident with other approaches to diagnosis. Multivariate approaches apply various statistical procedures (e.g., factor analysis, cluster analysis) to identify symptoms that tend to go together in children. With statistical approaches, parents or teachers usually are asked to complete checklists that encompass a large number of symptoms that children may show. The statistical techniques are used to identify the types of symptoms (items) that go together (correlate). In this way, larger groups or constellations of symptoms are identified. By assessing large numbers of symptoms and large numbers of children of different ages, one can identify consistencies in the types of dysfunctions that children evince. Across a large number of studies using different measures, child samples, and methods of statistical analysis, several consistencies have emerged. Table 2.2 provides some of the patterns that have emerged quite consistently across studies and the characteristic

Table 2.2

Dimensions Arising in Multivariate Statistical Analysis with Frequently Associated Characteristics of Each

Conduct Disorder	*Socialized Aggression*
Fighting, hitting	Has "bad" companions
Disobedient, defiant	Truant from home
Temper tantrums	Truant from school
Destructiveness	Steals in company of others
Impertinent, impudent	Loyal to delinquent friends
Uncooperative, resistant	Belongs to a gang
Attention Problems	*Anxious-Depressed Withdrawal*
Poor concentration, short attention span	Anxious, fearful, tense
Daydreaming	Shy, timid, bashful
Clumsy, poor coordination	Withdrawn, seclusive
Preoccupied, stares into space	Depressed, sad, disturbed
Fails to finish, lacks perseverence	Hypersensitive, easily hurt
Impulsive	Feels inferior, worthless
Motor Overactivity	*Schizoid-Unresponsive*
Restless, overactive	Will not talk
Excitable, impulsive	Withdrawn
Squirmy, jittery	Sad
Overtalkative	Stares blankly
Hams and makes other odd noises	Confused

From Quay, H.C. (1986). A critical analysis of DSM III as a taxonomy of psychopathology in childhood and adolescence. In T. Millon & G. Klerman (Eds.), *Contemporary issues in psychopathology.* New York: Guilford.

symptoms of each. A comparison of Tables 2.1 and 2.2 shows some overlap (e.g., conduct disorder, attention deficit disorder). In general, results from multivariate approaches have helped test the diagnostic entities proposed in clinically derived methods such as the DSM (Achenbach, 1985).

Advances in current work on delineating childhood disorders and developing specific diagnostic criteria have set the stage for treatment research on specific disorders. Yet, the late development of this information has had a two-fold effect. First, without the delineation of various disorders, the full range of children's treatment needs has been unclear. Many problems (e.g., autism, mental retardation) have been recognized and subjected to close scrutiny for some time. Yet delineating a larger set of disorders with subtypes can help focus treatment needs.

Second, the absence of an agreed-upon diagnostic system has delayed the accumulation of information about specific dysfunctions. Rather than referring to children in a standardized way, investigators adopted idiosyncratic terms to refer to problems of their child samples. Indeed this tradition has continued. For example, child treatment studies have focused on "emotional disturbance," "problems in self-management," "social adjustment disorders," and "social skills deficits," which are all nonstandardized terms that have no uniform meaning beyond the specific definitions of individual studies. Use of idiosyncratic terms also hinders a

Table 2.3

Prevalence of Selected Behavior Characteristics in a Sample of 482 Children Ages 6–12 as Reported by their Mothers

Behavorial Problem	Percentage
Fears and worries, 7 or more present	43
Bed wetting within the past year:	
All frequencies	17
Once a month or more	8
Nightmares	28
Food intake:	
Less than "normal"	20
More than "normal"	16
Temper loss:	
Once a month or more	80
Twice a week or more	48
Once a day or more	11
Overactivity	49
Restlessness	30
Stuttering	4
Unusual movements, twitching or jerking (tics)	12
Biting nails:	
All intensities	27
Nails bitten down (more severe)	17
Grinding teeth	14
Sucking thumb or fingers:	
All frequencies	10
"Almost all the time"	2

Adapted from Lapouse, R., & Monk, M. A. (1958). An epidemiologic study of behavior characteristics in children. *American Journal of Public Health, 48*, 1134–1144.

constant set of referents for epidemiological studies to identify the incidence and prevalence of specific disorders.

DEVELOPMENTAL CONSIDERATIONS

Several developmental considerations make investigation of childhood disorders and the evaluation of treatment especially difficult. First, several behaviors that characterize maladjustment or emotional disturbance are relatively common in childhood (Lapouse & Monk, 1958; MacFarlane et al., 1954; Werry & Quay, 1971). Table 2.3 conveys a small sample of problem behaviors and their relative frequency for children ages 6–12. Although several behaviors identified by parents and teachers as problems early in childhood are relatively common, a major question is whether these child behaviors portend maladaptive behavior or dysfunction later in adulthood. Fortunately, as most children mature, they do not suffer serious psychiatric or psychological dysfunction. Thus, early signs of problems may not necessarily be clinically significant.

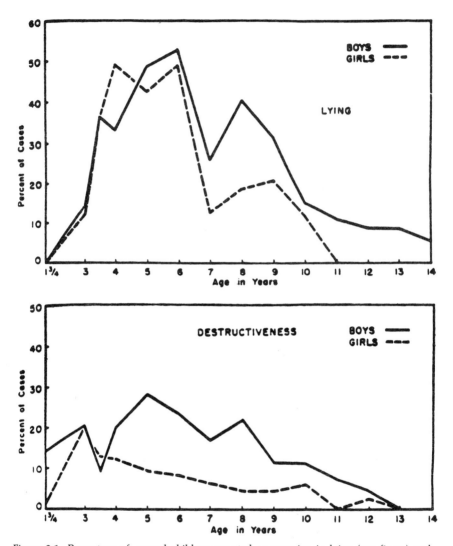

Figure 2.1. Percentage of normal children reported as engaging in lying (top figure) and destructiveness (bottom figure) as a function of age and sex. (From: MacFarlane, J. W., Allen, L., & Honzik, M. P. (1954). *A developmental study of the behavior problems of normal children between 21 months and 14 years.* Berkeley and Los Angeles: University of California Press.

Second and related children are undergoing rapid changes, and problem behaviors wax and wane at different ages (MacFarlane et al., 1954). The usual pattern is an attenuation of problematic behaviors over the course of childhood and adolescence; for example, consider lying and destructiveness, two behaviors that are often seen in children diagnosed as antisocial. Figure

2.1 conveys differences in the extent to which these are reported as problems as a function of age. As evident in Figure 2.1, lying was reported as a problem in the majority (53 %) of normal boys at age 6. Yet by age 12, this percentage had dropped to only about 10 %. In girls, the pattern is more dramatic with a high rate of lying (approximately 48 %) at age 6 and no lying reported as a problem after age 11. A similar pattern is evident for destructiveness. As evident by these two behaviors, marked changes may occur over time.

The fact that marked changes may occur in problematic child behaviors over the course of devopment has contributed to the difficulty in demarcating the full range of childhood disorders. Many problematic behaviors in childhood may not be appropriate or at least high priorities for treatment because they tend to disappear over the course of development. The course of such behaviors takes the urgency out of identifying treatments. It may be better to "wait and see" if children will grow out of their bothersome behaviors rather than to intervene. Of course, with significant clinical dysfunction (e.g., psychoses, mental retardation), a wait-and-see attitude is obviously less wise. Yet, part of the hesitancy in conducting research is in deciding which child problems will remit over the course of normal development and which ones require intervention. The ambiguity is obviously greater in this regard with children than it is with adults.

In addition, there are methodological implications of the marked changes in problem behavior. These marked changes require a clear understanding of the base rates and course of change of specific behaviors or symptoms at different ages and developmental levels. Without understanding the base rates of behavior and the course of behavior change, improvements that occur as a function of maturation are easily misattributed to intervening treatments that might have been administered. When the base rates of improvements are relatively high, any investigation designed to evaluate treatment must include large samples and extremely strong treatment effects to demonstrate a significant effect over and above a no-treatment control condition (Barrett, Hampe, & Miller, 1978).

Third, because of the changes over the course of development, it is possible that a particular clinical problem may disappear and be replaced by another problem at a different age. This phenomenon, referred to as *developmental symptom substitution* (Levitt, 1971), has not been well-studied, but can be illustrated by everyday experience. For example, young children may tease, threaten, and shove other children when they do not get their way. Years later, these children or young adolescents may show none of the original behaviors, but continue to be aggressive. Aggressive behavior, or fighting, may be manifest in quite different and more age-relevant ways such as fighting and confronting others with a weapon. Administration of the same assessment devices over time to see if persons have responded to treatment, a common practice in treatment evaluation with adults, is slightly more evaluation of treatment difficult. Although a few studies have evaluated progressions of behavior, that is, how behaviors may change or evolve into other behaviors (Edelbrock, 1983; Patterson, 1982), little is actually known. Thus, insufficient data are available to suggest how an assessment battery designed to evaluate treatment at one age might need to change over the course of posttreatment and follow-up assessment to identify related problems that may emerge.

The fact that problem behaviors can vary over the course of development has important implications for implementing and evaluating treatment. Many problems may simply remit over time. Rather than treatment, perhaps patience and education of those concerned with the problem (e.g., parents) are required. For example, many parents are impatient with the child who is not yet toilet trained. Yet, the long-term implications of early or late toilet training, within the period of a couple of years for most children, do not seem to be clinically significant. This is suggested by the fact that most adults do not suffer toileting problems, which indicates that the problem may remit over time. Also, other psychological problems in adulthood do not seem traceable to early or late toilet training. Procedures have been developed to help train children in toileting skills and to make the period of training earlier than it might otherwise be (Azrin & Foxx, 1974). However, the benefits of the treatment may be more for frustrated parents than for their children.[2] For many problems, treatment may perhaps accelerate change, but may be a relatively low priority in terms of clinical research if the long-term consequences do not seem to be clear or adverse. The higher priority obviously is to focus on dysfunctions that do not emerge as part of normal development and/or that do not remit without special treatment.

There are other developmental considerations that have served as obstacles to treatment evaluation. Assumptions about what children can and cannot experience have detracted from the examination of alternative dysfunctions and their treatment. For example, for years it was believed that children could not suffer Major Depressive Disorder analogous to the dysfunction experienced by adults (Mahler, 1961; Rie, 1966). Major Depressive Disorder consists of a constellation of symptoms that include dysphoric mood (sadness), loss of interest or pleasure in usual activities, changes in appetite, weight, or activity (e.g., increases or decreases), sleep difficulties, loss of energy, feelings of worthlessness, slowed thinking or poor concentration, and recurrent thoughts of death. According to orthodox psychoanalytic theory which had dominated thinking on this point,

[2]There are children for whom toileting skills are and remain a significant problem. The development of procedures to develop these skills has been an important breakthrough (Azrin & Foxx, 1971). The point of the present discussion is to note that for children within a "normal" range of functioning, there are many domains of functioning that parents may identify as problematic. The bulk of the problems remit over time and do not have long-term consequences related to adjustment or psychological dysfunction.

depression as a disorder is a phenomenon of the superego. Because the superego is hypothesized to develop in adolescence, the emergence of depressive disorder in childhood was considered to be impossible. This assumption has been put to rest with repeated demonstrations that major depression can be readily diagnosed in children (Cantwell & Carlson, 1983). However, assumptions about the psychological development of children and limits in their capacities had delayed identifying child cases and applying and evaluating treatments.

In general, developmental considerations have served as obstacles to the examination of alternative treatments. Lack of information about the course of dysfunctions and recognition that children may grow out of them have reduced the priority of treatment for many problems of childhood. Also, because of the changes associated with maturation, evaluating change and demonstrating that a treatment effect surpasses the impact of "mother nature" are difficult.

REFERRAL OF CHILDREN FOR TREATMENT

The manner in which clinical problems are identified in children raises obstacles for treatment research. To begin with, children rarely refer themselves for treatment. Other persons such as parents and teachers play a central role in referral, evaluation, and treatment. Children usually do not identify themselves as patients who suffer emotional or behavioral problems. Up to adolescence, youths are likely to see such problems as caused by environmental, social, family, and parental problems (Compas, Friedland-Bandes, Bastien, & Adelman, 1981; Dollinger, Thelen & Walsh, 1980). Late in adolescence, youths are more likely to see problems as a result of internal factors such as their own thoughts and feelings.

From the standpoint of treatment and treatment research, the application of various interventions such as "talking about one's problems" may be more difficult than it would be with adults. Consequently, the value of psychological treatment may not be apparent to children. In addition, maintaining children in therapy and sustaining their motivation may be problematic. Special efforts may be needed such as involving youth actively in treatment decisions which can enhance their motivation for treatment or increase their positive evaluations of treatment (Adelman, Kaser-Boyd, & Taylor, 1984; Kazdin, 1980a).

There may be a broader issue that relates to the retarded development of the child treatment outcome literature. Children are obviously in positions of limited power, and hence do not represent a strong "pressure" group to lobby for their own interests in the way that various adult groups act. In the United States, many governmental agencies, special task forces, and commissions have focused on the mental health needs of children (U.S. Congress, OTA. 1986). However, the commitment of resources to the problems of child mental health and to treatment research might be further along if children as a group were like many adult interest groups and could lobby for their needs.

DIVERSITY OF CLINICAL
PROBLEMS

The types of problems children can bring to treatment vary widely. As with adults, there are many identifiable disorders (e.g., depression and anxiety) in which the child is the primary focus of treatment. But there are other types of problems as well. Children are often seen in treatment when they are the victim, as in cases of physical or sexual abuse. Reactions to events in the home (divorce) may fall into this category. Detection of many child problems is difficult because the child may not seek outside help. Moreover, parents may purposely hide maladaptive practices or not consider them to warrant concern.

Many other problems emerge as part of normal development. They are not inevitable, but they are sufficiently familiar to be canonized such as the "terrible two's" or the "identity crisis" of adolescence. The range of problems, obstacles to their identification, and ambiguity if not confusion about knowing what warrants treatment, have hindered research.

A major issue, mentioned previously, is the fact that clinical problems are rarely identified by the children themselves. Rather, significant others such as parents refer children for treatment. This means that treatment may be administered to the child who feels there is no special problem. Because of the referral process, the extent to which there is a problem with the child's behavior can be questioned.

A parent's referral and evaluation of the child cannot be assumed to mirror the child's functioning. Parent perception of deviance and evaluations of their children on standardized rating scales are significantly related to their own symptoms of psychopathology (especially depression and anxiety), marital discord, expectations for child behavior, parental self-esteem, and reported stress in the home (e.g., Forehand, Lautenschlager, Faust, & Graziano, 1986; Mash & Johnston, 1983). The more severe the depression or anxiety of the mother, or the worse the other characteristics noted here are, the more likely the child is to be seen as deviant. Moreover, parental symptoms and daily experiences such as negative social contacts outside the home can influence their behavior, their reactions to their children, and the severity of deviant behavior in the children (e.g., Forehand et al., 1986; Wahler, 1980). Thus the source of the clinical problem and interpretation of referral information raises special complexities.

FOCUS OF TREATMENT

The focus of treatment for childhood disorders raises novel issues. First, there is the question of the person(s) to whom treatment should be directed. Even though the impetus for treatment may be a specific child problem, this leaves open the best (most effective) place to intervene. Major options to which the interventions can be directed include the child, parents, and/or family. A child focus, of course, would be exemplified by individual psychotherapy. A parent and family focus would be evident in family therapy or parent management training. It is likely that several domains may be targeted for change and incorporated into treatment. In one survey of psychologists and psychiatrists ($N = 110$), 94% reported that most parents are seen concurrently with children as part of the child's treatment (Koocher & Pedulla, 1977). In addition, 21% reported they consulted with teachers on all of their child cases. These figures suggest that professionals frequently see the need to incorporate parents and teachers into treatment of children.

From the standpoint of evaluating treatment, the diversity of persons and settings involved in treatment raises multiple problems. Comparison of a given set of treatments.(e.g., relationship therapy vs. cognitive therapy) is relatively straightforward in a study with adults. Such a comparison raises other design decisions and problems when conducted with children. Decisions need to be made regarding what is to be provided to the parents and teachers (e.g., such as providing parents and teachers with a standard program to hold these features constant). But the research design is a bit "messy" as a result.

A related dimension is whether treatment should be administered by the clinician directly to the child (e.g., individual and group therapy) or to others (parents, teachers, peers) with whom the child interacts (e.g., parent management training, behavioral programs conducted by teachers at school). The issue raises questions of the most effective place to intervene in producing change for a given clinical problem. In addition, if persons other than the clinician directly implement treatment with the child, then issues of training of paraprofessionals (parents, teachers, hospital aides) and monitoring their execution of treatment outside of the usual office visit pose new obstacles.

The options regarding the appropriate focus of treatment raise problems for evaluation. Although evaluation of the child's functioning would seem to be the primary basis for evaluating treatment, this is not necessarily the case. For example, in applications of family therapy, the child is usually viewed as the "identified patient," but not the appropriate focus of treatment or treatment evaluation. How should the efficacy of treatment be evaluated? Assessment of the problem entails communication and interactional patterns of the family. Here the focus of treatment may be on the family and evaluation of outcome may neglect the specific problems for which the child was referred.

GENERAL COMMENTS

The previously discussed issues do not exhaust the range of obstacles that have delayed development and evaluation of treatments for children. Several other influences have been identified. The unavailability of subjects in clinical settings has been noted as an obstacle (Kovacs & Paulauskas, 1986). Certainly for many types of dysfunctions (e.g., gender identity disorder, psychoses), this has been true. The routine appearance of children with many conditions without active recruitment for special projects is too infrequent to stimulate large-scale treatment trials. Yet for other types of dysfunction (e.g., aggressive behavior, hyperactivity), clinic samples are abundant. The absence of standardized criteria for identifying populations has thwarted drawing upon plentiful treatment populations.

Interest in the protection of children's rights and welfare may also have delayed treatment research. Because children do not seek treatment and submit in an informed and knowledgeable way to the interventions, there are reservations in designing and implementing research projects for them. The hesitancy is related as well to the possibility that treatment may produce untoward side effects. Side effects and placement of youths at risk have been concerns in the delays in pharmacological interventions for children. However, psychosocial interventions, as reflected in alternative forms of treatment and prevention, occasionally produce untoward side effects or increase rather than decrease the behavioral problems they were designed to improve (e.g., Fo & O'Donnell, 1975; Hackler & Hagan, 1975; McCord, 1978; O'Donnell, Lydgate, & Fo, 1979). Thus, there may be appropriate caution in intervening without considering the possibly deleterious effects on persons (children) who have not even requested treatment or are fully knowledgeable of its implications. For some small number of cases and clinical problems, it may be better to leave well enough alone. The difficulty is in knowing which cases these are.

Another source of delay in investigating treatments for children has been the difficulty in translating treatments developed for adults into techniques for children. Most forms of psychotherapy have been developed for adult populations. A number of them have been translated for use with children. For example, psychoanalytic and client-centered treatments for adults have been translated in different ways for child populations (Axline, 1947; A. Freud, 1946). The translation of treatments to children is a legitimate enterprise; its ultimate value can only be determined empirically. However, the approach conveys that child treatments are often an afterthought. Beginning with techniques for adults and reshaping these to fit children is not necessarily the best way to proceed. It might be better to begin with theory and research on the nature of specific childhood problems and then to consider the extent to which developmental stages and domains of functioning (e.g., cognitive, affective) may influence the emergence or amelioration of the dysfunction. On the basis of these sources of information, specific techniques might be developed for children.

CONCLUSIONS

Special issues emerge in the evaluation of alternative forms of treatment for children and adolescents. Diagnosis of various disorders in children has been an especially salient issue. Until recently, childhood disorders have been accorded relatively little attention. Recent attention has not only elaborated different types of dysfunction, but assessment techniques to measure these dysfunctions have been developed as well.

Developmental changes have raised a variety of obstacles for treatment evaluation. An initial obstacle stems from the need to consider age-based norms to decide if seemingly dysfunctional adjustment is aberrant and warrants identification and clinical attention. The presence and remission of problematic behaviors over the course of development make the identification of psychopathology complex. Because many problems wax and wane over the course of childhood, it is not clear whether interventions are necessary. Increased research on the course of normal behavior has helped to clarify when interventions may be warranted.

The diversity of children's problems also raises problems for evaluation of alternative treatments. Apart from the usual types of dysfunction (e.g., anxiety, depression, antisocial behavior), many sources of dysfunction emerge as a function of significant others (e.g., in response to abuse, divorce). Identification of many problems is difficult because children do not usually seek treatment. Other problems may be difficult to detect. Here too, advances in assessing areas of dysfunction, particularly those in which the child may be a victim, also have been made in recent years.

Finally, the appropriate focus of treatment for children raises a number of problems. Even within therapy for adults, there are debates about the appropriate focus of the intervention (e.g., on intrapsychic functioning, overt behavior, present events, past experiences). All of these extend to children as well. In addition, debates are more likely for children regarding the relative merits of treating the child, parents, and family. Where the best place(s) to intervene in order to help the child remains unclear for a given problem.

The preceding issues have contributed to delays in the study of alternative therapies for children and adolescents. More than that, they point to areas that need to be considered in the evaluation of specific treatments. Consequently, we will return to these issues again in the context of evaluating treatments and suggesting methodological improvements.

Chapter 3

The Effectiveness of Child Psychotherapy

The number of treatment techniques currently in use and the number of disorders to which they are applied have not been as well documented or traced over time for children as they have been for adults. Although it is difficult to identify precisely the number of techniques currently in use for children and adolescents, a search of key resource material yields a conservative estimate of over 230 alternative psychosocial treatments.[1] Needless to say, the vast majority of these treatments have never been subjected to controlled outcome studies. Yet, there have been evaluations of therapies for children over the course of the last few decades.

The effectiveness of psychotherapy has been examined in different ways. The most frequently used method is a *narrative or qualitative review* of the field where an individual sifts through all or most of the available research and draws conclusions about the effects of treatment. More recently, *quantitative reviews* have emerged as an alternative method of evaluating a body of research. In this method, referred to generally as *meta-analysis*, the effectiveness of treatment is examined by quantifying the effectiveness of treatment using a common metric among different studies. Conclusions about the effects of treatments and about the impact of alternative variables on outcome are integrated across many studies. Both narrative reviews and

[1]The count of alternative treatments for children and adolescents was obtained by examining several different sources (e.g., Bellack & Hersen, 1985; Corsini, 1981; Gumaer, 1984; Herink, 1980; Johnson et al., 1986; Morris & Kratochwill, 1983; Schaefer, 1979; Schaefer et al., 1982, 1984, 1986; Schaefer & Millman, 1977). In each source, a technique was included only if it was specifically applied to or stated to be in use with children or adolescents. Excluded from the count were treatments based on biological/medical interventions (e.g., psychopharmacology) and interventions of any kind with a focus limited to educational, academic, or communication (language, speech) objectives. The final count must be interpreted cautiously because often, very similar treatments were named quite differently by proponents and very different treatments were named quite similarly. The list of treatments extracted from the above literature is provided on pages 41–44.

29

meta-analyses have enjoyed widespread use in the context of adult treatment but much less attention for treatments with children and adolescents. This chapter evaluates the effectiveness of psychotherapy by examining the results of narrative reviews as well as meta-analyses.

HISTORICAL OVERVIEW: A REVIEW OF THE REVIEWS

Narrative Reviews

The evaluation of psychotherapy has been marked by provocative literature reviews, incisive critiques, and balanced appraisals (although there is some disagreement about which one is which). Well-known in the adult psychotherapy literature is the review of Eysenck (1952) which invariably is a starting point in modern evaluations of psychotherapy. Eysenck's review suggested that traditional forms of psychotherapy were no better than "spontaneous remission," that is, improvements that result without receiving formal treatment. The impact of Eysenck's review has been phenomenal in terms of the rebuttals, critiques, rereviews, and other types of works that were stimulated; the effects continue to be evident in contemporary writings (Garfield & Bergin, 1986; Rachman & Wilson, 1980; Smith et al., 1980). The specifics of the review, the treatises that followed, and the impact of the exchanges need not be traced here (Kazdin, 1978a). Suffice it to say that Eysenck's original papers probably accomplished the most that one can hope for in a review, namely, to provoke thought and discussion and to influence the quality of research that follows.   In the child literature, parallel reviews have been completed, although their impact has not been as jarring or productive in stimulating thought or treatment research. The reviews begin with Levitt (1957) who evaluated 18 studies of child psychotherapy. The review focused on youths whose problems could be classified generally as neuroses. Studies that focused on delinquents, mentally retarded persons and psychotic patients were excluded. Levitt's analysis indicated that improvement among children who received psychotherapy was approximately 67 to 78% at posttreatment and follow-up, respectively. Children who did not receive treatment improved at about the same rate (73%). Thus, the general conclusion was that the efficacy of traditional forms of psychotherapy for children had not been demonstrated.

The clarity of the summary statements resulting from the initial review masked a number of problems. To begin with, the "children" encompassed by the studies were quite diverse in age (preschool to 21 years old) and clinical dysfunction. Second, baseline or improvement rates of nontreated youths were derived from two studies and from children who received treatment but who terminated treatment early. Thus, the "control" or comparison groups to which treated children were compared were children who dropped out of treatment. Youths who fail to complete treatment are likely to differ systematically from youths who complete treatment and hence do not provide an adequate picture of the base rate of improvement without treatment. Third, improvement rates were based on evaluation of children by the therapists at the end of treatment. Therapist ratings alone, especially by current methodological standards, certainly are limited as a measure of outcome.

As might be expected, Levitt's review generated a number of rebuttals and re-evaluations of the data (Eisenberg & Gruenberg, 1961; Heinicke & Goldman, 1960; Hood-Williams, 1960). The rebuttals raised cogent points that not only challenged Levitt's conclusions, but also drew attention to methodological issues in designing outcome studies such as the need to consider diagnoses of children and family factors as moderators of treatment, and to use multiple measures to examine treatment outcome. Essentially, the rebuttals conveyed that the original method of analysis, criteria, and research reviewed by Levitt did not permit clear conclusions about the effects of treatment or no treatment.

Levitt's (1963) subsequent review evaluated 22 additional studies and addressed a number of criticisms such as consideration of different diagnoses. The conclusions essentially remained the same. Summing across diagnostic groups, Levitt's analyses showed improvements in treated and untreated youths to be approximately 65% and slightly below the rate of children who did not receive treatment (73%). Rebuttals and re-evaluations of these later reviews continued (Barrett et al., 1978; Heinicke & Strassmann, 1975).

Over the period covered, the need for greater specificity in evaluating treatment became quite apparent. One sign of this was the initial effort to distinguish different diagnostic groups in which the outcomes of treatment and so-called spontaneous remission rates differed. For example, Levitt (1963) noted that improvement rates were greater for neurotic patients relative to those who were delinquent or psychotic. However, the number of dimensions upon which treatment effects are considered to depend and the level of specificity have continued to expand. Currently, analyses of psychotherapy effects suggest that outcomes may depend on many different characteristics of treatments, patients, therapists, and measures (Casey & Berman, 1985; Smith & Glass, 1977; Smith et al., 1980; Weisz, Weiss, Alicke, & Klotz, 1987).

General Comments

The preceding comments do not address the reviews or rebuttals in depth. In so doing, there is no intention to slight the prominent place the reviews occupy historically nor the significance of the issues they raise. Indeed, we will return to many of the methodological issues in greater detail later (chapter 5). However, from the standpoint of providing a verdict on alternative forms of treatment, reviews of early research in the field have been wanting. Major issues were repeatedly raised in these reviews noting the paucity of studies, methodological shortcomings, and neglect of the range of variables that are likely to influence treatment outcome (e.g., child age, clinical problem). Thus, even within the criteria to evaluate research invoked at the time, difficulties were identified that precluded clear verdicts on treatment. Perhaps of even greater importance, in the ensuing years, the criteria for evaluating treatment outcome in individual patients and for conducting outcome research more generally have changed. Early reviews did not focus on the level of specificity now considered essential, namely, evaluating different treatments as applied to different types of problems and across different measures, and at different points in time.

CONTEMPORARY EVALUATIONS

Given the changing standards for conducting and evaluating outcome research, the value of reworking previous reviews and the majority of their constituent studies is questionable. Other literature reviews have emerged that focus on a wide range of treatments (e.g., Kadushin, 1974; Robins, 1973; Rutter, 1982; Tramontana, 1980). Firm conclusions are difficult to draw from these reviews in large part due to the limited outcome evidence. However, the nature of the task, namely, to review the literature across a large number of treatments and clinical problems, has created obstacles for identifying the status of current research. Progress has been made in the range of outcome studies now available and the different types of reviews that sift through their findings. Two sorts of literature can be cited to reflect current evaluations, namely, meta-analyses of treatment and narrowly focused reviews of selected approaches.

Meta-analysis

A major development in the last decade is the emergence of meta-analysis as a means of evaluating the literature. The method is an alternative to traditional narrative and qualitative evaluation (i.e., a review of the literature) where an author synthesizes multiple studies and derives conclusions about alternative techniques and the variables of which their effectiveness is a function. A striking feature of qualitative reviews has been the varied conclusions that are drawn about the same literature (Smith et al., 1980). Indeed, the controversy surrounding the effects of child psychotherapy reflect some of the pitfalls of the narrative method of reviewing. Part of the problem is the absence of established rules for evaluating, combining, and weighing alternative studies based on their merit or strength of effects or for drawing conclusions about the effects of a given treatment when the data from different studies are not in agreement.

Meta-analysis refers to a set of quantitative procedures that can be used to evaluate multiple studies. The essential feature is to provide an "analysis of analyses" (Smith et al., 1980, p. 809). Information within a given study (i.e., the results) are quantified in such a way as to permit the combination and comparison of results from different studies. Quantification of the results of a study permits a more reliable and consistent way of extracting the findings and integrating different studies than the usual narrative review permits. In addition, meta-analysis is designed to improve upon the information that can be culled from a body of research in terms of the range of information that is obtained and the range of questions that can be addressed (Kazdin, 1986b).

The most common way of evaluating the literature through meta-analysis is to compute *effect size* which provides a common metric across a variety of investigations. Effect size is calculated as the difference between means of an experimental (treatment) and control (no-treatment) group, divided by the standard deviation of the control group (or of the pooled sample of both groups). Effect size constitutes the dependent measure for the meta-analysis and is used as a summary statistic to examine the impact of other variables. Characteristics of the investigations (e.g., age of the subjects, the different types of treatment, duration of treatment) become the independent variables. The effect of a large number of variables (treatment technique, therapist and patient characteristics) can be studied, because investigations can be combined for the meta-analysis (Glass, McGaw, & Smith, 1981).

There have been numerous meta-analyses of the adult psychotherapy literature (see Brown, 1987), beginning with the seminal work of Smith and Glass (1977; Smith et al., 1980). In the 1980 study, the more comprehensive of the two, 475 controlled treatment outcome studies were evaluated. An effect size was calculated separately for each dependent measure in each study, yielding a total of 1760 different effect sizes. From the studies by Smith and Glass, several conclusions were drawn. Two of the more general conclusions were that alternative psychotherapies produce greater therapeutic change than no-treatment control conditions and that different treatments, based on alternative models or approaches (e.g., psychodynamic, behavioral), tend to be equally effective.[2] The conclusions

[2]Since the original studies by Smith and Glass, several replications have been completed using portions of the original set of studies alone or supplemented with additional research (e.g., Andrews & Harvey, 1981; Landman & Dawes, 1982; Prioleau, Murdock, & Brody, 1983; Shapiro & Shapiro, 1982; Steinbrueck, Maxwell, & Howard, 1983). These analyses have addressed a variety of questions about psychotherapy including the effects of treatment relative to no-treatment and placebo-control conditions, the impact of alternative treatments, and others. Other meta-analyses have appeared that focus more narrowly on specific types of techniques, patient populations, or clinical disorders (e.g., Davidson, Gottschalk, Gensheimer, & Mayer, in press; Dush, Hirt, & Schroeder, 1983; Miller & Berman, 1983; Straw, 1983).

Table 3.1
Characteristics of Reviewed Studies

Characteristics	Mean[a]	Range
No. of subjects at posttreatment	42.0	7–184
Percentage male subjects	60.0	0–100
Subject age	8.9	3–15
Grade level	3.7	0–6
Weeks of therapy	9.5	1–37

From: Casey, R. J., & Berman, J. S. (1985). The outcome of psychotherapy with children. *Psychological Bulletin, 98,* 388–400.
[a]Each mean is based on at least 45 studies.

do not sound revolutionary or particularly strong. Indeed, many had believed that psychotherapy was effective and that specific approaches did not yield starkly different results. The strength of the evaluation came not from the conclusions but by a method that seemed heir to less bias than the usual narrative review.

Few meta-analyses of child therapies have been reported. The original work of Smith and Glass included studies with children but separate effects of child vs. adult psychotherapy were not evaluated. In fact, from the list of studies upon which the meta-analysis was based, approximately 90 focused on children or adolescents. Interestingly, almost half of these studies were unpublished dissertations or theses. Hence, a significant portion of this relatively small literature is not easily available for review.

Casey and Berman (1985) completed a meta-analysis of the child psychotherapy literature. The review included 75 studies published between 1952 and 1983 in which some form of psychotherapy with children was compared with a control group or another treatment. Studies were included with children (ages 3-15) across a wide range of clinical problems. Selected treatment techniques were excluded (drug therapy, peer counseling, family therapy). Yet a wide range of traditional therapies (e.g., psychodynamic, client-centered), and behavioral therapies (e.g., behavior therapy, cognitive-behavioral treatments) were included.

Apart from evaluating the efficacy of treatment, the descriptive characteristics of the research are important to highlight in their own right. Table 3.1 includes characteristics of the studies. As the table shows, a broad range of characteristics were evident (e.g., the number of weeks of treatment ranged from 1–37). Based on "means" provided in the table, the typical treatment outcome study was conducted with slightly over 40 youths, most of whom were boys near the age of 9 and probably slightly behind in their grade level and who received 9 to 10 weeks of therapy.

There are a number of characteristics not included in the table that convey the type of outcome research that is conducted. The majority of child studies

(57%) included as their clients school children who did not seek treatment. Clinical samples from outpatient or inpatient facilities were used in a small percentage of studies (16% and 8%, respectively). Although clinical problems were not always described in sufficient detail in the original studies, the largest segment of dysfunction encompassed by the research was aggressive and withdrawn behavior (in 40% of the studies), followed by hyperactive or impulsive behavior (13%) and phobias (12%).[3] Finally, some form of behavior therapy (e.g., desensitization, modeling) was included in most of the studies (56%). Client-centered therapy and psychodynamic therapy were included in a small percentage of the studies (29% and 9%, respectively).

The preceding information is of interest because the characteristics of child psychotherapy studies are not generally known. However, the major purpose of conducting the meta-analysis and referring to it here pertains to the conclusions that can be reached about the efficacy of treatment. Summing across different therapies to reach general conclusions, Casey and Berman (1985) reported that there was a significant effect size due to treatment when compared to control conditions.

More specifically, an effect size of .71 was obtained across all techniques. This number is based on standard deviation units and means that the average outcome of child psychotherapy was slightly more than 2/3 of a standard deviation better than that of untreated control children. An overall effect size of this magnitude, as Casey and Berman (1985) noted, is comparable to the effects obtained in meta-analyses of psychotherapy with adults (Shapiro & Shapiro, 1982).

To translate effect size into more clinically meaningful terms, consider the differences in means that the effect represents and the impact of treatment on the average client. Based on the results of the Casey and Berman meta-analysis, two hypothetical distributions of scores might be drawn to reflect performance of children who do not receive treatment (controls) and those who do. The distributions reflect hypothetical scores on some measure of treatment outcome (e.g., parent ratings, clinical evaluations). Assume for the moment that a bell-shaped (normal) curve reflects the performance of children on the measures at posttreatment assessment within the individual groups. The bell-shaped curve not only provides a reasonable assumption about the likely distribution of scores but also facilitates evaluation of the impact of treatment on the average child.

Figure 3.1 shows the type two hypothetical distributions and that the mean difference in outcome is separated by .71 standard deviation units (i.e., mean

[3]Aggressive and withdrawn behavior was a single category for the analysis. Separation of the behaviors in this category would be desirable because aggression and withdrawal are usually regarded as fundamentally different types of problems such as undercontrolled (externalizing, or outward directed) versus overcontrolled (internalizing or inward directed) dysfunctions.

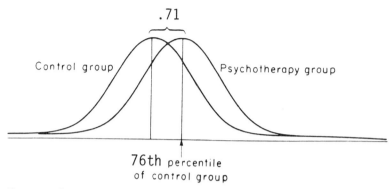

Figure 3.1. Representation of the effect of psychotherapy across outcome measures based on meta-analysis completed by Casey and Berman (1985).

effect size). This difference or degree of separation in standard deviation units can be converted into differences in percentages of children at a given point or level of improvement on the measure. One can compare how persons in the treatment group are likely to fare relative to persons in the no-treatment group. Given the effect size, the average child who is treated is better off at the end of therapy than 76% of the persons who did not receive treatment. Therapy is clearly effective on the average in improving children.

The effect sizes could be delineated for separate treatment techniques. Table 3.2 presents the mean effect sizes for the alternative treatments and the number of studies upon which this information is based. Behavioral therapies led to greater effect sizes than nonbehavioral therapies. However, the differences appeared to be associated with the use of different types of outcome measures and clinical problems in studies of behavioral and nonbehavioral techniques. When these latter effects were controlled, the superiority of behavioral techniques was no longer significantly different from nonbehavioral techniques.

A major advantage of meta-analysis is that it permits evaluation of a number of variables aside from treatment technique that might relate to outcome. Casey and Berman (1985) found that alternative techniques (e.g., play vs. nonplay therapy; individual vs. group therapy; child vs. parent focused treatment) and characteristics of the therapist (e.g., experience, education, sex) did not influence the effects of treatment (effect sizes). Characteristics of the children did make a difference in effect size. In general, treatments were less effective with problems of social adjustment (aggressive or withdrawn behavior) than for other problems (hyperactivity, phobias, somatic complaints). Also, studies with a greater proportion of boys yielded smaller effect sizes.

A more recent meta-analysis (Weisz et al., 1987), included a larger number of studies than those included in the Casey and Berman (1985) evaluation.

Table 3.2
Effects of Psychotherapy With Children

Treatment	Number of Studies	Effect Size	
		Mean	SD
All therapies	64	0.71[a]	0.73
Behavioral therapies	37	0.91[a]	0.77
Behavioral	26	0.96[a]	0.79
Cognitive behavioral	14	0.81[a]	0.84
Nonbehavioral therapies	29	0.40[a]	0.37
Client centered	20	0.49[a]	0.65
Dynamic	5	0.21	0.22

From: Casey, R. J., & Berman, J. S. (1985). The outcome of psychotherapy with children. *Psychological Bulletin, 98,* 388–400.
*The number of studies does not sum to 64 because some studies examined more than one form of therapy. In the table, SD refers to standard deviation.
[a]The mean effect size differs reliably from zero ($p < .05$).

Specifically, 108 controlled studies were chosen which encompassed youths from ages 4–18. The analysis was not redundant because only 32 (29.6%) of the studies were the same as those examined by Casey and Berman. Also, a slightly different age range was included than by Casey and Berman (ages 4–18 vs 3–15). The results were quite similar in many ways. Weisz et al. found that the mean effect size across different treatments, clinical problems, and patient samples was .79. Effect sizes tended to be greater for behavioral than for nonbehavioral techniques, and for children (ages 4–12) than adolescents (ages 13–18), but no different for boys than for girls.

From both the preceding meta-analyses, the main general conclusions are important to note. First, psychotherapy appears to be better than no treatment. Second, the magnitude of these effects closely parallels those obtained with adults. Third, treatment differences, when evident, tend to favor behavioral rather than nonbehavioral techniques. However, there are difficulties in reaching this latter conclusion because of the paucity of studies of nonbehavioral techniques and because of the finding that specific kinds of problems and outcome measures often are associated with these different techniques.

Limitations of the Analyses

The use of meta-analysis within the adult psychotherapy literature has been a major source of controversy (see Garfield, 1983; Michelson, 1985; Prioleau et al., 1983). One point of contention is the hazards of combining studies differing greatly in methodology. Another concern is the few studies available for some of the variables (treatment comparisons) of interest. The child psychotherapy literature may be particularly heir to this latter criticism because of the paucity of studies and the very weak base to draw conclusions about specific techniques or clinical measures. For example, in the Casey and Berman (1985) review, 75 studies were included but a number of conclusions were based on markedly fewer studies (see Table 3.2).

Meta-analyses yield general conclusions which can be reached only by combining studies. The combination or groupings of studies can be questioned. For example, it is very useful at some level to discuss "behavioral therapies." However, the constituent techniques (e.g., modeling, systematic desensitization, operant conditioning) are conceptually and procedurally quite different and are applied often to quite different problems. A general conclusion about behavior therapy really has little meaning.

Similarly, the preceding meta-analysis summed across outcome measures within a given study to obtain a single effect size for that study. A summarization here also is of unclear value because the efficacy of different treatments may vary across different measures. Moreover, the conclusions regarding improvements on different measures may vary with the point in time that behavior is assessed (e.g., Heinicke & Ramsey-Klee, 1986; Kolvin et al., 1981; Rachman & Wilson, 1980).

Nevertheless, the current meta-analyses (Casey & Berman, 1985; Weisz et al., 1987) improve in many ways upon early reviews of the literature on the effects of psychotherapy. The ground rules for inclusion or exclusion of studies in a meta-analysis, including how the different studies are evaluated and weighted, are made explicit. In fact, meta-analyses of psychotherapy have been amenable to criticism in part because assumptions underlying the evaluation of the research are usually quite explicit.

Focused Narrative Reviews

A problem with early reviews in the field, and even with more contemporary reviews and meta-analyses, is their attempt to reach summary conclusions across a large number of treatment techniques. The question such reviews address follows in the tradition of the global question, "Does psychotherapy work?" The question is analogous to the obviously more ridiculous one of "Does the practice of medicine or surgery work?" No doubt these latter treatments, as the case with psychotherapy, depend on a number of conditions including the specific version of treatment as applied to particular problems and patients, as evaluated with respect to specific outcome measures, and so on. Reviews that address the question of whether psychotherapy works include studies of a number of different techniques.

In recognition of the greater need for specificity, several focused literature reviews have concentrated on individual *treatment techniques* or "families" of conceptually or procedurally related procedures. Thus, there are now separate reviews of individual, group, family, behavior, and traditional psychotherapies (e.g., Abramowitz, 1976; DeWitt, 1980; Hobbs & Lahey, 1983; Kovacs & Paulauskas, 1986; Meador & Ollendick, 1984; Tuma & Sobotka, 1983). Reviews that are limited to specific techniques can identify potentially unique substantive and methodological issues that emerge. Even so, the individual categories (e.g., verbal psychotherapy or family therapy) are often broad and the constituent techniques might be applied widely across clinical problem areas.

Clinically, the major concern is not what the effects are of a particular treatment across a host of problem areas, but rather what the options are and what "works" for a specific clinical problem. In recognition of this priority, other reviews have focused on specific *clinical problems* and have examined alternative techniques for that problem. Thus, separate reviews of the effects of treatment for specific problems such as hyperactivity, anxiety and phobias, depression, oppositional behavior, and conduct disorder are available (e.g., Gard & Berry, 1986; Kazdin, 1985; Reynolds, 1985). The focus on problem areas is valuable in examining the extent to which any form of treatment has been shown to produce change.

Finally, a number of sources are available that evaluate several specific *techniques by individual areas of child dysfunctions* (Bornstein & Kazdin, 1985; Morris & Kratochwill, 1983).[4] In these sources, the complexity of reviewing the evidence is conveyed because multiple techniques have been applied to individual problem areas. The efficacy of each treatment is examined in relation to these problem areas.

The more focused reviews, by individual treatment techniques, clinical dysfunctions, or techniques by dysfunction, represent a desirable move toward greater specificity in examining the evidence. Yet, there is an obvious inherent limitation in seeking this specificity. With a small number of controlled outcome studies to begin with, finer subdivisions do not necessarily yield any more informative conclusions.

The hazards of making finer distinctions in a sparse outcome literature can be illustrated by examining the current status of family therapies. Several reviews have evaluated family therapies, an approach involving a variety of separate techniques (e.g., DeWitt, 1978, 1980; Gurman & Kniskern, 1981; Gurman, Kniskern, & Pinsof, 1986; Masten, 1979; Wells & Dezen, 1978; Wells, Dilkes, & Burckhardt, 1976). Of relevance here are those instances in which the child is the "identified patient," that is, has served as the initial impetus for treatment referral. Reviewers have invoked slightly different

---

[4]There are many other sources that review treatment techniques by individual problem areas (e.g., Harrison, 1979; Schaefer et al., 1982, 1984, 1986; Schaefer & Millman, 1977). They are not referred to here because they do not systematically review or evaluate the outcome evidence.

criteria in their selection of studies based on their definitions of family therapy and "well controlled research," but the conclusions have been similar.

For example, DeWitt (1978, 1980) included in her comprehensive review 31 outcome studies of family therapy; 23 of which did not utilize comparison groups to which family therapy could be contrasted. Of the eight remaining studies, five included a no-treatment or minimal treatment group. Only one of these studies included a condition (attention placebo) that would permit attribution of treatment effects to a family therapy focus. The conclusion of this review was that family therapy appeared to be more effective than no treatment. However, beyond this, little could be said about the effectiveness of family therapy relative to other treatments, the specific child problems for which family therapy is well suited, or the therapist, patient, and treatment factors that may contribute to change. Needless to say, from this one study, it could not be inferred whether some family therapy techniques were more effective for particular problems than another family therapy technique.

In another review, Masten (1979) included 14 studies where the child was the identified patient. She reported only two studies that were well-controlled; one of these ($n = 4$) did not permit analysis of treatment effects. The conclusions were appropriately guarded, namely, that there were few well-controlled studies and inferences about treatment effects are premature. These conclusions echoed those of several prior reviews. In a more recent review, several controlled studies of family therapy were identified, but were restricted largely to parent management training and functional family therapy (Gurman et al., 1986). The two forms of treatment (examined in greater detail in chapter 4) are very special versions of family therapy and out of the mainstream of usual family therapy practice. Beyond these techniques, the authors more generally concluded that ". . . little can be gleaned from this aggregate body of research that carries either significant theoretical meaning or clinical implications" (p. 576).

The case of family therapy is informative but not novel. The task of identifying a set of controlled studies is difficult, ignoring for the moment a critical point that there are quite different variations of a given type of treatment (e.g., several different family therapies) and they should not be grouped together to evaluate their impact in relation to specific clinical problems. Scrutinizing the literature in highly focused reviews is a valuable direction, but the outcome studies are in too short of supply to support the task. As the number of reviews of this literature approach or surpass the number of controlled outcome studies, it is clear that drastic improvements are needed. In the case of the family therapy outcome literature, the reviews have still made important contributions. Apart from pointing repeatedly to the empirical void, reviewers have frequently mapped the course towards improved research (Dewitt, 1980; Wells & Dezen, 1978).

CONCLUSIONS

Reviews of the child therapy literature are plentiful. The reviews to date support a number of general conclusions. Based on reviews of mulitple techniques (Casey & Berman, 1985; Tramontana, 1980; Weisz et al., 1987), evidence suggests that psychotherapy is better than no treatment for various childhood problems (e.g., anxiety, hyperactivity, social withdrawal and aggression). However, the statement requires considerable qualification. Too few controlled studies are available and the claims about the efficacy of a particular technique for a particular clinical problem are commensurately weak.

Part of the problem of reaching conclusions may derive from the task and method of reviewing the literature, whether they are narrative (qualitative) reviews or meta-analyses. Each type of review has liabilities and can gloss over gains that have been made in the evaluation of treatment. There are other levels of analysis of the child therapy literature and these are illustrated in the next chapter.

Appendix 3-A
List of Psychosocial Treatments for Children and Adolescents[a]

Activity-interview group therapy
Activity group therapy
Adlerian group counseling
Adlerian group psychotherapy
Adlerian psychotherapy
Anger control training
Anxiety management training
Art therapy
Assertiveness training
Attitude therapy
Autogenic feedback
Automated hypnosis
Aversion therapy
Aversive conditioning
Awareness training
"Bark" technique
Behavioral engineering
Behavioral family therapy
Behavioral group counseling
Behavioral rehearsal
Behavioral social skills training
Behavioral weight control
Bell and pad conditioning
Bereavement counseling

Bibliotherapy
Biofeedback
Brief focal family therapy
Brief parent therapy
Brief psychotherapy
Broad-spectrum behavior therapy
Catalyst therapy
Chemical aversion
Client-centered play therapy
Client-centered therapy
Co-therapy
Cognitive coping techniques
Cognitive restructuring
Cognitive therapy
Color-your-life technique
Communication therapy
Community based treatment
Companionship therapy
Comprehensive family therapy
Conditioned avoidance
Conflict resolution therapy
Confrontation reality therapy
Conjoint family therapy
Conjoint group therapy

Contact desensitization
Contingency contracting
Contingency management
Contingent aromatic ammonia
Correspondence therapy
Costume play therapy
Counterconditioning
Covert extinction
Covert modeling
Covert punishment
Covert reinforcement
Covert response cost
Covert sensitization
Creative aggression
Crisis intervention
Crisis therapy (crisis-oriented
  family therapy)
Cue-controlled relaxation
Cuento therapy
Dance therapy
Day treatment
Developmental play
Developmental therapy
Differential reinforcement of low
  rate behavior
Differential reinforcement of other
  behavior
Direct decision therapy
Direct family therapy
Directed day dreaming
Directive therapy
Drama therapy
Dry-bed training
Dynamic cognitive therapy
Dynamic here-and-now focused
  psychotherapy
Emotive imagery
Encounter therapy
Encouragement therapy
Eriksonian therapy
Exaggeration therapy
Experiential treatment
Exposure

Extinction
Facial screening
Fair play therapy
Family council
Family crises therapy
Family play therapy
Family problem solving
Feedback (video, verbal)
Filial therapy
Flooding
Focused time-limited psychotherapy
Functional family therapy
Goal-directed therapy
Good behavior game
Group anger control training
Group art therapy
Group contingencies
Group skills training
Group therapy
Guided affective imagery
Guided fantasy
Guided group interaction
Habit reversal
Home-based reinforcement
Horticultural therapy
Hypnosis
Imagotherapy
Impasse/priority therapy
Implosive therapy
In vivo desensitization
Interpersonal problem solving skills
  training
Interpersonal process recall
Kinetic psychotherapy
Kleinian technique of therapy
Lemon juice treatment
Life skills counseling
Logotherapy
Marathon therapy
Massed practice
Meditation
Milieu therapy
Morita therapy

Modeling
Multimedia treatment
Multimodal therapy
Multiple conjoint family therapy
Multiple impact therapy
Multiple-family therapy
Music therapy
Mutual story telling
Naikan psychotherapy
Negative reinforcement
New identity process therapy
Nurture groups
Office network therapy
Overcorrection
Paradigmatic psychotherapy
Paradoxical intention
Paraverbal therapy
Parent counseling
Parent counseling-teacher
  consultation
Parent management training
Participant modeling
Past lives therapy
Personal construct therapy
Permission-limited information-
  specific suggestions-intensive
  therapy
Pet psychotherapy
Physical punishment
Play group therapy
Play therapy
Poetry therapy
Positive practice
Positive reinforcement
Primary relationship therapy
Provocative therapy
Psychoanalytic play therapy
Psychoanalytic therapy
Psychoanalytically oriented milieu
  therapy
Psychoanalytically oriented therapy
Psychodrama
Psychodynamically oriented
  therapy

Psychomotor therapy
Puppet therapy
Radical therapy
Rational-emotive therapy
Reality therapy
Reattachment therapy
Reinforcement of incompatible
  behavior
Relationship enhancement
  therapy
Relationship therapy
Relaxation therapy
Release therapy
Required relaxation
Residential treatment
Response cost
Response deprivation
Response prevention
Response satiation
Responsibility-reinforcement
  treatment
Restricted environmental
  stimulation therapy
Retention control training
Role taking training
Roleplaying therapy
School-based psychotherapy
Self-control training
Self-correction
Self-evaluation
Self-hypnosis
Self-instruction training
Self-monitoring
Self-punishment
Self-puzzle
Self-reinforcement
Semantic play therapy
Sensitivity training
Shadow therapy
Shaping
Shock therapy
Short-term family therapy
Social reinforcement

Social system psychotherapy

Social work groups

Sports groups

Squiggle technique

Staggered wakening technique

Stimulus control

Stimulus satiation

Strategic therapy

Stress inoculation

Structural family therapy

Structural learning

Suggesting therapy

Supportive psychotherapy

Systematic desensitization

Talking-feeling and doing game

Task-oriented group therapy

Theme-centered interactional
  groups

Therapeutic community

Theraplay

Time out from reinforcement

Token reinforcement

Transactional analysis

Twenty-four hour therapy

Wholistic family therapy

World technique

Yoga

Zaraleya psychoenergetic technique

Z-process therapy

[a]The techniques were culled from several sources (e.g., Bellack & Hersen, 1985; Corsini, 1981; Gumaer, 1984; Herink, 1980; Johnson et al., 1986; Morris & Kratochwill, 1983; Schaefer, 1979; Schaefer et al., 1982, 1984, 1986; Schaefer & Millman, 1977). To be included, the procedures or illustrations were required to note that the technique was applied to children and/or adolescents. As noted previously (footnote 1), ambiguities emerged in constructing this list in part because similar and overlapping treatments were occasionally given different names and different treatments often shared similar names. Several decision rules were adopted. Synonyms for a given technique were occasionally identifiable. When these seemed clear (e.g., assertion training and assertiveness training), only one term was used for the list. In some cases, one or more techniques (e.g., covert modeling, participant modeling) appeared to be subtypes of a broader category (e.g., modeling). Separate entries were included if a distinction could be made in the procedures that were described. Because of the difficulties in distinguishing various techniques and the absence of data on interjudge agreement on the decisions, the specific count and entries must be viewed cautiously.

Chapter 4

Promising Approaches to Treatment

There are problems with reviews of the child therapy literature, particularly when a single approach or treatment technique serves as the focus. Reviews attempt to integrate the evidence which consists of studies varying widely in methodological quality. Few studies include appropriate controls, careful and well-specified selection of homogeneous subjects, and broad-based outcome assessment. With the sparse high-quality studies from which to draw, it is difficult to reach firm conclusions. Analyses of diverse techniques in narrative reviews of meta-analyses, even if focused on individual treatments, fail to capture some of the excellent progress that has been achieved.

Beyond the reviews, outcome research can be examined at two molecular levels, namely, exemplary individual studies and programs of treatment outcome research. A great deal can be learned from illustrations of research at these levels. Indeed, substantive conclusions not easily reached from qualitative or quantitative reviews can be made from these more molecular levels of analysis. This chapter identifies individual studies and programs of research to illustrate current progress and to raise issues for broader consideration.

INDIVIDUAL STUDIES

The individual studies highlighted here were not selected haphazardly. After all, the population of studies that meet reasonable methodological desiderata of current research (e.g., control conditions, follow-up assessment) is rather restricted. Two studies were selected for presentation because they are large-scale investigations that included a number of important methodological features not frequently seen in research on child treatments and because they encompass diverse treatment approaches and child problems. The publication of each study in book form facilitated

45

evaluation of both substantive and methodological features. The present studies set important standards, yield significant conclusions, and convey difficulties in carrying out high quality outcome research.

School-based Treatments of Neurotic and Antisocial Behavior

Description. Kolvin et al. (1981) conducted an ambitious outcome study in England between 1972 and 1979 to evaluate different interventions for maladjusted children in the schools. The objective was to examine the impact of different treatments, on different types of clinical problems, with children at different stages of development and dysfunction. Thus, the study began with the more elaborate (or "ultimate") question that is often considered to be important as a guide to treatment research, that is what techniques work, for whom, under what conditions, and so on.

Two different types of child dysfunction were investigated, namely, *neurotic* and *conduct disorder*. Neurotic disorder was defined broadly to include internalizing types of dysfunction (e.g., neuroses, depression, anxiety); conduct disorder was defined to include externalizing types of dysfunction (e.g., disruptive behavior, bullying, delinquency). Because of the potential significance of developmental stage on the nature of child dysfunction and response to treatment, two different age levels were selected. Children ages 7–8 and 11–12 were included and referred to, respectively, as juniors and seniors. Screening of 4300 children was undertaken to identify the final group (slightly less than 600) of children included in the study. Screening criteria were invoked to identify children who showed maladjustment problems at school and were at risk for psychiatric impairment (juniors), or who already evinced psychiatric disturbance (seniors). Multiple measures involving parent, teacher, peer, and clinician evaluations were used to conduct screening and to evaluate treatment outcome. Major characteristics of the study are highlighted in Table 4.1.

Once identified, children were assigned randomly to one of four conditions. The conditions varied slightly for younger and older children (see Table 4.1); but for each group there was a no-treatment control group that provided the basis for comparison over the course of treatment and follow-up. *Parent-counseling plus teacher-consultation* consisted of social work consultation with parents and teachers in an effort to coordinate school and home activities, casework with the family, and support for the teacher. *Nurture work* consisted of providing enrichment activities for the children, close interaction with the child, and behavioral shaping for individual child goals. *Group therapy* was based on client-centered principles and practices and consisted of play group therapy (for younger children) or discussion (more traditional) group therapy for older children. In each case, the focus

Table 4.1
Selected Characteristics of the Outcome Study Conducted by Kolvin et al. (1981)

Domain	Major Characteristics
Sample	Ages 7–8 (juniors) or 11–12 (seniors)
Sample Size	60–90 youths per group ($N = 574$)
Screening	Multi-stage screening to identify dysfunctional youths
Setting	Regular public schools
Treatments (Juniors)	Parent counseling/Teacher consultation
	Nurture work
	Group (play) therapy
	No-Treatment
Treatments (Seniors)	Parent counseling/Teacher consultation
	Group (nondirective, discussion) therapy
	Behavior modification
	No-Treatment
Treatment Sessions	Number and duration varied for each treatment.
Source of Data	Parent, teacher, peer, self, and clinician ratings
Assessment Domain	Adjustment, psychopathology, cognitive, and social functioning
Major Outcome Measures	Rutter Teacher and Parent Scales, parent interview to assess neurotic, antisocial, and psychosomatic behavior, Junior Eysenck Personality Inventory, Devereax Elementary School Behavior Rating Scale, measures of vocabulary, intelligence, and reading ability, sociometric data
Assessment Periods	Pretreatment, posttreatment, follow-up (18 months after treatment ended)
Training of Therapists	Special programs for trainers involving formal and informal instruction and supervision, varying as needed by condition.

was on the expression of feelings, acceptance of the child, warmth, and the therapeutic relationship. The *behavior modification* program (for seniors only) consisted of classroom reinforcement systems relying on social and token reinforcement to improve deportment and classroom performance.

The treatments involved different models of care delivery and different personnel (e.g., social workers, teachers, teacher aides). The treatments were carefully developed, structured, and implemented. Training of staff provided formal and informal supervision and discussion, and reading background information on the principles and practices underlying treatment.

The effects of treatment are not easily summarized given the large number of outcome measures and different sources of information. In general, for the younger children, play group therapy and nurture work led to significantly greater changes than no-treatment controls and the parent–teacher condition. These effects were evident primarily for neurotic rather than conduct problem behavior. For the older children, group therapy and behavior modification led to greater changes than controls and the parent–teacher condition.

Among the different treatments, children with neurotic disorders, as defined earlier, responded better than children with conduct disorders. Also, girls responded better to treatments than did boys. There were no consistent interactions between the type of treatment and type of child disorder nor between treatment and child sex. However, neurotic behavior appeared to be more amenable to change in boys than girls, whereas conduct problems appeared to be more amenable to change in girls than boys.

The treatments sampled different dimensions of interest in contemporary work. One dimension is the extent to which treatment is *direct vs. indirect.* Direct treatments consists of face-to-face interaction with the child (e.g., group therapy), whereas indirect treatment consists of working with significant others (e.g., parents and teachers) who treat the child (e.g., parent–teacher consultation). Another dimension is whether treatment focuses on *intrapsychic process vs. overt behavior* (e.g., group therapy vs. behavior modification, respectively). Finally, treatments varied markedly in duration and intensity with a *brief vs. more extended treatment* (e.g., 10 sessions of group therapy versus 20 weeks of daily behavioral treatment).

In the present project, each of these dimensions was not fully represented or extensively sampled. Nevertheless, at the end of the project tentative conclusions could be drawn. Indirect treatment (parent–teacher consultation) did not appear to produce major changes; more direct treatments including group therapy and behavioral approaches produced the most significant changes. Treatment focus, whether intrapsychic or behavioral, did not seem to be the crucial determinant given the impact of both group therapy and behavioral approaches. Duration of treatment did not seem to be an issue, because relatively shorter and longer treatments (e.g., group therapy and behavior modification) led to greater change. Again, each of the dimensions of possible interest was not carefully sampled, so the conclusions of the study can be applied only to the specific condition.

Overall Evaluation. There are a number of excellent features of this study. The use of multiple measures for screening, a comparison of separate treatments with a randomly comprised no-treatment control group, assessment of multiple domains of functioning (maladjustment, cognitive functioning, social relations with peers), the evaluation of follow-up, and other features make this study truly outstanding. Also, in both adult and child therapy literatures, studies rarely include a sufficient number of subjects to provide a sensitive (i.e., statistically powerful) test of treatments (see Kazdin, 1986a). The sample size (60–90) in each group is almost without peer.

Few studies have attempted to examine the effects of different treatments on alternative problems and with children of different ages. Kolvin et al. (1981) addressed treatment at the level of complexity that avoids highly diluted and diffuse conclusions. The focus on different ages within a single study may serve as an excellent basis for drawing conclusions about treatment. Qualitative or quantitative literature reviews that attempt to piece together conclusions with inadequately designed studies as a data base are unlikely to do as well.

Community-based Treatment for Antisocial Youths

Description. Feldman, Caplinger, and Wodarski (1983) conducted a community-based treatment project for antisocial youths. Community-based treatment, unlike treatment derived from traditional mental health models, attempts to take advantage of the resources in the everyday environment that can support prosocial behavior. Integration of treatment in existing community programs increases the likelihood that prosocial behavior will extend from treatment to community settings. It is likely that carry-over problems will arise if the youths are removed from the community (e.g., being placed in a psychiatric hospital or juvenile correctional facility) for their treatment.

Another characteristic of community-based treatment is an effort to expose problem youths to their prosocial peers. If positive peer group influences are to be fostered in treatment, it is critical that the peers not be restricted to other deviant youths. Segregation of deviant youths in residential settings in particular provides them with models for further deviant behavior.

Feldman et al. (1983) conducted a large-scale community-based program that was integrated with activities of the Jewish Community Centers Association in St. Louis, Missouri. The St. Louis Experiment, as it was called, included youths (ages 8–17) who were referred for antisocial behavior (referred youths), or who normally attended the regular activities programs and were not identified as showing problem behavior (nonreferred youths). The project began with approximately 700 youths; this number declined to approximately 450 by the end of treatment.

The design of the study was complex because of the interest in evaluating the separate and combined effects of different influences on outcome (see Table 4.2). The study evaluated the effects of three types of treatment, two levels of therapist experience, and three different ways to compose the groups. The three treatments were *traditional group social work* (focus on group processes, social organization and norms within the group), *behavior modification* (use of reinforcement contingencies, focus on prosocial behavior), and *minimal treatment* (no explicit application of a structured treatment plan; spontaneous interactions of group members). Activity

Table 4.2
Selected Characteristics of the Outcome Study Conducted by Feldman et al. (1983)

Domain	Major Characteristics
Sample	Referred for antisocial behavior (ages 8–17, M = 11.2)
Sample Size	N = 452 participants, N = 54 at follow-up
Screening	Severity of antisocial behavior on checklists completed by referral agent and parent.
Setting	Jewish Community Center
Treatments	Traditional Group Social Work; Behavior Modification; Minimal Treatment (no explicit or structured plan)
Treatment Sessions	Range from 8–29 sessions (M = 22.2 sessions) 2–3 hours each
Sources of Data	Referral agency, parents, children, therapists
Assessment Domain	Antisocial, prosocial, nonsocial behavior
Major Outcome Measures	Checklist questions designed to measure prosocial, antisocial, and nonsocial behavior completed by professionals at referral agencies, parents, therapists, and youths; direct observations of youths in the groups designed to measure prosocial, antisocial, and nonsocial behavior; therapist and observer completed measures of group norms, child and peer relations; aggression scale completed by youths
Therapists	Experienced (social work graduate students) versus inexperienced (undergraduates)
Training of Therapists	In-service training; prior course work and practical training for "experienced" therapists.

groups within the center were formed and assigned to one of these three interventions. The groups were led by trainers, some of whom were *experienced* (graduate students of social work with previous experience) and others who were *inexperienced* (undergraduate students). Finally, the groups were comprised in three ways: (a) all members were youths *referred* for antisocial behavior, (b) all members were *nonreferred* ("normal") youths, and (c) members were a mixture of *referred and nonreferred.*

The main objective was to evaluate changes in antisocial behavior of referred youths over the course of the intervention. Measures were obtained from parents, referral agents, the youths, and group leaders as well as direct observations of the groups. The intervention was conducted over a period of a year in which the youths attended sessions and engaged in a broad range of activities (e.g., sports, arts and crafts, fund raising, discussions). The specific treatments were superimposed on the usual activity structure of the community facility. Treatment sessions ranged from 8 to 29 sessions (mean = 22.2 sessions), each lasting about 2 – 3 hours.

The results indicated that treatment, trainer experience, and group composition exerted impact on at least some of the measures. Youths showed greater reductions in antisocial behavior with experienced rather than inexperienced leaders. Referred (antisocial) youths in mixed groups (that included nonreferred children) showed greater improvements than similar youths in groups comprised of only antisocial youths. Treatment also differed; behavior modification led to greater reductions in antisocial behavior than did traditional group treatment. Traditional treatment led to some decrements in antisocial behavior relative to the minimal contact group. However, treatment accounted for only a small amount of variance in predicting outcome.

Overall, antisocial youths benefitted from the program, especially those who received the most favorable intervention condition (i.e., behavior modification with an experienced leader and in a mixed group of referred and nonreferred peers). For a small subsample ($n = 54$), follow-up data were available 1 year later. The follow-up data revealed nonsignificant increases in antisocial behavior based on data from parent and referral agent reports. Yet, the small size of the follow-up sample precluded evaluation of the effects of treatment, trainer experience, and group composition.

Overall Evaluation. There remain some ambiguities regarding the impact of alternative treatments. Checks on how treatment was carried out revealed a breakdown in treatment integrity. For example, observations of treatment sessions revealed that approximately 35% of the leaders did not implement the behavior modification procedures appropriately for two of the three sessions observed; approximately 44% of the minimal-treatment leaders carried out systematic interventions even though none was supposed to; finally, only 25% of the leaders in the traditional group treatment condition carried out the intervention appropriately. It is difficult to draw conclusions about the relative impact of alternative treatments. It is so rare for studies to even assess treatment integrity. Consequently, attention should be directed to this superb methodological feature rather than faulted on the departures from the intended interventions. Nevertheless, it is still possible that there would be greater differences in outcome when the treatments are conducted as intended and even substantially different conclusions about individual treatment conditions.

The absence of stronger follow-up data raises other problems. Follow-up was restricted to ratings on nonstandardized measures of antisocial behavior and was available for only 12% (54/450) of the sample. From these data, it is not possible to tell how the vast majority of youths fared. Follow-up data are critical given the possibility that the results might differ from, and even be diametrically opposed to, the pattern evident immediately after treatment (see chapter 5). Nevertheless, the St. Louis Experiment represents a major contribution to the treatment literature. The project shows that interventions can be delivered on a relatively large scale and can provide benefits for referred (and nonreferred) youths.

General Comments

The two previously noted studies illustrate very special efforts to evaluate alternative treatments. The studies share several characteristics such as the evaluation of multiple treatments, the reliance upon multiple measures and perspectives to examine outcome, and the sampling of different "types" of youths to examine the differential responsiveness of clients to treatment. More than the specific commonalities, both studies focus on questions involving the interaction of treatment outcome with other variables (e.g., clinical problem, child age, referral status). This level of specificity is what is needed in outcome research, which is a fact widely recognized but rarely translated into action in the child therapy literature. The results of these studies could be included in a meta-analysis of treatment but such an analysis would fail to represent their rich findings.[1] The analysis of each study on its own provides a clearer statement of the effects of the constituent treatments along with the requisite qualifications based on design issues.

ILLUSTRATIONS OF RESEARCH PROGRAMS

Even more than individual studies, programs of research convey the advances and promise of current treatments for children. Typically, programs refer to systematic and consecutive studies by an individual investigative team that explores a particular treatment technique. A program of research by an individual investigator or research team is laudatory. For present purposes, the broader issue of the systematic accumulation of information among researchers is primary. Consequently, it is useful to extend the definition of programmatic research to include the accumulation of findings among separate researchers who have explored a particular treatment approach. Research programs, in this broader sense, are worth highlighting because they convey the progress over time in understanding particular clinical problems and developing treatments in a systematic fashion.

As with the individual studies, the programs highlighted here are illustrative. There are, of course, many other programs in various stages of development that could be identified as well. Programs selected for review are focused primarily on externalizing behaviors (aggression, disruptive behavior). Diverse treatment techniques have been developed that vary in focus, procedures, and goals to address these behaviors.

Parent Management Training

Background and Underlying Rationale. Parent management training (PMT) refers to procedures in which a parent or parents are trained to interact

---

[1]Interestingly, the two studies highlighted here were not included in the meta-analyses of child treatments reviewed earlier (Casey & Berman, 1985; Weisz et al., 1987).

differently with their child. PMT has been evaluated in hundreds of outcome studies with behavior–problem children varying in age and degree of severity of dysfunction (Kazdin, 1985; Moreland, Schwebel, Beck, & Wells, 1982). The work of Patterson and his colleagues, spanning more than two decades, exemplifies the programmatic outcome research on parent training with antisocial youths. Over 200 families have been seen that include primarily aggressive children (ages 3-12 years) referred for outpatient treatment (Patterson, 1982). The effectiveness of treatment has been evaluated in several controlled studies where progress in developing the procedures and sophistication of the research questions are readily apparent.

PMT is based on the general view that aggressive child behavior is inadvertently developed and sustained in the home by maladaptive parent–child interactions. In fact, research has shown that parents of aggressive youths engage in several practices that promote aggressive behavior and suppress prosocial behavior. These practices include directly reinforcing deviant behavior, frequently using commands and harsh punishment, and failing to attend to appropriate behavior (Patterson, 1982).

Coercive interaction patterns in particular play a central role in promoting aggressive child behavior. *Coercion* refers to deviant behavior on the part of one person (e.g., the child) which is rewarded by another person (e.g., the parent). The notion of coercion is designed to explain a particular type of interaction, often referred to as a *reinforcement trap*. Aggressive or other deviant behaviors performed by a child and directed toward a parent, usually the mother, may be reinforced when the parent gives in or complies. The trap is that the parent may acquiesce to end the child's aversive behavior in the short-run, but inadvertently increases the likehood that the behavior will recur in the future. Essentially, the parent's own behavior is sustained (negatively reinforced) because of its success in terminating the child's aversive behavior in the short-run. However, the child's aversive behavior is maintained through positive reinforcement because of compliance of the parent. Through the reinforcement trap, children are inadvertently rewarded for their aggressive interactions and their escalation of coercive behaviors.

PMT is designed to alter the pattern of interchanges between parent and child so that prosocial rather than coercive behavior is directly reinforced and supported within the family. This requires developing several different parenting behaviors such as establishing the rules for the child to follow, providing positive reinforcement for appropriate behavior, delivering mild forms of punishment to suppress behavior, and negotiating compromises.

Characteristics of Treatment. Although many variations of PMT exist, several common characteristics can be identified. First, treatment is conducted primarily with the parents who directly implement several procedures in the home. There usually is no direct intervention of the therapist with the child. Second, parents are trained to identify, define, and observe problem behaviors in new ways. Careful specification of the problems is essential to delivery of reinforcing or punishing consequences and to evaluate if the program is working.

Third, the treatment sessions cover social learning principles and the procedures that follow from them. Considerable time is devoted to such techniques as positive reinforcement (e.g., the use of social praise and tokens or points for prosocial behavior), mild punishment (e.g., use of time out from reinforcement, loss of privileges), negotiation, contingency contracting and other procedures. Fourth, the sessions provide opportunities for parents to see how the techniques are implemented, to practice using the techniques, and to review behavior change programs in the home. The therapist uses instructions, modeling, role-playing, and rehearsal to convey how the techniques are implemented.

The immediate goal of the program is to develop specific skills in the parents. This is usually achieved by having parents apply their skills to relatively simple behaviors that can be easily observed and that are not enmeshed with more provoking interactions (e.g., punishment, battles of the will, coercive interchanges). As the parents become more proficient, the focus of the program can address the child's most severely problematic behaviors and encompass other problem areas (e.g., school behavior) as well.

Overview of the Outcome Evidence. Several controlled studies completed by Patterson and his colleagues have demonstrated marked improvements in child behavior over the course of treatment. Moreover, these changes surpass those achieved with variations of family-based psychotherapy, attention-placebo (discussion), and no-treatment conditions (Patterson, Chamberlain, & Reid, 1982; Walter & Gilmore, 1973; Wiltz & Patterson, 1974). Spanning different programs of research, the effects of treatment have also been shown to bring the problematic behaviors of treated children within normative levels of nonreferred peers who are functioning adequately (Eyberg & Johnson, 1974; Patterson, 1974; Wells, Forehand, & Griest, 1980). Follow-up assessment has shown that the gains are often maintained 1 year after treatment (Fleischman & Szykula, 1981). The continued benefits of treatment have been evident up to 4.5 and 10.5 years later (Baum & Forehand, 1981; Forehand & Long, in press).

The impact of PMT is relatively broad. To begin with, the effects of treatment are evident for child behaviors that have not been focused on directly as a part of training. Also, when parents are trained to alter the behavior of the child identified as in need of treatment, the behavior of the other children in the home improve, even though they are not directly focused on in treatment. In addition, maternal psychopathology, particularly depression, has been shown to decrease systematically following PMT. These changes suggest that PMT alters multiple aspects of dysfunctional families (see Kazdin, 1985; Moreland et al., 1982; Patterson & Fleischman, 1979).

Factors that Contribute to Outcome. Several characteristics of the treatment and the families who participate contribute to treatment outcome. First, among the treatment characteristics, duration appears to influence outcome. Brief and time-limited treatments (e.g., < 10 hours) are less likely to show benefits with clinical populations. More dramatic and durable effects have been achieved with protracted or time-unlimited programs extending up to 50 or 60 hours of treatment (Kazdin, 1985). Second, specific training components such as providing parents with in-depth knowledge of social learning principles and utilizing time out from reinforcement in the home enhance treatment effects (e.g., McMahon, Forehand, & Griest, 1981; Wahler & Fox, 1980). Third, some evidence suggests that therapist training and skill are associated with the magnitude and durability of therapeutic changes (Fleischman, 1982; Patterson, 1974), although these have yet to be carefully tested.

Parent and family characteristics are also related to treatment outcome. As might be expected, families characterized by many risk factors associated with childhood dysfunction (e.g., marital discord and parent psychopathology) tend to show fewer gains in treatment than families without these characteristics (e.g., Strain, Young, & Horowitz, 1981). Moreover, when gains are achieved in treatment, they are unlikely to be maintained in families with socioeconomic disadvantage (Wahler, Berland, & Coe, 1979).

The social support system of the mother outside of the home also contributes to the efficacy of PMT (Dumas & Wahler, 1983). Mothers who are insulated from social supports outside the home (i.e., have few positive social contacts with relatives and friends) are less likely to profit from treatment. Thus, variables beyond the specific parent–child interactions need to be considered in treatment. In fact, when PMT addresses many of the family problems (e.g., parental adjustment, marital adjustment, and extrafamilial relations), the efficacy of treatment in terms of child behavior change is enhanced (Dadds, Schwartz, & Sanders, 1987; Griest et al., 1982).

Overall Evaluation. Several features of PMT make it one of the more promising treatments for aggressive behavior. First, the treatment has been effective with children varying in severity of clinical dysfunction. Treatment effects have been maintained up to one year after treatment is terminated, and occasionally longer. Moreover, changes at home and at school can bring deviant behavior of treated children within the range of children functioning normally. Second, the benefits of treatment often extend beyond the target child to siblings and parents.

Third, along with treatment outcome investigations, basic research has been conducted on family interaction patterns and influences outside of the home that affect treatment outcome. This research has enhanced our understanding of the emergence of antisocial behavior (Patterson, 1986). Fourth, a major advantage is the availability of treatment manuals and training materials for parents and professional therapists (see Ollendick & Cerny, 1981, for a list). These materials make this modality of treatment potentially widely available for further research as well as clinical application.

Several limitations of PMT can be identified as well. First, some families may not respond to treatment. Explicit procedures may need to be included in treatment to address family and parent conflicts that influence the parent–child interactions in the home. Second, PMT makes several demands on the parents such as mastering educational materials that convey social learning principles, systematically observing deviant child behavior, implementing specific behavior change procedures at home, attending weekly sessions, and responding to frequent telephone contacts made by the therapist. For some families, the demands may be too great to continue in treatment. Third, and related, for many children PMT is simply not a viable option. PMT requires at least one parent who is available, willing and capable of following through with treatment. Some parents cannot participate because of their own dysfunction; others will not participate because they feel they have reached their limits in trying to help their children.

On balance, PMT is clearly a promising treatment for aggressive youths. Among treatments for problem children, this technique has one of the strongest bases in controlled outcome research. Also, much has been learned about family processes that sustain antisocial behavior and about the parent, family, and treatment variables that influence outcome.

Functional Family Therapy

Background and Underlying Rationale. Family therapies are widely advocated for problems where the child is the identified patient. As noted previously, few controlled outcome studies are available to evaluate their impact. An exception is the work of Alexander, Barton, Parsons and their colleagues who have developed and evaluated functional family therapy (FFT) for the treatment of delinquent youths (Alexander & Parsons, 1982; Barton & Alexander, 1981). Research underlying FFT has found that families of delinquents show higher rates of defensiveness in their communications, both in parent–child and parent–parent interactions, and also lower rates of mutual support compared to families of nondelinquents (Alexander, 1973). Improving these communication and support functions is a central goal of treatment.

FFT reflects an integrative approach to treatment that has relied on two perspectives of human behavior and therapeutic change. The first perspective is a *systems approach*, in which clinical problems are conceptualized from the standpoint of the functions they serve in the family as a system, as well as for individual family members. The assumption is made that problem behavior evident in the child is the only way some interpersonal functions (e.g., intimacy, distancing, support) can be met among family members. Maladaptive processes within the family are considered to preclude a more direct means of fulfilling these functions. The goal of treatment is to alter interaction and communication patterns in such a way as to foster more adaptive functioning.

The second perspective is an *operational behavioral perspective*. This is based on learning theory, and focuses on specific stimuli and responses that can be used to produce change. Behavioral concepts and procedures for identifying specific behaviors for change and reinforcing new appropriate adaptive ways of responding, and empirically evaluating and monitoring that change are included in this perspective.

More recent formulations of FFT have included a third perspective which emphasizes *cognitive processes* (Morris, Alexander, & Waldron, in press). This perspective focuses on the attributions, attitudes, assumptions, expectations, and emotions of the family. Family members may begin treatment with attributions that focus on blaming others or themselves. New perspectives may be needed to help serve as the basis for developing new ways of behaving.

Characteristics of Treatment. FFT requires that the family see the clinical problem from the relational functions it serves within the family. The therapist points out interdependencies and contingencies between family members in their day-to-day functioning with specific reference to the problem that has served as the basis for seeking treatment. Once the family sees alternative ways of viewing the problem, the incentive for interacting more constructively is increased.

The main goals of treatment are to increase reciprocity and positive reinforcement among family members, to establish clear communication, to help specify behaviors that family members desire from each other, to negotiate constructively, and to help identify solutions to interpersonal problems. The family members read a manual that describes behavioral principles (e.g., reinforcement and extinction) to develop familiarity with the concepts used in treatment. In therapy, family members identify behaviors they would like others to perform. Responses are incorporated into a reinforcement system in the home to promote adaptive behavior in exchange for privileges. However, the primary focus is within the treatment sessions where family communication patterns are altered directly. During the sessions, the therapist provides social reinforcement (verbal and nonverbal praise) for communications that suggest solutions to problems, provide information to clarify problems, or offer feedback to other family members.

Outcome Evidence. Only a few studies of FFT have been reported. But these have been well-designed studies that reflect a clear progression in the information they yield. The initial study included male and female delinquent adolescents referred to juvenile court for a variety of behaviors such as running away, truancy, theft, and unmanageability (Parsons & Alexander, 1973). Cases were assigned to the FFT, an attention-placebo condition (group discussion and expression of feeling), or to a no-treatment control group. Posttreatment evaluation, following 8 treatment sessions, revealed that the family therapy condition led to greater discussion among family members, that family members spoke more equitably, and that frequency and duration of spontaneous speech increased. The changes were significantly greater than in the attention-placebo and no-treatment groups.

In an extension of this program, Alexander and Parsons (1973) compared FFT, client-centered family groups, psychodynamically oriented family therapy, and no treatment. The results indicated greater improvement on family interaction measures and lower recidivism rates from juvenile court records up to 18 months after treatment for the FFT group. Follow-up data obtained $2\frac{1}{2}$ years later, revealed that the siblings of those who received FFT showed significantly lower rates of referral to juvenile courts (Klein, Alexander, & Parsons, 1977). Thus, the results suggest significant changes on both index children as well as their siblings.

Overall Evaluation. Given these outcome studies, FFT shows obvious promise. Clearly, additional replications are needed. Albeit few studies exist, some important statements can already be made about the treatment. First, the effectiveness of treatment appears to be influenced by the relationship (e.g., warmth, integration of affect and behavior) and structuring (e.g., directiveness) skills of the therapist (Alexander, Barton, Schiavo, & Parsons, 1976). Second, process measures of family interactions at posttreatment are related to subsequent recidivism (Alexander & Parsons, 1973). This finding adds credence to the model from which treatment was derived. Finally, in the outcome studies, client-centered and psychodynamically oriented forms of family-based therapies have not achieved the positive effects of FFT. Thus, treatment of the problem at the level of the family per se does not appear to be sufficient to alter antisocial behavior.

Table 4.3
Interpersonal Cognitive Problem-Solving Skills

---

1. *Alternative Solution Thinking* – the ability to generate different options (solutions) that can solve problems in interpersonal situations.

2. *Means-Ends Thinking* – awareness of the intermediate steps required to achieve a particular goal.

3. *Consequential Thinking* – the ability to identify what might happen as a direct result of acting in a particular way or choosing a particular solution.

4. *Causal Thinking* – the ability to relate one event to another over time and to understand why one event led to a particular action of other persons.

5. *Sensitivity to Interpersonal Problems* – the ability to perceive a problem when it exists and to identify the interpersonal aspects of the confrontation that may emerge.

Adapted from Spivack et al. (1976).

Cognitive Problem-solving Skills Training

Background and Underlying Rationale. Problem-solving skills training (PSST) focuses on the child's cognitive processes (perceptions, self-statements, attributions, expectations, and problem-solving skills) that are presumed to underlie maladaptive behavior. The assumption of PSST is that children with deviant behavior suffer deficiencies in particular processes or from an inability to use or apply cognitive skills. Impulsive cognitive style, deficits in taking the perspective of others, and misattribution of the intentions of others are some of the processes implicated in externalizing child behavior (Dodge, 1985; Ellis, 1982; Kendall & Braswell, 1982).

The relationship between cognitive processes and behavioral adjustment has been evaluated in programmatic studies by Spivack and Shure (1982; Shure & Spivack, 1978, 1982; Spivack, Platt, & Shure, 1976). These investigators have identified different cognitive processes or interpersonal cognitive problem-solving skills that underlie social behavior (see Table 4.3). Spivack and Shure have completed several investigations which show that the ability to engage in these problem-solving steps is related to behavioral adjustment, as measured in teacher ratings of acting-out behavior and social withdrawal. Disturbed children tend: (a) to generate fewer alternative solutions to interpersonal problems, (b) to focus on ends or goals rather than the intermediate steps to obtain them, (c) to see fewer consequences associated with their behavior, (d) to fail to recognize the causes of other people's behavior, and (e) to be less sensitive to interpersonal conflict (Spivack et al., 1976).

Characteristics of Treatment. Spivack and Shure have developed and evaluated their interpersonal cognitive problem-solving skills program for several years and with a variety of child and adult populations (e.g., Spivack et al., 1976; Spivack & Shure, 1982). Many variations of problem-solving skills training have emerged from other research programs as well (e.g., Camp & Bash, 1985; Kendall & Braswell, 1985). The variations share many characteristics.

First, the emphasis is on how the child approaches situations. Although it is obviously important that the child ultimately select appropriate (prosocial) means of behaving in everyday life, the primary focus is on the thought *processes* rather than the *outcome* or specific behavioral acts that result. Second, the treatment attempts to teach the child to engage in a step-by-step approach to solve problems. The method is usually achieved by having the child make statements (self-instructions) to himself or herself that direct attention to certain aspects of the problem or task that lead to effective solutions. Third, treatment utilizes structured tasks involving games, academic activities, and stories. Over the course of treatment, the cognitive problem-solving skills are increasingly applied to real-life situations. Fourth, the therapist usually plays an active role in treatment. He or she models the cognitive processes by making verbal self-statements, applies the sequence of statements to particular problems, provides cues to the child to prompt use of the skills, and delivers feedback and praise to develop correct use of the skills. Finally, treatment usually combines several different procedures including modeling and practice, role-playing, and reinforcement and mild punishment (loss of points or tokens). .

Overview of the Outcome Evidence. A number of researchers have conducted programmatic series of studies showing the efficacy of PSST (see Kendall & Braswell, 1985; Spivack & Shure, 1982). Research has established the efficacy of alternative variations of treatment. The majority of studies, however, have evaluated the impact of training on cognitive processes and laboratory-task performance, rather than deviant child behavior (see Gresham, 1985; Kazdin, 1985).

Spivack et al. (1976) have demonstrated with different age groups that developing interpersonal problem-solving skills leads to improved ratings of behavioral adjustment in the classroom, as well as increased interpersonal attributes such as popularity and likeability. Studies of impulsive or aggressive children and adolescents have shown that cognitive based treatment can lead to significant changes in behavior at home, at school, and in the community and that these gains are evident up to 1 year later (Arbuthnot & Gordon, 1986; Kazdin, Esveldt-Dawson, French, & Unis, 1987; Kendall & Braswell, 1982; Lochman, Burch, Curry, & Lampron, 1984). However, the magnitude of the changes may need to be greater than those currently achieved to return children to normative or adaptive levels of functioning at home and at school.

Few studies have elaborated the factors that contribute to treatment outcome. Some evidence has suggested that the greater the level of child aggression, the less effective treatment is (Kendall & Braswell, 1985). Duration of treatment influenced outcome in one study with longer treatment (> 18 sessions) leading to greater change than shorter treatment (Lochman, 1985). However, further tests of the effects of duration are needed among different treatments. Age and cognitive development may influence outcome as well, although these have yet to be explored in the context of clinical treatment trials (Cole & Kazdin, 1980).

Overall Evaluation. PSST at this point in time has not been shown to be an effective treatment for externalizing behaviors such as impulsiveness, hyperactivity, and aggression. Nevertheless, several features make this one of the more promising psychosocial approaches to the problem. First, PSST draws on theory and research in developmental psychology. Theory and research on the emergence and maturation of cognitive processes and the relationship of these processes to adjustment provide an important foundation for generating and testing treatment techniques. Also, maladaptive cognitive processes have been shown to relate to parental child-rearing practices that are correlated with the development and maintenance of child maladjustment (Shure & Spivack, 1978).

Second, developmental differences may need to be considered in designing effective treatments. Processes highly significant at one age (e.g., means–ends thinking in adolescents) may be less critical at other ages (early childhood) (Spivack et al., 1976). Third, a major feature of PSST for both purposes of clinical application and research is that variations of the approach are available in manual form (e.g., Camp & Bash, 1985; Kendall & Braswell, 1985; Spivack et al., 1976). Specification of treatment procedures in manual form helps promote further research on the efficacy of treatment.

There are clear limitations to the application of PSST as well. Research to date has generally adopted the view that children with problems of adjustment, broadly conceived, have cognitive deficits. There has been little attempt to relate specific cognitive deficits to particular types of clinical dysfunction. For example, Spivack et al. (1976) have found similar cognitive deficits between acting out and socially withdrawn children. Their work with adolescents and adults has also shown that drug addicts, delinquents, and schizophrenic patients evince cognitive deficits compared to normals matched on various demographic variables. Finer distinctions need to be explored to delineate the cognitive correlates or underpinnings of specific clinical problems.

Existing studies show that various forms of PSST can produce relatively consistent changes on a variety of measures that reflect cognitive style, thought processes, perception, aspects of intelligence, and academic performance. Additional efforts to alter specific clinical problems on measures of dysfunction at home, at school, or in the community are needed before the efficacy of treatment can be decided. Nevertheless, major advances have been achieved in developing variations of PSST for application to child dysfunctions.

General Comments

Parent management training, functional family therapy, and problem-solving skills training illustrate programs of research that are exemplary in the psychosocial treatment literature, whether for child or adult therapies. Of course, many questions remain regarding the effectiveness and limits of these specific treatments. Yet, highlighting such questions detracts from the purpose of their illustration. Each research program evaluates the nature of the dysfunction to which treatment is directed and the processes and outcomes of treatment. The programs help to convey that developing effective treatments requires an interface of studies on the nature of the processes underlying the clinical problem and treatment outcome.

In passing, the specific techniques that were identified may be of some concern. The bulk of clinical practice is devoted to relationship, insight-oriented, play, and family (other than FFT) therapies (Gould et al., 1980; Koocher & Pedulla, 1977; Tuma & Pratt, 1982). Yet these more familiar approaches were not used to illustrate the programmatic lines of work. Programs of work are difficult to identify that evaluate generic and eclectic forms of individual, group, and family therapy that are commonly used in clinical practice. It is still the case that the techniques that are probably most commonly used in practice (e.g., insight-oriented, relationship based, and client-centered treatments) are not well evaluated in the child treatment outcome research (Casey & Berman, 1985; Weisz et al., 1987).The programs of research outlined previously convey the type of programmatic evaluation from which these other treatments would profit.

CONCLUSIONS

The previous discussion provides a narrow and selective review of the child psychotherapy literature. The focus on individual studies and programs of research reflects a more molecular level of analysis than the evaluation of narrative reviews and meta-analyses. The more molecular analysis has much to offer in terms of evaluating progress toward empirically based treatments for children and adolescents. To begin with, the individual studies provide a model for the type of research that is needed. Two studies were outlined that included several important design practices such as careful screening of the cases explicitly specifying the clinical problem, using multiple outcome measures, and employing relatively large sample sizes. Also, the studies went beyond merely comparing alternative treatments, and examined child (e.g., age, sex, type of dysfunction), therapist (level of experience) and treatment variables (type of peers included in the groups) that may interact with the intervention. At the level of the individual study, it is also important to identify the methodological problems that emerge. In a global literature review it is easy to discount a particular study because of ubiquitous "methodological problems." It is important to see how various obstacles emerge (e.g., maintaining the integrity of treatment, retaining a sufficient number of subjects at follow-up to evaluate treatment).

Programs of research convey other points that large-scale reviews omit. Research programs not only illustrate the progress evident with a particular technique, but also convey the conceptual foundations, basic research on the processes and outcome studies examining the technique, and factors that may interact with treatment. Outcome studies that might find their way into a literature review may not provide a complete appraisal of the technique. In terms of long-term investment for developing and identifying effective treatments, different types of studies are quite relevant.

Although previous chapters in this book have lamented the state of child psychotherapy, there are actually many promising leads. Examined at a molecular level, individual studies, specific treatments, and programs of research raise a great deal of hope. A difficulty for developing progress is that the studies and programs remain relatively isolated in the sense that they are not part of a larger conceptualization of what is needed to make progress. Few studies build upon each other in terms of conceptual or methodological advances.

Improvements that are needed for individual studies and the accumulation of systematic information about child therapies do not emerge in an obvious way from the reviews of the literature. Several issues can be identified that are likely to influence the quality of the conclusions that are drawn from child therapy outcome research. Substantive and methodological issues that reflect the variables selected for study and the manner in which they are evaluated are discussed in the next chapter.

Chapter 5

Methodological and Substantive Issues in Child Therapy Research

High quality individual outcome studies and programs of research are important to highlight because they illustrate the type of work that needs to be fostered. Exemplary studies that address substantive questions of significance often introduce methodological advances worth highlighting as well. Yet the outcome research on child treatments is relatively weak. The difficulties not only stem from the paucity of studies, but also from the failure to address critical issues.

Several issues can be identified that have both substantive and methodological implications. For example, in a treatment outcome study, the manner in which patients are selected, the investigation of moderating variables, and the conceptualization underlying treatment not only affect the methodological quality of the experimental test but also the sophistication of the questions that are asked about treatment. The issues addressed in this chapter, if incorporated into child treatment research, can greatly advance progress toward the "ultimate" question, that is what treatments work with what problems, under what circumstances, and so on.

PATIENT ISSUES

Identification of Clinical Dysfunction

Interpretation of current treatment research is obfuscated by the failure to specify crucial information about the children and their families. In many treatment studies, children are referred to informally as *emotionally disturbed, impulsive, socially withdrawn*, or having *conduct problems*. Although such terms imply that the children suffer impairment, the severity, duration, and scope of dysfunction are rarely discussed.

Separate problems are evident in research in the use of such terms. First, the terms are often quite general so that heterogeneous groups of children are included. For example, a common procedure is to recruit children for a study based on teacher referrals for "classroom problems." In a given study, the children may be referred for out-of-seat behavior, aggressiveness, reading problems, or noncompliance. The investigator may intentionally invoke very broad inclusion criteria to obtain a sufficient number of subjects to complete the study. Yet the absence of treatment effects or presence of weak effects at the end of the study might be due to the heterogeneity of the sample. The treatment may have been effective with a subsample of children, but the variability (individual differences) within the treatment group is relatively large.

A second problem is that the use of general terms to define the subject sample tends to be idiosyncratic across studies. Because definitions for emotionally disturbed, maladjusted, and conduct problem children are not standardized, studies using the same term might be referring to very different types of children. Thus, the accumulation of information about a particular clinical problem in a consistent fashion across studies is difficult.

One of the issues resulting from the lack of specification of the sample has to do with the severity of the dysfunction. Across studies, operational criteria to define severity of the clinical problem may not be reported. The failure to use standard diagnostic criteria or widely used assessment devices make it difficult to draw conclusions about the severity of dysfunction relative to other samples and to "normal" (nonreferred) peers.

Interpretation of treatment trials also requires specification of greater details about the parents, family, and home situation. Such variables as single-parent families, parent psychopathology, family size, and marital discord are quite relevant because they may be related to long-term prognosis of child behavior and influence the extent to which treatment can have impact (Rutter & Giller, 1983). These variables are also often unreported.

For any given clinical problem, it may be difficult to agree on the full range of parent and family variables that might be relevant. Thus, a consistent set of measures may be unrealistic to demand from researchers. Nevertheless, increased attention to parent and family variables that are likely to have impact on the child is essential to understand the type of persons and situations to which treatments have been and can be effectively applied.

Potential Moderating Variables

Moderating variables refer to those factors that may influence treatment in producing therapeutic change. Most outcome studies neglect moderating variables in evaluating treatment effects. The neglect of such influences tacitly assumes that patients are homogeneous and are likely to respond in a similar way to treatment, which is a belief referred to as a *uniformity myth* (Kiesler, 1971). The search for moderating variables to delineate children in meaningful ways has as its objective the prediction of responsiveness to treatment. If variables can be identified that interact with treatment, children can be directed to specific forms of treatment for which they are likely to be suited. Among a broad range of domains (e.g., personality, demographic, parent, family, socioeconomic, and other characteristics), an indefinite number of potential moderating variables could be identified.

Perhaps the primary patient variable that is likely to mediate treatment effects is the type of clinical dysfunction. Obviously, a given treatment is likely to be effective with particular types of problems rather than all types of child dysfunction. Child diagnosis or another measure that delineates type of dysfunction would be important to consider in a particular investigation. This can be accomplished by including two or more types of clinical problems in a study of a given treatment to see if patients vary in their responsiveness.

To extend this further, two or more clinical problems can be evaluated in a study examining two or more treatments. For example, in the Kolvin et al. (1981) study reviewed earlier, the impact of alternative treatments was evaluated for children with one of two types of dysfunction (neurotic or conduct disorder). Interactions of treatment with different types of problems did not emerge. Yet, this is one of the few studies that provided a careful test to determine if treatments varied in their effectiveness among clinical problems.

With improved diagnostic criteria available for childhood disorders, it is likely that future outcome studies will be able to select reasonably homogeneous populations. In such cases, type of dysfunction may not be studied as a moderator variable because all patients will meet criteria for the dysfunction. Even so, symptom patterns may be important moderators. Subtypes of dysfunctions, associated features, and secondary diagnoses may have important implications. For example, among delinquent or antisocial samples, some evidence suggests that those who also show symptoms of anxiety may respond better to treatment (Jesness, 1971). This information, if replicated, obviously is extremely important in identifying a moderator of treatment.

Apart from clinical dysfunction, developmental level of the child may be an important moderator of treatment (Achenbach, 1985). Although there is considerable agreement on the significance of developmental level in the abstract, few researchers involved in treatment studies operationalize the concept in any way other than chronological age. Level of development can be examined in many ways based on different psychological (e.g., moral reasoning of Kohlberg; stages of Piaget) and physical stages (e.g., Tanner). In general, efforts to identify a particular theoretical framework for stages and to incorporate these into treatment trials are difficult to find.

The task, of course, is not merely to measure specific stages and to evaluate their role in treatment outcome. Rather, the goal is to make and test predictions in relation to alternative stages and to propose how or why these stages might influence outcome for a specific clinical function or treatment technique. A possible point to begin such work would be in the application of cognitively based interventions where the level of cognitive development (e.g., stage of moral reasoning at pretreatment) could conceivably affect responsiveness or amenability to treatment.

Although chronological age is not a substitute for stages derived from a specific theoretical position, it represents a moderating variable of potential importance. It is already known that problem behaviors in children vary greatly as a function of age (Achenbach & Edelbrock, 1983; MacFarlane et al., 1954). Less well-studied is responsiveness to treatment as a function of child age. For example, Miller, Barrett, Hampe, and Noble (1972) compared alternative treatments (systematic desensitization vs. psychotherapy) for the treatment of phobias. Younger children (6-10 years old) showed greater improvement than older children (age 11 and older). In fact, age contributed more to the outcome (i.e., accounted for more variance) than did treatment technique.

The selection of youths of different ages and evaluation of age X treatment interactions is a very important focus in child treatment research. There are frequently voiced assumptions that treatment and/or preventive efforts are likely to be more effective with younger rather than older youths because of the amenability of younger children to various influences, particularly adult influences. Even such basic assumptions free from theories about specific clinical disorders have yet to be well tested.

Child gender is another variable that warrants inclusion and evaluation as a moderator of treatment effects. Boys and girls are known to differ in the types of dysfunctions they bring to treatment. Boys more frequently show externalizing disorders, whereas girls tend to (but do not invariably) show more internalizing disorders (Gould et al., 1980; Graham, 1977). Sex differences are known to play a significant role in the emergence of clinical dysfunction over childhood, adolescence, and adulthood. Now that many such differences are established, it remains important to relate them to treatment outcome. Inclusion of the child's sex as a moderator variable is an excellent lead for identifying patient X treatment interactions. For example, it might well be, based on findings from developmental psychology, that boys and girls are differentially responsive to various techniques, therapeutic strategies, tasks, and therapist characteristics because of the different sex-typed experiences to which they are exposed early in childhood. Here too, theories of child development provide an excellent point of departure for generating hypotheses about factors that moderate treatment effects.

To date, sex differences have been infrequently studied in child treatment outcome research. One reason is the preponderance of boys in many studies. Also, with small samples in many studies, the further division of the sample to examine sex × treatment interactions would yield relatively weak (insensitive) tests. Yet, in some cases where such analyses have been completed, provocative results have emerged. For example, Kolvin et al. (1981) found that girls responded better to various treatments than did boys. More interestingly, neurotic behaviors were more easily changed in boys than in girls, but antisocial behaviors were more easily changed in girls than in boys.

Beyond the child, characteristics of the parents and family are likely to moderate the effects of treatment. For example, parent management training does not produce change in all families. Families with low socioeconomic status, marital discord, greater parental psychopathology, and poor social support systems show fewer changes with treatment and are less likely to maintain treatment gains (Kazdin, 1985). This information is critical in making treatment recommendations for the individual clinical case. More generally, identification of the importance of such factors as mediators of therapeutic change has led to incorporation of parental dysfunction into these programs (Dadds et al, 1987; Griest et al., 1982).

The preceding text cannot begin to identify the range of patient variables that might moderate treatment effects. The main point here is not to lobby for the uncritical inclusion of diagnosis, age, and gender as moderating variables in any particular study. To be sure, the field would profit from systematic data on these basic variables. However, the primary objective is to argue for the inclusion of moderating variables and for testing specific hypotheses about characteristics of patients or their clinical problems that might plausibly influence outcome. For example, in the treatment of antisocial behavior, early onset of dysfunction and range of symptoms are patient characteristics known to predict poor clinical course (Kazdin, 1987a). Delineation of youths by such factors may reveal patient characteristic × treatment interactions. In the general case, specific features of the clinical problem, child level of development, and the treatments that are tested may suggest highly specific hypotheses.

TREATMENT ISSUES

Representativeness of Treatment

An initial issue in designing a treatment outcome study is ensuring that the treatment will be fairly and faithfully represented. This issue needs to be addressed before the study begins to ensure that the test is not a unique or idiosyncratic application of the treatment that has little relation to the treatment as usually conceived or practiced. The need to address this issue before conducting the treatments has become especially clear in comparative outcome studies (e.g., DiLoreto, 1971; Paul, 1966; Sloane, Staples, Cristol, Yorkston, & Whipple, 1975). The results of such studies are often discounted by critics after the fact because the specific treatments, as tested, did not represent their usual application in practice (e.g., Boy, 1971; Ellis, 1971; Heimberg & Becker, 1984; Rachman & Wilson, 1980; Roback, 1971).

There are, of course, many different reasons why treatments evaluated in research may not faithfully represent their counterparts in clinical practice (Parloff, 1984). Perhaps the main issue is that rarely is there a single agreed upon or standardized method that can be gleaned from prior research or clinical practice. Thus, investigators usually need to develop treatment guidelines and manuals and to make explicit those procedures that are poorly specified or highly variable in clinical work. Also, in clinical work, the therapist has the luxury and obligation to vary critical dimensions of treatment (e.g., number of sessions, focus of content) in response to changes or lack of changes in the patient. Some of the departures in research are intentional to help standardize treatment or to evaluate treatment by itself without the addition of many accoutrements or other interventions that clinicians are apt to introduce.

Prior to the investigation, those features of treatment that might depart from standard practice to permit experimental investigation should be specified. Even more importantly, it is essential to ensure that treatment reflects or represents a reasonable variation or approximation of the treatment of interest. There currently are no standard ways to evaluate at the inception of a study whether the treatment faithfully represents the intervention(s) of interest. One alternative is to develop the treatment in manual form and to submit the manual to proponents and practitioners of the technique (Sechrest, West, Phillips, Redner, & Yeaton, 1979). The experts can examine whether specific procedures are faithfully represented and whether the strength and dose of treatment (e.g., duration, number of sessions) are reasonable. The information so gained might be useful to revise the manual to represent treatment better. It would be useful to have some assurance initially that the study provided a reasonable test of that treatment.

Specification and Integrity of Treatment

Conceptualization of Treatment. Whether a new or currently available treatment is to be investigated, several features need to be carefully specified. To begin, the *conceptual basis of treatment* as applied to the specific clinical problem is critical. It is important to identify those factors in treatment that address the child's dysfunction and/or that explain how underlying processes (e.g., intrapsychic, familial, or social) contribute to the dysfunction. The conceptualization points to the specific treatment components or techniques that are likely to alter behavior and the processes through which they may operate. For example, in alternative family therapies, the functions of various behaviors, the roles of parents and children in relation to each other, and specific patterns of communication may be hypothesized to account for the problem behaviors evident in the child (as the identified patient). Specific structures and functions in the families should serve as the basis for the focus of treatment. The initial question would be to determine if the treatment produces greater changes than those associated with the passage of time (no-treatment or waiting-list control group). Early in the progression of research, it is also important to measure the family processes considered to relate to the problem(s) and to show changes in these processes over the course of treatment.

Procedural Specification. It is critical to specify what the treatment procedures are, to the extent possible, and to ensure that the treatment was conducted as intended. If possible, treatments should be delineated in *manual* form that includes materials to guide the therapist in the procedures, techniques, topics, themes, therapeutic maneuvers, and activities that will attain the specific goals of treatment (Luborsky & DeRubeis, 1984). Obviously, some treatments (e.g., systematic desensitization) are more easily specified in a manual than others (e.g., psychodynamically oriented psychotherapy). For childhood problems, several treatment manuals are available for parent management training, problem-solving skills training, and social skills training, to mention select techniques (Camp & Bash, 1985; Kendall & Braswell, 1985; Michelson, Sugai, Wood, & Kazdin, 1983; Ollendick & Cerny, 1981). For traditional variations of child psychotherapy (e.g., psychodynamically oriented therapy, client-centered psychotherapy and family therapies), manuals are less readily available. This is unfortunate because the techniques are among the most frequently used in clinical practice (Gould et al., 1980; Koocher & Pedulla, 1977; Tuma & Pratt, 1982), but the least well-investigated in controlled outcome studies (Casey & Berman, 1985; Weisz et al., 1987).

Treatment Integrity. The specification of treatment is not an end in itself, but rather, serves a larger purpose. An essential prerequisite of outcome research is to ensure the integrity of treatment, i.e., that the procedures are carried out as intended (Quay, 1977; Yeaton & Sechrest, 1981). Treatments can depart from the intended procedures in many ways. In perhaps the most dramatic examples where integrity has been sacrificed, none of the intended treatment sessions was actually held with the clients (see Sechrest, White, & Brown, 1979).

The breakdown of treatment integrity is one of the greatest dangers in outcome research. Interpretation of outcome assumes that the treatments were well-tested and carried out as intended. Consider hypothetically, a study in which two treatments are equally effective at posttreatment. The two treatments, if implemented as intended, may in fact be equally effective. However, a pattern of no difference might result from a failure to implement one or both of the treatments faithfully. Large variation in how individual treatments are carried out across patients within a given condition and failure to implement critical portions of treatments may also lead to no differences between two or more treatment conditions. Even when two treatments differ, it is important to rule out the possibility that the differences are due to variations of integrity with which each was conducted. One treatment, perhaps because of its complexity or novelty, may be more subject to procedural degradation and appear less effective because it was less faithfully rendered. Thus, integrity of treatment is relevant in any outcome study independent of the specific pattern of results.

There are several steps that can be performed to address treatment integrity. To begin with, the specific criteria, procedures, tasks, and therapist and patient characteristics that define the treatment need to be specified as well as possible. Second, therapists need to be trained to carry out the techniques. Training is usually defined by the number of cases the therapist has seen or amount of time (years of experience) using the techniques, rather than proficiency in the constituent skills (Kazdin, Kratochwill, & VandenBos, 1986). The training experience, however defined, obviously has important implications for how faithfully treatment is likely to be rendered. Third and related, when treatment has begun, it may be valuable to provide continued case supervision. Listening to or viewing tapes of selected sessions, meeting regularly with therapists to provide feedback, and similar monitoring procedures may reduce therapist drift (departure) from the desired practices.

Whether treatment has been carried out as intended can only be evaluated definitively after the treatment has been completed. This evaluation requires measuring the implementation of treatment. Audio or video tapes of selected treatment sessions from each condition can be examined. Codes for therapist and/or patient behaviors or others specific facets of the sessions can operationalize important features of treatment and help decide whether treatment was conducted as intended (DeRubeis, Hollon, Evans, & Bemis, 1982).

Treatment integrity is not an all-or-none matter. Hence, it is useful to identify what a faithful rendition of each treatment is and what departures fall within an acceptable range. On some variables, decisions may be difficult to defend, but making them explicit facilitates interpretation of the results. For example, to consider a relatively simple characteristic, treatment may consist of 20 sessions of individual therapy. The investigator may specify that treatment is administered adequately (i.e., is reasonably tested) only if a client receives 15 (75%) or more of the sessions. For other variables, particularly those within-session procedures that distinguish alternative treatments, specification of criteria that define an acceptable range may be more difficult. In some cases, the presence of select processes (e.g., discarding irrational beliefs, improving one's self-concept) might be sufficient; in other cases, a particular level of various processes (e.g., anxiety or arousal) might be required to denote that treatment has been adequately provided.

THERAPIST ISSUES

Training

Therapist as a Factor in the Design. Treatment usually is administered by a therapist, trainer, counselor, or some mediator, all of whom for present purposes are encompassed by the term *therapist.* Although many substantive questions about therapist influences can be studied, there are manifold methodological considerations that must be addressed. It is important to make implausible the possibility that treatment outcome differences can be attributed to differences in therapist competence or other characteristics, unless evaluation of these differences reflects an objective of the study. There are different methodological issues that emerge depending upon the type of outcome study. If one treatment is being tested (e.g., treatment vs. no-treatment or waiting-list control condition), the major issue is ensuring that more than one therapist provides treatment in the study. With only one therapist, any intervention effects might really reflect an effect unique to that therapist. That is, treatment may only be effective (or ineffective) with the particular therapist that was used, perhaps because of some special but not clear characteristic of that therapist. This amounts to a treatment × therapist interaction that cannot be detected by the design. If two or more therapists are utilized, then the effect of the therapist and therapist × treatment can be evaluated as part of the results.

In a study with two or more treatments, other issues emerge. Depending on many practical issues as well as the specific treatments that are studied, a decision needs to be made whether therapists as a factor should be *crossed with* or *nested within* treatment. When therapists are crossed with treatment, each therapist administers each of the treatment conditions in the investigation. Therapists can then be identified as a "factor" in the data analysis. Such analyses permit evaluation of the impact of therapists alone (as a main effect) and in combination (interaction) with treatment.

If therapists are nested within treatments, separate sets of therapists are used to administer the separate treatments. Thus, therapists only administer one of the treatments rather than all of the different treatments. The impact of therapists as a group cannot be separated from treatment effects. Any treatment difference can be reinterpreted as a difference in the therapists who provided the respective treatments. The alternative hypothesis of therapist effects cannot be treated lightly because different sorts of therapists might be attracted to different treatments. It is important to try to rule out the alternative hypothesis that therapist variables accounted for the results. To that end, such characteristics as age, gender, and professional experience should be similar across the sets of therapists administering alternative conditions. It may be difficult to match other characteristics that in a given case might differentiate groups of therapists, because the number of such therapists in any single outcome study typically is small (e.g., two or three therapists for each treatment condition). The small contingent of therapists may also preclude meaningful statistical evaluation of therapist attributes in relation to outcome.

Purely from the standpoint of experimental design, crossing therapists with treatment is preferable because that portion of the patient change associated with therapists (therapist variance) can be separated from the portion due to treatment technique (treatment variance). Yet in outcome studies, overriding reasons may dictate the nesting of therapists within treatments. An obvious advantage of nesting therapists is that therapists of a given technique can be selected for their background, skill level, commitment to, and enthusiasm for a specific technique. The alternative of having all therapists administer all techniques raises other problems such as the differential skill level and background for the different techniques within a given therapist and across therapists. Also, each therapy technique may require considerable training and experience. Consequently, it may be unreasonable to attempt to train novices to master each technique. Furthermore, it may not be feasible to conduct such training because professional therapists, unlike therapists in training, may have less time available or be less willing to learn multiple treatments for a research project.

Even when therapists are selected for their expertise or proficiency within a given technique, the multiple considerations related to treatment integrity should be addressed. Therapist training in the specific version that is to be tested should be provided, supervision should be ongoing to avoid drift from the treatment guidelines or manual, and selected sessions should be assessed to evaluate treatment integrity.

Therapist Characteristics

It seems reasonable that there will be differences among persons who administer treatment and that some of these differences will influence therapeutic change. Indeed, characteristics of therapists have been studied rather extensively in the context of treatment for adults (Beutler, Crago, & Arizmendi, 1986). Significantly less work has been completed in the context of child treatment. Available evidence suggests that therapist characteristics can play an important role in treatment outcome. It is not very meaningful to discuss therapist characteristics that have been generally shown to influence the efficacy of various child treatments. Specific therapist characteristics (e.g., openness, assertiveness, and directness) have been found to be important in relation to specific techniques (e.g., group therapy) (Kolvin et al., 1981).

Of interest here are the methodological considerations raised by the study of therapist characteristics. First, many different types of characteristics can be studied, and these may raise different sorts of problems. Subject and demographic characteristics (e.g., age, experience, treatment orientation) may be of interest. Alternatively, characteristics that emerge over the course of treatment (e.g., expressions of warmth, self-disclosure) can be evaluated as well. Selection of characteristics for study ideally rely upon theory about the treatment, clinical problem, and youth to whom treatment is applied. Theoretical guidelines are sparse for selection of therapist characteristics that would be predicted to relate to outcome.

Second, the study of therapist characteristics requires a sufficient number of therapists to evaluate different levels or degrees of the characteristic of interest. For example, evaluation of the impact of therapist warmth (high vs. low) is not well-studied by utilizing two therapists to administer treatment. Several therapists would be needed and they may need to be carefully selected for their initial characteristics.

Third, there is a special feature of therapist characteristics that warrants mention. In child treatment, many techniques are not administered directly by a therapist in the usual sense. Paraprofessionals often administer treatment. These may include parents, teachers, or peers outside of the context of treatment sessions where therapist characteristics are usually studied. Characteristics of persons who deliver treatment (e.g., parents) as moderators of outcome also are difficult to conceive simply as therapist characteristics. Such characteristics often have important implications for the development and maintenance of the clinical problem. For example, parent management training appears to be less effective when applied to mothers who have lower socioeconomic standing and who are isolated from positive social contacts (Dumas & Wahler, 1983). These characteristics may have a great deal to do with how well specific parenting techniques are grasped and applied. The characteristics may be more properly conceived as patient-related variables (family characteristics) that moderate treatment effects or features that affect treatment integrity.

ASSESSMENT ISSUES

Selection of Outcome Measures

The assessment of treatment outcome has received extensive discussion in the adult therapy literature. There is some agreement that outcome assessment needs to be multifaceted, involving different perspectives (e.g., patients, significant others, mental health practitioners), different facets of the individual (e.g., affect, cognition, and behavior), and different methods of assessment (e.g., self-report, direct observation) (Kazdin & Wilson, 1978a; Lambert et al., 1983; Strupp & Hadley, 1977). In relation to the treatment of children, assessment should include evaluation of performance and adjustment in different settings (e.g., at home, at school, and in the community) and different perspectives (e.g., parent, teacher, child, peers). Additional domains and settings may be dictated by the specific clinical problem. For example, the social impact of treatment (such as participation in school activities for social phobic children or contacts with the police for antisocial children) may assume special importance.

There are special issues that may emerge in the assessment of children. With adults, self-report plays a central role in identifying the clinical problem and evaluating treatment. With children, parent and teacher reports usually provide the primary outcome measures. Although children can report on their symptoms, they often underestimate their dysfunction (Kazdin, Esveldt-Dawson, Unis, & Rancurello, 1983; Orvaschel, Puig-Antich, Chambers, Tabrizi, & Johnson, 1982). Research has shown that there are many discrepancies between reports of children and significant others. For example, reports obtained from parents and children on the children's emotional and behavioral problems often show a very low correlation (Achenbach, McConaughy, & Howell, 1987). Thus, data from these different sources may vary in the extent to which they can reflect therapeutic change. Evidence suggests that children are better reporters than parents on their internal states (e.g., anxiety, depression) but may not recognize several overt behaviors (e.g., tantrums, stealing) as being problematic (Edelbrock, Costello, Dulcan, Conover, & Kalas, 1986). Given the lack of correspondence of measures and the differential reporting of symptoms between parents and children, it is likely that outcome effects would vary for measures completed by these different raters.

Reducing Symptoms and Increasing Prosocial Functioning

The impetus for seeking treatment usually is the presence of various symptoms, or maladaptive, disturbing, or disruptive behaviors. Naturally, the effects of treatment would be measured by the extent to which the problems identified at the outset of treatment are reduced when treatment is completed. Often assessment includes other symptom areas to see if treatment reduced dysfunction in other domains than those initially identified as problematic. The reduction of symptoms, whether identified at the outset of therapy or evident at pretreatment assessment, is obviously central to the evaluation of outcome.

In addition to symptom reduction, it is important to assess prosocial functioning or positive experience of the child. Prosocial functioning refers to the presence of positive adaptive behaviors and experiences such as participation in social activities, social interaction, and making friends. With children and adolescents, adjustment may depend heavily on the positive adaptive behaviors or skills, given the significance of the peer group and prosocial experiences outside the home.

Reducing symptoms no doubt can improve a person's functioning. Yet, the overlap of symptom reduction and positive prosocial functioning may not be great. Separate lines of work can be brought to bear on the issue. To begin with, depressive affect of children is negatively correlated with positive affective experiences such as enjoyment and pleasure (Kazdin, 1987b). The correlation between these two measures, whether completed by children ($r=-.38$) or parents ($r=-.53$) is negative, as expected. However, the small amount of shared variance between the scales indicates that the presence of depressive symptoms is not tantamount to the absence of positive experience and vice versa.

The relation of symptoms and prosocial behavior was also elaborated in a study of changes made among psychiatric inpatient children (ages 6-12) over the course of brief hospitalization (Kazdin, in press a). Ratings were available from parents who evaluated their children before and after hospitalization , using the Child Behavior Checklist (Achenbach & Edelbrock, 1983). The measure includes total symptom and total prosocial (social competence) scores. At prehospitalization, the correlation between a child's total symptoms and total prosocial behavior was $r=-.36$ ($p<.001$, $N=306$). The negative correlation reflects the predictable inverse relationship between symptoms and prosocial behaviors. In addition, over the course of treatment, change in total symptoms correlated $r=-.15$ ($p<.05$, $N=185$) with a change in total prosocial behavior. The low magnitude of the correlation suggests that the reductions in symptoms are not tantamount to improvements in prosocial functioning.

The above findings suggest that prosocial functioning and symptom reduction are not the same. Prosocial functioning may be an important indicator for treatment evaluation in separate ways. It is possible that treatments that appear equally effective in reducing symptoms vary in the extent to which they promote and develop prosocial behaviors. In addition, for children whose symptom reduction is similar, the prognosis may vary as a function of prosocial behaviors evident at treatment outcome. For these reasons, assessment of prosocial behavior needs to be incorporated into treatment outcome.

The assessment of prosocial functioning is not as well developed in scales for children and adolescents as is the assessment of various symptoms. Some measures that currently enjoy widespread use and focus primarily on symptoms have scales to evaluate prosocial functioning. For example, the Child Behavior Checklist, mentioned previously, includes a number of scales to assess a wide range of symptom areas (e.g., anxiety, social withdrawal, depression, aggression, hyperactivity). In addition, a social competence scale is included that assesses participation in social activities, social interaction, and progress at school.

Other measures are available and are devoted exclusively to social behavior. For example, the Matson Evaluation of Social Skills with Youngsters evaluates positive (e.g., conversation skills, making friends) and negative (e.g., social isolation, expression of hostility) social skills (Matson, Rotatori, & Helsel, 1983). Other measures of prosocial functioning may be culled from studies of peer relations and child acceptance and rejection at school (see Parker & Asher, in press). Such measures, including sociometric ratings of various kinds, have infrequently been used as outcome measures in treatment trials.

Other Types of Measures

The emphasis of outcome measures overlooks many other types of measures that may contribute as much or more information about the relative utility and value of alternative treatments. One type of measure worth including pertains to the *processes* within the treatment sessions. The value of such measures is that they can shed light on the processes leading to therapeutic change and serve as a partial test of the model that underlies treatment. Thus, it is valuable to show that changes in, say, cognitive processes occur during treatment when such processes are assumed to mediate change (Spivack et al., 1976).

Another type of measure that is important to include in outcome studies might be referred to generally as *client reactions to treatment.* These measures may reflect dimensions that do not necessarily refer to the adjustment or dysfunction of the clients, but still may distinguish alternative treatments (Kazdin & Wilson, 1978a). For example, attrition, untoward side effects, adherence to the prescribed regimen, attendance, and satisfaction with and acceptability of treatment might vary among treatments. Even if the outcomes of alternative treatments were identical, the treatment of choice might be determined by one or more of these other criteria. Indeed, these other criteria may be of such significance that one treatment that is slightly less effective than another might still be preferred because the loss in effectiveness is much less than the gain in other benefits. For example, a treatment that clients find quite acceptable and easy to comply with might be the treatment of choice over an alternative that is more effective but without these characteristics.

Finally, and related to the above, measures concerning the *administration of treatment* need to be included in outcome studies. Such measures as cost of the treatments, requirements for training therapists, ease of application of procedures by paraprofessionals, resistance of treatment to violations of integrity, and other measures, are quite relevant. Again, treatments similar in outcome may differ on these measures. In general, the extent to which treatment leads to improvements on outcome measures is obviously of central importance. Yet, the exclusive focus on outcome neglects many other significant measures that professionals, parents, teachers, and children alike would consider as important distinctions among alternative treatments.

Timing of Follow-up Assessment

Assessment immediately after treatment is referred to as *posttreatment* assessment; any point beyond that ranging from weeks to years typically is referred to as *follow-up* assessment. Follow-up raises important issues for psychotherapy outcome research such as whether gains are maintained and whether conclusions can be reached at all given patient attrition.

Conclusions about the efficacy of a treatment or relative effectiveness of alternative treatments may vary greatly depending on when assessments are conducted. For example, in the Kolvin et al. (1981) study, two of the interventions (group therapy and behavior modification) used with maladjusted children showed different effects depending on the point in time that assessment was completed. Immediately after treatment, relatively few improvements were evident in the areas of neuroticism, antisocial behavior, and total symptom scores. These areas improved markedly over the course of follow-up which was approximately 18 months after treatment ended. The authors discussed a *sleeper effect*, that is, improvements that were not evident immediately after treatment but emerged and/or increased over time.

Several other studies involving child and adult samples point to the significance of the timing of outcome assessments (e.g., Craighead, Stunkard, & O'Brien, 1981; Deffenbacher & Shelton, 1978; Heinicke & Ramsey-Klee, 1986; Jacobson, 1984; Kingsley & Wilson, 1977; Patterson, Levene, & Breger, 1977; Wright, Moelis, & Pollack, 1976). In these studies, conclusions about the effectiveness of a given treatment relative to a control condition or another treatment differed at posttreatment and follow-up.

Thus, the treatment that appeared more or most effective at posttreatment did not retain this status at follow-up.

Not all studies find that the pattern of results and conclusions about a given treatment relative to another treatment or control condition vary from posttreatment to follow-up assessment. Indeed, a review of treatment studies has suggested that as a rule the pattern between treatments evident at posttreatment remains evident at follow-up (Nicholson & Berman, 1983). However, the number of clear exceptions suggests that the conclusions about a given treatment in any particular study might well depend on when the assessment is conducted. The possibility of quite intricate relationships between timing of assessment and outcome results exists when one considers that changes on different types of measures (e.g., self- or parent-report, psychophysiology) and measures of different constructs (e.g., specific symptoms, adjustment) may also vary with the point in time that assessments are administered (cf. Rachman & Hodgson, 1974).

The possible dependence of conclusions on the timing of follow-up assessment has different implications. To begin with, it is important to determine whether therapeutic changes are maintained and whether they surpass the gains that may be associated with the passage of time without that particular treatment. More than that, it is important to identify the function, curve, or course of change on the outcome measures associated with different techniques. If a few assessment points were obtained during follow-up, the function might be extrapolated so that whether change continues and how change continues can be inferred.

Decisions regarding the timing of follow-up assessment may be influenced by several considerations (Hartmann, Roper, & Gelfand, 1977; Robins, 1973). First, the nature of the treatments may be a critical consideration. Some treatments may be expected to produce a more rapid rate of change, whereas others, possibly equally or more effective in the long run, may be initially slower in their rate of therapeutic change. The occasional finding that treatment effects are delayed (Heinicke & Ramsey-Klee, 1986; Kolvin et al., 1981) and that changes at follow-up are often greater than those immediately after treatment (e.g., Wright et al., 1976) underscores the possibility that a given treatment may vary in outcomes at different assessment points.

Second, characteristics of the symptoms or dysfunction may influence the decision regarding when to conduct follow-up assessment. For behaviors or problems that are expected to be relatively stable (e.g., autistic behavior), the timing of follow-up assessment may be less central than if the behaviors (e.g., depressive symptoms) are episodic and transient. For low frequency events (e.g., firesetting), long follow-up periods may be needed to allow for the accumulation of the behaviors over time to examine differences between treated and control groups of children. Ideally, information on the natural course of the disorder could be used to help decide when to conduct follow-up. The assessment would be planned for the time when the disorder, symptoms, or behavior would be expected to be present.

Third, age or developmental stage of the sample may influence timing of follow-up. If special milestones (e.g., entry into adolescence) follows treatment, follow-up assessment may be planned to avoid or consider the impact of any changes. Also, the normal rate of change in various behaviors may dictate the evaluation period. If marked changes are expected over a follow-up interval as a function of maturation, a briefer follow-up interval may be selected.

OTHER DESIGN ISSUES

Power to Detect Group Differences

A critical research issue is the extent to which an experiment can detect differences between groups when differences exist. This notion, of course, denotes the *power of the test*, which can be estimated quantitatively.[1] Although power is an issue in all research, it raises special issues for treatment studies.

For many studies, the goal may be to compare treatment with a no-treatment or waiting-list control condition. In such investigations, the impact of treatment is expected to be great relative to changes expected to occur without treatment. This is the usual model of research with adult samples. Untreated adults change and these changes vary as a function of the clinical problem, period of time in which change is monitored, and no doubt many other factors. The general view is that if left untreated, clinical problems of adults are less likely to change than if they are treated.

In research with children, a comparison of treatment versus no treatment needs to be considered more cautiously. Depending on the age of the children and the specific dysfunction, marked improvements may occur with no formal treatment. As a general rule, the rate of symptom change is likely to be greater in childhood than in adulthood. Thus, some of the strongest influences on child behavior (history, maturation) may have significant impact on adjustment and dysfunction in the short and long run.

For example, in one treatment study, children were referred by teachers for their aggressiveness, inattention, impulsiveness, lack of motivation and reading or math difficulties (Kent & O'Leary, 1976). Children were assigned to a behavioral treatment or no-treatment control condition. At posttreatment, treated children improved on a variety of measures of deviant

---

[1]Power (1-beta) is the probability of rejecting the null hypothesis when it is false. Stated differently, power is the likelihood of finding differences between the treatments that are being tested when, in fact, the treatments are truly different in their outcomes. The power of a test is a function of sample size, alpha (significance level), and the differences between the conditions that are compared (effect size).

behavior and social and academic functioning relative to untreated controls. However, at the time of follow-up 6 and 9 months later, control children had improved as much as treated children on most of the outcome measures. These findings point to the importance of including no-treatment control children. They also raise the possibility that detecting differences between treatment and no treatment may be more difficult in child than in adult treatment outcome research. Larger sample sizes or highly potent treatments may be needed to detect differences if improvements without treatment can be relatively large.

Considerations related to the power of the investigation become especially salient when outcome studies evaluate two or more active treatments, rather than treatment versus a no-treatment condition. When both interventions are expected to produce change, the investigation must be sufficiently powerful to detect what might prove to be relatively small differences. In the vast majority of outcome studies that contrast two or more treatments, the power is extremely weak due largely to the very small samples sizes (Kazdin, 1986a).

There are many reasons to suspect that outcome studies, as a general rule, provide weak tests. Over 25 years ago, Cohen (1962) completed an analysis of the power of clinical research and concluded that most studies were very weak in detecting small or medium effects (see also Cohen, 1977). Cohen's analysis examined clinical research published in the *Journal of Abnormal and Social Psychology* for a 1-year period (1960). Over 2000 statistical tests were identified (from 70 articles) that were considered to reflect direct tests of the hypotheses of the investigations. To evaluate power, Cohen examined different effect sizes, i.e., the magnitude of the differences between alternative groups based on standard deviation units. Cohen distinguished three levels of effect sizes (small = .25; medium = .50; and large = .75) and evaluated the power of published studies to detect such differences. The results indicated generally that power was extraordinarily weak to detect differences equivalent to effect sizes of the different magnitudes. For example, the median probability of the studies to detect a difference reflecting medium effect size was .48. This means that on the average studies had less than a 50-50 chance to detect group differences when there was a medium size effect. Cohen concluded in general that the power of the studies was weak and that sample sizes in future studies routinely should be increased (see also Cohen, 1977).

A more recent analysis was completed to evaluate the acceptability of these conclusions 20 years later (Rossi, Rossi, & Cottrill, 1984). These investigators sampled research from the *Journal of Personality and Social Psychology* and the *Journal of Abnormal Psychology* journals which were descendants of the journal Cohen analyzed. The data were obtained from 142 articles in the 1982 volumes of these journals. The conclusions were quite similar to those reached by Cohen. Although slight increases in power were evident for detecting small and medium effects, the more recent evaluation led to similar conclusions to those of Cohen. Studies are quite weak for detecting such effects. Although there are no definitive criteria for deciding when power is adequate, power at or above .80 is often provided as a general guideline. In both of the previous evaluations, the vast majority of studies had power below .80 for detecting small and medium effects, respectively.

The applicability of the findings to the present topic might be questioned. Both Cohen (1962) and Rossi et al. (1984) surveyed studies for only a 1-year period. Moreover, the studies did not focus on psychotherapy outcome exclusively or primarily.

There are some problems of psychotherapy outcome studies that may make the preceding analyses of clinical research across diverse areas too conservative. For example, a major problem in treatment research is attrition. Apart from the selection biases that attrition can introduce, power may diminish over the course of follow-up. Sample sizes (and power) at the beginning of an investigation may be markedly reduced by the end of treatment and follow-up assessment. For example, in one large-scale outcome study discussed earlier, almost 90% of the cases (396/450) that completed treatment were lost at follow-up 1 year later (Feldman et al., 1983). The small sample ($n = 54$) divided among several different conditions precluded evaluation of the impact of treatment.

Whether outcome studies are sufficiently powerful to detect differences depends on a number of factors. Among these factors, of course, are the actual differences between treatments on the outcome criteria. When two or more active treatments are included in a given study, each of which is expected to produce change, a very large sample per group (e.g., $n > 100$) may be needed to detect differences when differences exist (Kazdin, 1986a). Needless to say, contemporary outcome studies do not usually include sufficient sample sizes. Although occasionally 25 or more subjects per group are included (e.g., Sloane et al., 1975), typically, the number averages 20 or fewer per group (e.g., Cross, Sheehan, & Khan, 1982; Diloreto, 1971; Liberman & Eckman, 1981; Rush, Beck, Kovacs, & Hollon, 1977). Indeed, in the child therapy literature it is not difficult to find studies comparing alternative treatment and control conditions where the sample sizes are 10 or fewer children per condition (e.g., Forman, 1980; Yu, Harris, Solovitz, & Franklin, 1986). Even with a larger number, the sample may decline considerably over the course of treatment and follow-up. In fact, in some child treatment programs between 40% and 50% may drop out of treatment (Fleischman, 1981; Patterson, 1974; Viale-Val, Rosenthal, Curtiss, & Marohn, 1984). Thus a study beginning with a modest sample of, say 20 per group, would have substantially less than a 50/50 chance of detecting small or medium effects between groups at the time of posttreatment, leaving aside the inevitable attrition over the course of follow-up. Outcome studies as currently conducted may have relatively low power and would be expected to show little or no differences among treatments.

The importance of considering power in advance of designing an investigation has been frequently discussed and helpful guidelines have been available for some time (Cohen, 1977). The use of such guidelines requires considerations of the likely differences (effect size) among treatment and control conditions. Investigators seem to be reluctant to estimate the likely effect size in advance. Rather, they often choose sample sizes based on other considerations such as convenience or standard practice. Yet the option of providing more informed estimates of the requisite sample size is available. Approximations of the likely effect sizes between alternative treatments or treatment and control conditions can be obtained from meta-analyses of psychotherapy (Casey & Berman, 1985; Weisz et al., 1987). Once effect size is estimated, guidelines for sample sizes are easily obtained (see Cohen, 1977).

The power of a test of course goes beyond considerations of effect size and includes sample size and alpha. Because effect size depends on within-group variability of the observations, any facet of the experiment that can reduce the variability can augment power. Attention to methodological issues such as therapist training, treatment integrity, and selection of a homogeneous set of subjects are examples pertinent to outcome research that can increase precision of the test.

Clinical versus Statistical Significance

Typically, conclusions about the relative effectiveness of alternative psychotherapies are based on statistical evaluation of treatment outcome. Statistically significant differences may be important when testing alternative theories or isolating and identifying variables that may have conceptual significance if they lead to different results. In clinical trials where alternative treatments are compared, the primary interest is in outcome. It is not important to show merely that treatments differ (although that may have important value), but rather that there is some clear benefit of a more practical nature favoring one treatment over another.

Several different measures of clinical significance have been posed for psychotherapy research including measurement of the extent to which treatment returns clients to normative levels of functioning, the degree to which change is perceptible to significant others in the clients' everyday lives, and elimination of the presenting problem (Hugdahl & Ost, 1981; Jacobson, Follette, & Revenstorf, 1984; Kazdin & Wilson, 1978a; Kendall & Norton-Ford, 1982; Yeaton & Sechrest, 1981). As yet, there is no standard or uniformly adopted procedure or measurement strategy to assess clinical significance.

Relatively few psychotherapy studies, whether with child or adult populations, incorporate any of the measures designed to evaluate the clinical significance of change. Among those studies that do, one of the most frequently used measures is the extent to which treated patients are returned to normative levels of functioning. To invoke the criterion, a comparison is made between treated patients and peers who are functioning well or without problems in everyday life. Prior to treatment, the patient sample presumably would depart considerably from their well-functioning peers in the area identified for treatment (e.g., anxiety, social withdrawal, aggression). One measure of the extent to which treatment produced clinically important changes would be the demonstration that at the end of treatment, the patient sample was indistinguishable from or well within the range of the normative, well-functioning sample on the measures of interest. A main issue for invoking this criterion is determining the level or range that defines "normal" functioning.

There are many examples of studies that could be cited in which the effects of treatment were evaluated by comparing posttreatment and follow-up performance with normative levels of behavior (e.g., Forehand & Long, in press; Patterson, 1974). As one illustration, Kazdin et al. (1987) examined the effectiveness of problem-solving skills training (PSST), relationship therapy, and minimal-treatment contact with hospitalized antisocial children. PSST consisted of 20 sessions in which children were seen individually. In the sessions, children were trained to apply problem-solving skills to interpersonal interactions that evoked prior aggressive and antisocial behavior. Relationship therapy consisted of sessions in which the therapeutic relationship was utilized to develop insight and to encourage expression of feelings. Minimal-contact children met briefly in sessions with a therapist and played games or engaged in other activities that provided contact, but no specific treatment regimen to alter antisocial behavior. The results showed significant improvements in antisocial behavior and other symptom areas for youths who received PSST, as reflected on parent and teacher checklists immediately after treatment and up to 1 year later. PSST youths were more improved than relationship therapy and minimal contact youths who did not reliably improve. The effects were statistically significant, but were they clinically important?

To answer that question, comparisons were made among treated youths and the normative data obtained for children of the same age and gender. For illustrative purposes, parent data are presented here for the Child Behavior Checklist (CBCL; Achenbach & Edelbrock, 1983) and teacher data are presented for the School Behavior Checklist (SBCL; Miller, 1977). Total scale scores for each of these measures (Total Behavior Problems and Total Disability, respectively) reflect an index of overall symptoms of dysfunction or psychopathology that are evident at home and at school, respectively.

Because the 90th percentile on the measure of total behavioral problems on the CBCL has been found to discriminate clinical and nonreferred samples, this percentile was adopted as the *upper limit for defining a normative range.*

The results in Figure 5.1 (upper panel) show the level of performance of each group in relation to the upper limit of the normative range. For the CBCL, marked changes from pretreatment to posttreatment were evident for the PSST group; yet the changes were of questionable clinical value. Both at posttreatment and follow-up, the means for all groups were well above (i.e., outside of) the upper limit of the normative range. Thus treatment did not move the mean level of the group within the normative level. The data for individual children in the PSST condition also reflected the lack of impact. At posttreatment and 1-year follow-up, approximately 18% and 23% respectively, of youths who received the PSST fell within the normal range for total behavior problems. Thus, the vast majority of children did not improve to the extent that their behavior fell within the normative range.

For the SBCL (Figure 5.1, lower panel), the data are slightly more encouraging. At posttreatment, the mean level of performance of the PSST group fell within the normal range. Unfortunately, by the 1-year follow-up, deviant behavior had increased and exceeded the upper limit of this range. The data for the individual children in the PSST group also convey the effects of this intervention. At posttreatment and 1-year follow-up, approximately 67% and 39% of the youths who received PSST fell within the normal range on the SBCL.

The point of the preceding example is only to illustrate the use of measures designed to evaluate the clinical, applied, or social importance of therapeutic change. Although there are no standard measures at this point, there is general agreement that outcome measures must move beyond those that reflect statistical significance alone (Jacobson et al., 1984). For the child psychotherapy literature, the case might be made that it is premature to examine the clinical significance of change. Relatively few studies have even begun to examine statistical significance of changes in controlled trials. Yet, the paucity of outcome research and the costs of conducting research increase the need to design individual studies in such a way that their yield is maximized. Measures of clinical significance provide important information about the impact of treatment and the need to further develop treatments. As such, clinical significance addresses questions other than those raised by statistical significance alone.

CONCLUSIONS

Several methodological issues and recommendations for psychotherapy research discussed in this chapter do not represent novel approaches or requirements. The issues have been addressed over years of research on

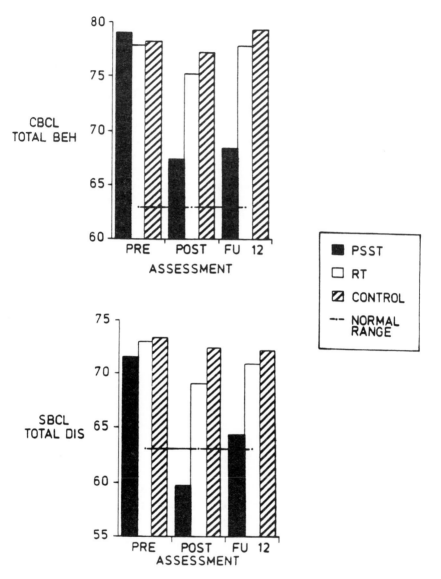

Figure 5.1. Means scores (T scores) for the Problem Solving Skills Training (PSST), Relationship Therapy (RT), and Contact Control groups for the Total Behavior Problem Scale of the CBCL (upper panel) and the Total Disability Scale of the SBCL (lower panel). The horizontal line in each graph represents the *upper* limit of the nonclinical (normal) range of children of the same gender and age. Scores *below* this line fall within the normal range. (From: Kazdin, A. E., Esveldt-Dawson, L., French, N. H., & Unis, A. S. (1987). Problem-solving skills training and relationship therapy in the treatment of antisocial child behavior. *Journal of Consulting and Clinical Psychology, 55,* 76–85).

psychotherapy with adults. A difficulty with child psychotherapy research is the frequent failure to meet basic methodological desiderata. Although there are novel issues that emerge in the investigation of techniques with children, many methodological and design demands for treatment research are approximately the same. Thus, there is no need for child therapy research to undergo the slow methodological evolution the adult therapy research has already passed.

This chapter focused on patient, treatment, therapist, and assessment issues. For the patient issues, emphasis was placed on the need to evaluate alternative types of diagnostic, child, parent, and family variables that may moderate treatment outcome. For treatment issues, special significance was accorded the need to ensure the representativeness of treatment, to specify the procedures and their conceptual bases, and to ensure treatment integrity. The discussion of therapist issues emphasized the importance of therapist training, evaluation of therapists in relation to outcome, and consideration of therapist characteristics that might be predicted as moderators of outcome. Finally, assessment issues were addressed including the range of outcome measures and measures other than outcome that may be relevant to evaluating treatments. The importance of follow-up assessment was also noted given the possible dependence of conclusions about the relative efficacy of alternative treatments on the point in time at which comparisons are made. Other issues of relevance in designing outcome research are the evaluation of statistical power of the test of interest and of the clinical importance of therapeutic change. Failure to attend to these issues will make progress in child psychotherapy continue at a very slow pace.

Chapter 6

Models of Treatment Outcome Research

The field suffers from a paucity of outcome studies on alternative forms of child psychotherapy, a statement that at this point should be fairly clear. Yet, the problem is not only limited in the number of investigations, but also by the inconsistent and weak methodological standards that they often reflect. Progress will be made as improvements emerge in assessment, design, and specification of treatments. As salient issues are addressed, as discussed in the previous chapter, further gains will no doubt be made.

Progress is likely to be accelerated more dramatically by expanding the models of treatment outcome research. *Model of outcome research* here refers to the investigator's conceptualization of the clinical problem and treatment, the specific type of question that is asked about treatment, and the methodological decisions affecting assessment and experimental design. The progress of current treatment research has been limited in part by the restricted model that is applied. Several alternative models are identified and illustrated in the following text. The separate models help delineate the different approaches for identifying and developing effective treatments.

ALTERNATIVE MODELS

Conventional Treatment Model

Description. In the typical psychotherapy outcome study, a specific intervention is applied to a clinically identified group for a specific, time-limited duration. The effects of treatment are evaluated immediately after treatment is terminated and usually over a period of follow-up. These characteristics are so much a part of current outcome strategies that they are difficult to conceive of as a special model of research. Yet, it is useful for the moment to identify these general characteristics as representing a *conventional model of treatment outcome research*. The purpose is not to oversimplify or demean the model, but rather to refer to it as a point of departure for identifying alternative models.

Isolated studies within the fold of the conventional model are easily identified. However, the strength of the approach stems from the set of questions that can be addressed and the cumulative knowledge they can yield. Different treatment evaluation strategies within the conventional model address alternative questions about therapy. Because the goal is to consider novel models, the specific approaches within the conventional model are only highlighted briefly here (see Kazdin, 1980b, for further details).

Perhaps the most basic question of the conventional model is to ask whether a particular treatment or treatment package is effective for a particular clinical problem. This question is asked by the *treatment package strategy* which evaluates the effects of a particular treatment as that treatment is ordinarily used. The notion of a "package" emphasizes that treatment may be multifaceted and include several different components. The question addressed by this strategy is whether treatment produces therapeutic change. To rule out the influence of change as a function of historical events, maturation, "spontaneous remission," repeated testing, and other threats to internal validity, a no-treatment or waiting-list control condition is usually included in the design.

For example, nondirective play therapy is frequently used as a treatment for young children. A treatment package study might test this in a controlled way by selecting children (e.g., $N = 60$) with a particular clinical problem and assigning them (randomly or unsystematically) to either the play therapy or control (waiting-list) condition. The effects would be evaluated on several measures administered after treatment. If the results favored play therapy, this would not, of course, explain why the differences occurred or precisely what aspect of the play therapy condition accounts for the findings. Yet a few such studies would establish that this is an effective treatment for a given clinical problem.

The *dismantling treatment strategy* consists of analyzing the components of a given treatment package. After a particular package has been shown to produce therapeutic change, research can begin to analyze the basis for change. To dismantle a treatment, individual components are eliminated or isolated from the treatment. Some clients may receive the entire treatment package while other clients receive the package minus one or more components. Dismantling research can help identify the necessary and sufficient components of treatment. For example, in the context of child treatment, child psychotherapy is often accompanied by counseling of the parent (Levitt, 1971). A dismantling approach might examine whether the combined components (parent and child contact) offer benefits beyond those associated with a focus on the parent or child alone.

The *constructive treatment strategy* refers to developing a treatment package by adding components that may enhance outcome. In this sense, the constructive treatment approach is the opposite of the dismantling strategy. A constructive treatment study begins with a treatment which may consist of one or a few ingredients or a larger package, and adds various ingredients to determine whether the effects can be enhanced. The strategy asks the question, "what can be added to treatment to make it more effective?"

The strategy of constructing an increasingly effective treatment was illustrated in a school-based program for 6th and 7th grade youths selected because of their discipline problems and low academic motivation (Bien & Bry, 1980; Bry, 1982; Bry & George, 1980). The youths were assigned randomly to one of three interventions or a no-intervention control condition. Each condition added various components to alter student behavior. In the first condition, teacher conferences were scheduled by program staff to focus attention and programs on individual children with problems. In the second condition, teacher conferences were held but group meetings with the children were also scheduled. In these meetings special behavioral programs were devised to help the children with school activities. In the third condition, teacher conferences and group meetings with the children were scheduled but parent conferences were also held.

Essentially, the group with all three ingredients, involving contact with teachers, students, and parents was the only condition preventing further deterioration in grades. Interventions without all three ingredients were no better than the no-intervention group. At follow-up assessments 1 and 5 years later, intervention youths evinced greater employment, less drug abuse, less reported criminal behavior, and fewer school problems than controls. This study nicely illustrates the accretion of ingredients that characterizes the constructive strategy.

The *parametric treatment strategy* refers to altering specific aspects of treatment to determine how to maximize therapeutic change. Dimensions or parameters are altered to find the optimal manner of administering the treatment. These dimensions are not new ingredients added to the treatment (e.g., as in the constructive strategy) but variations within the technique to maximize change. Increases in duration of treatment or variations in how material is presented are samples of the parametric strategy.

As an illustration of the parametric strategy, Heinicke (1969) compared two variations of psychoanalytic treatment for children (6-10 years old) referred for a learning disturbance with psychological difficulties. Intensity of treatment, as reflected in frequency and total amount of treatment, was varied between two groups. Children were seen either once a week or four times per week. Mothers were also seen separately once a week for children in each of the groups. At the end of treatment and up to a 2-year follow-up, children seen four times per week showed greater change in personality processes than those seen only once per week. Achievement gains for children seen four times per week were also superior at the 2-year follow-up. These results have been replicated (Heinicke & Ramsey-Klee, 1986).

The *comparative treatment strategy*, probably the most familiar approach, contrasts two or more treatments and addresses the question of which treatment is best for a particular clinical problem. Comparative studies attract wide attention because they address an important clinical issue and because they often contrast conceptually competing interventions. For example, and as mentioned previously (chapter 4), Alexander and Parsons (1973) compared three variations of family therapy (client-centered, psychodynamically oriented, and functional family therapies) and no treatment for delinquent youths. Posttreatment and an 18-month follow-up assessment showed improved family interaction and lower recidivism rates (court contacts) for youths in the functional family therapy group relative to other family therapies and no-treatment controls.

Comparative outcome studies have enjoyed widespread use, particularly in the psychotherapy literature with adults (Kazdin & Wilson, 1978b; Luborsky, Singer, & Luborsky, 1975). Among alternative treatment evaluation strategies, special difficulties often arise in comparative studies including obstacles in keeping the techniques distinct, in holding constant variables associated with treatment administration, and ensuring the integrity of the individual treatments (Kazdin, 1986a).

The previous strategies emphasize the technique as a major source of influence in treatment outcome. The effectiveness of treatments can vary widely as a function of characteristics of the patients and the therapists. The *client and therapist variation strategy* examines whether alternative attributes of the client (child, parent, family characteristics) or therapist contribute to outcome. The strategy is implemented by selecting clients and/or therapists on the basis of specific characteristics. When clients or therapists are classified according to a particular selection variable, the question is whether treatment is more or less effective with certain kinds of participants.

For example, questions of this strategy might ask if treatment is more effective with girls rather than boys, with children who are older rather than younger, or with children who vary in level of cognitive or intellectual development. Does treatment lead to greater change when administered by therapists who have more experience with children or who themselves are parents? Examples of the client and therapist variation strategy were provided in the discussion of individual treatment studies (chapter 4). The study by Kolvin et al. (1981) evaluated child age, gender, and clinical problem (neurosis vs. conduct disorder) to see if treatments varied as a function of these child characteristics. In their study of antisocial behavior, Feldman et al. (1983) investigated whether experience of the trainers affected outcome. As illustrated here, there are a host of client and therapist variables that might be selected. Ideally, a theoretical framework or special understanding of the treatment, nature of the population, or clinical problem serve as the basis for selecting specific variables for study.

General Comments. Viewed individually, the strategies of the conventional treatment models reflect a logical progression in the type of questions that are addressed about treatment. The progression can be seen in the specificity of questions and the type of control and comparison conditions they require. A very basic question about the effects of treatment can begin with the treatment package strategy. Other strategies elaborate the conditions under which the treatment is maximally effective. Of course, this progression does not necessarily characterize how research actually proceeds. For example, comparative outcome questions that examine the relative efficacy of alternative treatments often are conducted early in the development of a treatment and possibly before the individual techniques have been well-developed enough to warrant such a test.

The yield from the conventional model of psychotherapy evaluation has not been particularly great for the development of child psychotherapies. Yet, the model and the manifold questions that it can address should not be faulted. Relatively few studies have taken advantage of the conventional model. Of the many studies, methodological flaws have often interfered with the range of inferences that can be drawn. For example, the patient sample and the treatment are often poorly specified, randomization of children to groups is sacrificed, and treatment is not implemented as intended. The yield of an investigation of any treatment strategy requires that basic methodological requirements are met. Because of methodological limitations, the different strategies embraced by the conventional model have not been thoroughly mined.

Even if improvements in research methodology occurred immediately, there are several reasons to look beyond the conventional model of treatment evaluation. Additional models expand the approaches for developing effective treatments. These alternative models supplement rather than replace or compete with conventional outcome research (Kazdin 1987c).

High-strength Intervention Model

Description. In the conventional model, the treatment obviously is intended to have impact, but rarely is it explicitly designed to provide a potent version of treatment. An obvious direction would be to adopt a high-strength intervention model which consists of increasing the strength or intensity of treatments. The high-strength intervention model addresses the question, "What is the likely impact on the problem of the maximum or seemingly most potent treatment available?" This model is especially relevant to severe clinical problems where effective interventions have not been identified.

"Severe problems" might be defined here in part in relation to the stability or prognosis of the problem and the absence of clearly effective treatments. Examples of severe problems might include delinquency, autism, and severe mental retardation. These problems are severe because the problems are multifaceted and affect diverse areas of functioning. For such clinical problems, it is useful to evaluate interventions that provide the strongest versions of the currently available treatments. Such an evaluation conveys what we can accomplish at this point in the development of treatment. If the strongest version of treatment can produce significant therapeutic change, then one can begin to reduce the dose, intensity, cost and other factors to see if similar gains can still be achieved. On the other hand, if a strong version of treatment does not produce change or sufficient change for clinically significant improvement, this suggests that other treatments or components of treatment need to be considered.

For psychosocial treatments, strength and intensity of treatment are difficult to define. The problem stems in part from nebulous or poor conceptualizations of treatment. To vary or increase the strength of treatment, one must have some idea regarding the procedures or processes that account for therapeutic change. Only when these processes are identified and described can they be explicitly maximized in the context of treatment.

One way of conceptualizing the strength of treatment is with the notion of *therapeutic effort* (Newman & Howard, 1986). This refers to the amount of treatment that is provided, the degree of restrictiveness that is required of the patient (e.g., inpatient vs. outpatient care) or the extent to which treatment encompasses multiple aspects of the child's environment and daily life (e.g., inclusion of the intervention of behavior at home and at school, involvement of parents, teachers, peers), and the costs of providing treatment. A high-strength intervention might consist of a high dose of treatment, that encompasses diverse facets of the child's life, and that is costly in terms of the use of professionals and paraprofessionals involved in treatment.

Considering one facet of therapeutic effort conveys the need for pursuing a high-strength intervention model. One way of enhancing the strength of treatment might be to increase the amount of treatment. Current tests of treatment are relatively brief. In one review of child psychotherapy entailing a variety of psychosocial treatments and clinical problems, the mean duration of treatment outcome studies was 9.5 weeks (Casey & Berman, 1985). Although duration of treatment is not necessarily a sign of the likely strength of the intervention, 9 to 10 sessions provided once per week is relatively brief considering that many of the problems children bring to treatment are not transient. The adult psychotherapy literature has tended to show a duration or dose effect of psychotherapy (Howard, Kopta, Krause, & Orlinsky, 1986). Across a large number of patients and studies, more sessions were associated with greater improvements. As shown in Figure 6.1, 50% of

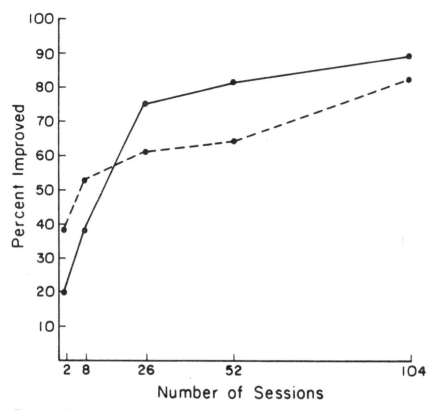

Figure 6.1. The relationship between the number of sessions of psychotherapy for adult patients and the percent of patients improved. The solid line reflects ratings at the end of treatment completed by researchers based on chart review. The broken line reflects patient self-report ratings during the course of treatment. (From: Howard, K. I., Kopta, S. M., Krause, M. S., & Orlinksy, D. E. (1986). The dose-effect relationship in psychotherapy. *American Psychologist, 41,* 159–164.)

the patients are evaluated as markedly improved by the eighth session (solid line) and 75% markedly improved by the 26th session. Thus, duration of treatment may be a significant factor. In the case of children, age, developmental stage, sex, clinical problem, and treatment technique may all determine the relative impact of a particular duration of treatment on outcome. The point here is not to focus on treatment duration, but rather on the broader set of variables that might contribute to the strength or potency of the intervention.

Illustration. It is difficult to specify the precise criteria that would constitute a high intensity dose or variation of treatment, but illustrations are clearly recognizable when they occur. For example, Lovaas (1987) reported the effects of a high-intensity intervention for young autistic children (under 4 years of age). Children with a diagnosis of autism were assigned to an experimental group that provided an intensive treatment program or to one of two control conditions. The treatment condition was a behavioral program that was conducted in the child's home, school, and community for an average of 40 hours per week for 2 or more years. Several college student-therapists who worked on a part-time basis administered the treatment over this period. In addition, parents were trained extensively, so that treatment could take place at home for almost all of the child's waking hours, 365 days a year.

Treatment focused on eliminating maladaptive behavior (e.g., self-stimulation, aggression) and developing a variety of prosocial (e.g., play) and cognitive/academic skills (e.g., language, reading, writing, and other tasks). A major goal of treatment was to place children into the normal classroom where they would function largely as other children. For youths who entered a normal first-grade class, treatment was reduced from 40 hours per week to 10 hours or less per week and eventually was terminated with minimal contact. For treated children who did not enter a normal first grade, the intervention continued at 40 hours per week for more than a total of 6 years (more than 14,000 hours of one-to-one treatment per child).

Two separate control groups were included. In the first control condition, 10 hours per week of treatment were provided but not all of the behavioral contingencies were invoked. In the second condition, children did not participate in treatment. Multiple measures were used to evaluate outcome but primary emphasis was on educational functioning at follow-up.

The results indicated that 47% of the treated group achieved normal intellectual and educational functioning, as reflected by scoring within the normal range on standardized intelligence tests and successfully completing first grade in the public schools. The two control groups did not differ from each other in educational functioning, and only 2% achieved normal educational functioning. The impact of the intensive treatment was dramatic. For example, the treatment group gained an average of 30 points on standardized intelligence tests (WISC-R, Stanford Binet, or other measures) over control subjects who did not participate in the treatment.

The Lovaas study (1987) clearly provided a high-strength treatment. One can make this evaluation of the strength of treatment largely independently of the outcome effects. The intensive focus within a given week (e.g., 40 hours of treatment) and protracted period of treatment (up to 6 years) greatly surpass other parallel efforts. It would be difficult to mount this type of treatment on a routine basis or in subsequent studies. Yet, the findings identify the sorts of changes that can be accomplished. It is possible that less intense treatment regimens might be developed to return high proportions of youths to public school classrooms. On the basis of the Lovaas study, it appears as if the goal can be attained.

The question of primary interest is whether a maximum treatment effort can produce change and whether change is clinically important. At a given point in time, theory and research may alter views about what a high-strength treatment might be for a particular clinical problem. Based on current conceptualizations and available procedures, the Lovaas test illustrates the model very well. The use of a control condition in which a highly abbreviated version of treatment was provided (e.g., 10 vs. 40 hours per week) and with fewer treatment components (e.g., exclusion of some of the contingencies to alter child behavior), also illustrates features of parametric and dismantling studies of the conventional treatment model.

General Comments. High-strength tests of treatment are rarely conducted and for reasons that are readily understandable. Several problems emerge in attempting to test a high-strength version of treatment. First, the dimensions that determine strength are unknown. Thus, well-intentioned clinical researchers would not necessarily know how to maximize the strength of treatment if they wanted to. Second, there are practical limits to increasing the strength of treatment as well including what consumers (children, parents, third-party payers, and grant funding agencies) will accept. The idea of protracted and intensive treatment for deviant behavior is not as familiar nor as well-accepted as protracted punishment for criminal acts. Third, patient attrition is another limitation that restricts how long treatments can be implemented. A reasonable assumption is that the longer patients are asked to remain in treatment, the greater the attrition rate. Yet, stronger treatments may not translate simply to more and longer sessions for reasons noted previously. Finally, a major objection to high-strength treatments is their cost. High strength is likely to be reflected in the cost of resources (e.g., therapists, therapist training, number of sessions, patient contact hours). Conducting a test of a high-strength treatment may be objected to because of these costs. Yet even if such a test were very expensive in terms of professional resources and patient care, in the long run the knowledge gained might save future costs derived from many other tests with weaker versions of treatment.

Amenability-to-treatment Model

Description. An obvious assumption in treatment research is that the specific technique that is applied to the clinical problem makes an important difference. Yet, implicit in much of treatment research is that the specific technique, at the exclusion of other factors, accounts for most of the change that is achieved. Much of the child psychotherapy literature is an array of different treatment techniques that are designed to produce change. There has been relatively little interest in evaluating the possible child, parent, and family factors that might interact with (i.e., moderate the effects of) treatment. The client and therapist variation strategy of the conventional treatment model consists of evaluating characteristics of the client (e.g., child, significant other) or therapist that might influence treatment outcome. For example, demonstration that child gender, age, or level of cognitive development affects treatment outcome would illustrate the client and therapist variation strategy.

There is a special version of this strategy that warrants delineation as a separate model. The goal of this model is to identify those individuals who are likely to be most amenable to treatment. The model requires the selection of youths on the basis of factors supposedly related to amenability to treatment and then evaluating the differential amenability of youths to treatment in a clinical trial. Once an effective treatment is identified with a group considered to be especially amenable to the treatment, the intervention can be extended in subsequent tests to less amenable cases. If treatment did not produce change with youths considered to be highly amenable cases, the likelihood of the procedures working with more recalcitrant cases is small.

The selection of youths who vary in their amenability to treatment will depend on the specific clinical problem and the factors related to its onset and continuation. For example, in the treatment of antisocial child behavior, several child characteristics (e.g., age of symptom onset, diversity of antisocial symptoms), parent characteristics (e.g., father alcoholism, criminal behavior), and family characteristics (e.g., size, presence of siblings with antisocial behavior) relate to continuation of the behaviors (Kazdin, 1987a). Based on epidemiological evidence, one could identify youths who are likely to vary in their responsiveness to treatment efforts. This would be important because to date, few techniques have been demonstrated to exert impact on the problem.

Illustration. An illustration of the amenability-to-treatment model has been provided in a study with delinquents. Adams (1970) evaluated individual psychotherapy with institutionalized older delinquents ($N=400$, age range 17-23 years) who were randomly assigned to treatment or a no-treatment control group. Youths were delineated as *amenable* or *nonamenable* to treatment on the basis of pooled clinical judgment derived from several characteristics of the youths. Amenable youths were more intelligent, verbal, anxious, insightful, aware of their problems, and interested in change. Treatment consisted of one or two weekly counseling sessions given for an average of 9 months. Some youths also received group therapy. After treatment and up to a 3-year follow-up, amenable youths who received treatment showed significantly less recidivism than controls. In contrast, nonamenable treated youths did worse in comparsion to controls. The study points to the potential benefits of delineating youths by their likely amenability to treatment.

General Comments. The approach of identifying youths who are more or less amenable to treatment can be integrated into existing controlled outcome research. Within a given study, youths can be identified as more or less amenable to the intervention based on characteristics of the sample and hypotheses about the interface of treatment and these characteristics. Analyses of outcome effects are then based on comparisons of subgroups within the investigation to assess responsiveness to treatment as a function of amenability. A major issue, of course, is identifying those factors that relate to amenability. Leads from research on the correlates of a particular disorder might serve as a point of departure. For example, children who are clinically depressed or show anxiety disorders are likely to have a parent with the respective disorders (e.g., Last, Francis, Hersen, Kazdin, & Strauss, 1987; Strober & Carlson, 1982). It may be that children with similar clinical dysfunction but who vary in their family history (loading) of the disorder will differ in their amenability to intervention.

If disorder specific leads are difficult to identify from current research, there are some more general variables that might be used as a tentative basis for selecting youths who are likely to be amenable to treatment. Family patterns of deviance and psychopathology, high levels of stressful events, and history of a "difficult" temperament are some of the variables that are implicated with the onset of clinical dysfunction and long-term course (Garrison & Earls, 1987; Johnson, 1986). These factors are not relevant to risk for all disorders, but do have a degree of nonspecificity for long-term risk for dysfunction. Hence, these factors might serve as a point of departure for identifying youths who are likely to vary in responsiveness to treatment.

Broad-based Intervention Model

Description. Clinical problems can vary in the extent to which they affect and encompass diverse aspects of the child's life. Some problems may be relatively circumscribed (e.g., enuresis, tics) and can be focused on directly with circumscribed or highly focused interventions. Other problems are relatively circumscribed but they may affect diverse areas of funtioning. For example, separation anxiety may keep a child home from school and isolated from interactions with peers. Once the anxiety is reduced, school and peer functioning may be quite adequate. Treatment of anxiety may have broad impact on other areas of functioning.

Yet, other problems, by their very nature, are quite broad; virtually all areas of functioning are related to the dysfunction (e.g., pervasive developmental disorder, severe mental retardation). One need not look to extremes of behavior to identify problems that have pervasive effects. For example, antisocial child behavior encompasses the child's functioning at home and at school, interactions with adults and peers, behavioral and cognitive processes related to social interaction, and academic performance. In the typical application of treatment, a particular intervention is implemented to alter an important facet of the child and/or the system in which the child functions. Psychic conflict, self-esteem, cognitive processes, and behavioral repertoires illustrate some of the foci of treatment. The facet that is targeted is considered on theoretical or clinical grounds to be central to the child's problem. Yet, in light of the range of deficits and pervasiveness of dysfunctions such as antisocial behavior, the scope of most treatments may not be sufficiently broad.

Continuing with the example of antisocial behavior, what can reasonably be expected from alternative techniques and would they be expected to be sufficient in the breadth of their effects? For example, if individual psychotherapy achieved the maximum benefits for those psychological domains that are altered, could one expect less aggressive behavior, more prosocial behavior at school, improved grades, or reduced temper tantrums? The connections between improved functioning in individual therapy, as defined by alternative approaches such as psychodynamically oriented or client-centered therapy, and changes in the many domains in which antisocial youths are deficient have not been established empirically. Similarly, for social skills training (a behavioral approach that focuses directly on interpersonal behavior), it seems unreasonable to expect changes in such domains as cognitive functioning, grades, and temper tantrums. One would hope for improved prosocial behavior. Yet, changes in other domains do not necessarily follow.

One direction for future research is to broaden the comprehensiveness or scope of interventions from their typical application to address a large set of domains relevant to the clinical problem and to the individual youth's dysfunction. Perhaps treatment should be conceived of in a *modular fashion*, where there are separate components that are woven into an overall treatment regimen. Separate areas of the child's dysfunction could be addressed including treatment for the family (parent management training, family therapy) and the child (e.g., individual or group psychotherapy). In addition, different aspects of the child's behavior may require special treatments (e.g., medication to gain control of aggressive acts, academic counseling, behavior modification contingencies for the classroom and community settings).

One area that warrants special mention for broad-based interventions pertains to academic performance. Academic difficulties are often the primary basis for which children are referred to clinics (Gilbert, 1957).

Children referred for treatment of emotional or behavioral dysfunction often have difficulties in academic work as reflected in grade or achievement level in reading, writing, and arithmetic.[1] For some clinical dysfunctions (e.g., enuresis, tics), academic performance may or may not be a problem. For other dysfunctions (e.g., attention deficit-hyperactivity disorder, conduct disorder), it is quite likely that the child is performing poorly in school.

School functioning is an important and perhaps neglected concomitant of psychiatric dysfunction and treatment. The importance is suggested by findings indicating that academic dysfunction in childhood predicts subsequent psychiatric impairment and, alternatively, early psychiatric impairment predicts subsequent academic dysfunction (Bachman, Johnston, & O'Malley, 1978; Hobbs, 1982). Also academic functioning at the end of treatment predicts maintenance of both academic and behavioral adjustment thereafter (Baenen, Stephens, & Glenwick, 1986). Current findings do not illuminate the relations of academic functioning to long-term prognosis for various disorders or treatment techniques. It is relatively clear that academic dysfunction including learning and reading disabilities are relatively stable and that these problems are correlated with other problematic behaviors (e.g., acting out) over time (see Clarizio & McCoy, 1983). The impact of broadening psychosocial treatments to address deficiencies in school performance remains in need of clarification. Nevertheless, it would seem advisable based on current, albeit incomplete, data to include specific and concrete academic interventions as part of treatment for children not functioning well at school.

Illustration. The need for a broad-based intervention has been suggested by recent studies on childhood depression. Depressive symptoms (e.g., sad affect, loss of interest in activities, feelings of worthlessness) have been effectively treated with tricyclic medication. Yet, current research suggests that depressed children show marked deficiencies in communications with their mothers and in peer relations, when compared to nondepressed children and nonreferred ("normal") children (Puig-Antich et al., 1985a, 1985b). After recovery from depression with the medication, mother-child interactions and peer relations remain deficient. The results suggest that deficient social functioning, often associated with depression, may not improve sufficiently with medication. It is likely that some form of additional treatment that focuses on social skills and interpersonal functioning would be helpful to address the broad range of symptoms and associated features.

---

[1]Several Developmental Disorders are recognized in DSM III-R that reflect a variety of dysfunctions in academic achievement in reading, writing, and arithmetic (Reading, Expressive Writing, and Arithmetic Disorders, respectively). The fact that these dysfunctions are recognized and diagnosed does not necessarily mean that they are specifically and concretely incorporated into treatment plans.

Indeed, research on depression with adults has suggested that psychosocial treatments (e.g., interpersonal psychotherapy) and medication often provide unique and complementary advantages in addressing different symptoms (Klerman & Schechter, 1982).

More is known about the range of dysfunctions that are reflected by antisocial behavior than childhood depression. Specific interventions often are applied that attend to a narrow range of areas where dysfunctions are evident. For example, parent management training focuses on parent-child interaction and its contribution to deviant child behavior. Many problems within the family (e.g., parent psychopathology and marital discord) are not usually treated, although they may be relevant to the success and outcome for the child. Perhaps even more obvious, parent management training does not focus on the child in the sense of improving his or her coping skills and interpersonal resources. Although the conceptual model upon which parent management training is based does not emphasize children's resources in responding to their environment, there is ample evidence that such children have special problems in their interpersonal repertoires (Dodge, 1985; Spivack et al., 1976). Treatment can be expanded to address this and other domains known to be deficient or problematic.

Most treatments are relatively narrow in their scope and focus. This has many desirable features. Hopefully, specific techniques do have specific effects on domains of functioning and should not be oversold as panaceas for child and family problems. On the other hand, many clinical problems are multifaceted and one can raise the question of whether a specific or single technique will alter the domains known to be problematic for a given clinical problem. This is not a rationale for a "shotgun" approach to treatment selection and application nor for an unspecified or loose eclecticism. Rather, the issue demands a reasoned and empirically based approach for selecting broad treatments, as the clinical problem and breadth of dysfunction demand.

General Comments. The idea of multifaceted treatments is not at all new. Indeed, clinical researchers have long recognized the multiple problems of children and their families and have proposed treatments that provide family casework, community mental health services, and vocational guidance, plus direct treatment of child and parental dysfunction (e.g., Glick, 1972). Some treatment regimens routinely provide such diverse services. As a prime example, residential treatment programs for emotionally disturbed children often include a wide array of interventions (e.g., music, art and recreational therapies), independently of their demonstrated efficacy (Kazdin, 1985).

There are other examples of broad-based treatments where a select number of components or modules are integrated. As an example, Massimo and Shore (1963, 1967) provided psychotherapy, vocational placement, and remedial education for antisocial adolescents. Similarly, in the Cambridge-Somerville Youth study, delinquent youths received individual and family counseling, academic tutoring, community programs, and psychiatric and medical attention (Powers & Witmer, 1951). These studies illustrate some of the many attempts to provide comprehensive treatments but they are *not* proposed here as models to guide future treatment research. There are difficulties with these and other studies that point to the need for fresh evaluation efforts of multifaceted treatments.

First, the different components have been provided unsystematically or on an "as needed" basis. Not all persons receive all components of treatment or the same amount of a given component. Individualization of treatment is fine, but decision rules need to be explicit to determine who receives what treatment, when, and why. Second, treatment components are rarely described in a fashion that permits their duplication in clinical work or replication in research. Finally, treatment integrity of the different components has not been assessed in most applications of multifaceted treatments, so that there is no assurance that treatments were tested or that individual components have been provided. In fact, assessment of treatment integrity may be particularly crucial in multifaceted treatments where deterioration of portions of the intervention are most likely. The complexity of treatment and the uneven abilities of trainers (therapists) to provide the various treatment components make the intervention especially vulnerable to decay.

The potential need for broad-based programs is not a rationale for the haphazard agglomeration of techniques selected for their intuitive appeal and face validity. The selection of the treatments for a more comprehensive focus needs to be based upon the best available conceptualizations and evidence. Constituent components of treatment need to have a strong warrant for inclusion. Many current treatments suffer from weak conceptual bases already. The combination of multiple techniques without regard to what they are supposed to accomplish and how they are to be administered potentially compounds the problem.

There is a tendency to reject the methodology inherent in a broad-based approach because of the lack of specificity of the conclusion that can be reached about treatment. At the end of the investigation, one cannot identify what component(s) accounted for change. Perhaps not all of the components are needed to produce change or perhaps the complexity of the intervention was unnecessary. There are separate responses to such objections. The broad-based intervention model is not proposed for situations where relatively circumscribed interventions have been effectively applied. For situations where the clinical problem is complex and multifaceted, and for which effective techniques have yet to be identified, the initial task is to produce therapeutic change. A multifaceted and broad-based treatment provides a point of departure for maximizing the likelihood of change. As such, the rationale of the broad-based treatment model closely resembles that of the high-strength intervention model. For the broad-based intervention, demonstration of initial change is the critical priority. Once such a multifaceted treatment is shown to produce change, it might be quite worthwhile then to begin to analyze the contributions of individual components with dismantling strategy research.

A Chronic Disease Model

The final model to be proposed as a guide to treatment research warrants some prefatory comments. There is, within psychology and other social sciences, a frequently voiced disdain for "the medical model" of psychopathology or deviant behavior. The model is proposed to help explain how a particular dysfunction came about, how it should be treated, and what might occur in the future with and without treatment. Actually, there are many different models of disease, injury, and dysfunction within medicine (Buss, 1966). It is not difficult to select one of these models (e.g., bacterial infection, systemic disease, trauma) and to convey how it is patently inappropriate as a model for a particular set of deviant or normal behaviors. There is no interest here in entering into the broader discussion about medical models and the strengths and limitations of their application within medicine or other areas (Kazdin, 1978a).

Evidence suggests that some problems (e.g., conduct disorder, attention deficit-hyperactivity disorder, major depression) may have lifelong consequences. The usual conventional model may not provide the appropriate guidelines for identifying effective interventions. There is one medical model among the many that may prompt an approach to the identification and development of psychosocial treatments, namely, that of chronic disease. There are, of course, many chronic diseases, and here too, one might distinguish different models based on etiology, clinical course, and response to treatment.

Among many diseases, diabetes mellitus is relatively familiar and one that illustrates selected issues that may be applicable to clinical dysfunctions such as conduct disorder or hyperactivity; problems that may continue from childhood into adulthood for many youths. Diabetes mellitus is a disorder of carbohydrate metabolism that results from the inadequate production or utilization of insulin. Characteristically, diabetes is viewed as a chronic condition that is not treated in such a fashion that it is expected to go away. Treatment is based on the assumption that the person suffers from a condition that requires continued care, management, and treatment.

The conventional model of psychotherapy research is to administer a particular intervention over a period of time (e.g., weeks or months), to terminate the treatment and to hope for and/or marvel at the permanent changes. For many clinical problems, this model *is* very much like an inappropriate medical model (e.g., bacterial infection) where the antidote (e.g., an antibiotic) is administered and is expected to eliminate (e.g., cure) the problem. Indeed, the model would also be inappropriate for a disease like diabetes where an effective treatment (e.g., insulin) administered for a delimited period would not, after termination, be expected to ameliorate the problem. It might be heuristically valuable to consider some types of childhood dysfunction as chronic conditions that require intervention, continued monitoring, and evaluation over the course of one's life.

Consider conduct disorder as an example of a childhood dysfunction where a chronic disease model may be relevant. First, research on conduct disorder suggests that it is very much like a chronic condition in terms of its development and course. Also, the dysfunction has broad impact both during childhood (e.g., in affecting behavior at home and at school; interpersonal, academic and cognitive spheres) and adulthood (e.g., psychological, social, and work adjustment).

Second, there are in fact a number of therapeutic procedures that can produce change in antisocial behaviors. Many behavioral treatments such as social skills training and reinforcement and punishment programs are effective in altering aggressive behavior (Kazdin, 1985). Comprehensive behavioral programs for antisocial youths (e.g., Achievement Place program initiated in Kansas) have been especially effective while they are implemented (Kirigin, Braukmann, Atwater, & Wolf, 1982). Yet, these programs have as a rule shown little long-term effects after treatment is terminated. The fact that treatments can achieve marked changes while they are in effect, using the conventional model of treatment application, is interpreted as representing failure (i.e., that the treatments are good but not good enough). Alternatively, the treatments could be viewed, within a chronic disease model, as quite effective. The treatments merely need to be applied in some form on a continuous basis.

There is no need to press the analogy of diabetes and various psychological or psychosocial disorders of childhood. However, diabetes helps to convey a very different model from the one usually implicit in conventional treatment outcome studies of childhood disorders. Also, there is an interesting aspect of the treatment of diabetes that may be relevant. Diabetes often requires continued administration of treatment (insulin), the model adopted here. Yet, current work on organ transplants suggests that there might well be a permanent cure of diabetes for many persons, although it may be premature to state within the next few years the actual effective application of the procedure. The point to underscore is that adopting a chronic disease model for alternative psychological disorders is not a permanent commitment to this model. The model points to the need for continued care and monitoring of functioning until the time that a better, more abbreviated, and more effective intervention is developed.

CONCLUSIONS

This chapter identified five alternative models that might be used to identify effective treatments for children. The *conventional treatment model* was identified as the approach evident in the vast majority of contemporary outcome studies. The model was identified not to demean its importance. Indeed, the model can address a large number of critical questions about treatments and factors that contribute to their efficacy. Specific strategies within the conventional model were noted including treatment package, dismantling, constructive, parametric, comparative, and client and therapist variation strategies. Although there are limits to the scope of these strategies, the conventional model has not been sufficiently exploited in the child psychotherapy literature. A number of methodological flaws that plague outcome research have sacrificed the yield from conventional outcome studies.

Even with improved methodology, there are other models of treatment that warrant serious attention. Such models can greatly accelerate advances in identifying effective interventions. Several models were presented including the *high-strength intervention model*, the *amenability-to-treatment model*, the *broad-based intervention model*, and a *chronic disease model*. The models are characterized by different ways of presenting treatment and identifying cases for inclusion in outcome studies.

One might argue that the models have been repeatedly applied and cite examples that reflect close approximations. For example, prevention studies focusing on high-risk youths and community interventions that provide multiple services to behavior problem children might be considered to reflect the *amenability-to-treatment* and *broad-based treatment models*. Yet, little work has focused on specific, well-operationalized disorders; addressed risk factors of known significance for long-term prognosis; combined multiple facets of treatment in a reasoned way; and then evaluated their subsequent impact on specific dysfunctions. In short, the models have not been applied in a way to address the issues noted here.

Similarly, a *chronic disease model*, as applied to mental health problems, is not new. There are already "mental health" problems that are viewed in this fashion (e.g., Alcoholics' Anonymous views of treatment for the alcoholic). Yet, specific dysfunctions of childhood (e.g., conduct disorder, attention deficit-hyperactivity disorder) are prime candidates for consideration because of the fact that they often reflect chronic conditions. A crucial feature of the model, yet to be applied, is to assess the youth's progress periodically (e.g., at home, school, and the community) to monitor the extent to which he or she is adjusting well, and to use the information to reapply treatment. Indeed, a key to treating diabetes mellitus is the assessment of the extent to which the patient has control over blood glucose levels. Whether treatment is to be increased, decreased or altered markedly depends upon the feedback that assessment provides. Assessment of a child or adolescent's progress does not raise insurmountable problems for application of a similar model. Before consideration of a chronic disease model, which calls for protracted treatment, further tests are needed of intensive treatment within conventional and other treatment models.

To date, little in the way of effective and empirically established treatments are available for disorders of childhood and adolescence. In chapter 4, several promising techniques were discussed, including parent management training, functional family therapy, and problem-solving skills training. Even with the most promising treatments, there are too few controlled trials with clinical populations. For a large number of other techniques that are applied clinically, the bulk of the information is anecdotal (Schaefer et al., 1982, 1984, 1986; Schaefer & Millman, 1977). Given the paucity of research and the methodological limitations of the available studies, it is obviously premature to abandon the conventional model of treatment evaluation. On the other hand, this may not be the time to restrict clinical trials to any singular model of applying and evaluating treatments. Given the empirical status of current treatments, new models warrant exploration.

Chapter 7

Recommendations and Future Directions

Previous chapters examined the current status of child psychotherapy research. The evidence was considered by examining narrative reviews of the literature, meta-analyses, individual outcome studies, and promising research programs. In addition, issues and methodological problems that have thwarted the development of research were elaborated as well. In the process of presenting the evidence, it is natural that the author's own interpretations greatly influenced the conclusions. The evidence was compiled to make the case for the central thesis that the current state of child psychotherapy research leaves a great deal to be desired and that "new and improved" directions for research are needed. The goal was set, albeit perhaps not attained, to present a reasonably fair rendition of the treatment outcome literature. This chapter consolidates major points in the form of recommendations for the field and for investigators who conduct outcome research on child treatment.

RECOMMENDATIONS AND ISSUES

Basic Theory and Research on Child Dysfunction

There are several specific areas that reflect needed emphases to accelerate the development and identification of effective treatments. Improved outcome studies obviously will be required to develop effective treatments. However, there are more fundamental areas upon which such gains will depend. Theory and research on the nature of childhood dysfunction are greatly needed. In this context, theory refers to conceptualizations of the development of the clinical problem and factors that lead to its expression and amelioration. It is unreasonable to expect sweeping theories derived from a single conceptual model (e.g., psychodynamic, behavioral) to explain

107

the development of "psychopathology" or even a particular disorder. Broad theories can provide coherent accounts or explanations of the problem but they have rarely generated *testable hypotheses.*

What is likely to be more profitable are "mini-theories", that is, models or explanations that are designed to address one or more components of a specific type of dysfunction. At the outset, a mini-theory only attempts to explain a circumscribed set of influences and their effects. By being more restricted in scope, mini-theories are more likely to be directly testable and to be subject to refutation and revision.

For example, Patterson (1986) has developed alternative models to explain the development and maintenance of antisocial behavior in children. Separate models are posed to explain how antisocial behavior begins in the home, how the child's antisocial behavior has impact on self-esteem, peer relations, and academic competence, and the factors that foster specific parent child-rearing practices.

Consider the model for how the child initially learns to engage in antisocial behavior. The model assumes that antisocial behavior is learned through family interaction sequences. The parents ineffectively punish mildly coercive interactions on the part of the child (e.g., noncompliance, whining, and teasing). According to the model, this leads to more coercive exchanges between the parent and child. Among the influences is the inadvertent reinforcement of the child's increased coercive (verbal and physical) actions. The parent unwittingly reinforces the child's coercive behavior by giving in or reducing the demand placed on the child. Escalation of aversive interactions on the part of both parent and child, ineffective discipline, and parent acquiescence to the child's coercive demands foster increased levels of coercion in the home and antisocial (aggressive) child behavior. Inept parental discipline, as reflected in excessive use of threats, physical abuse, attention to inappropriate behavior, among other practices, also contribute directly to coercive child behavior through modeling and direct reinforcement.

A diagram of the model appears in Figure 7.1. The open circles reflect the constructs of interest, the arrows reflect the direction of influence, and the rectangles include the specific ways in which the constructs are measured (operationalized). For example, antisocial behavior is defined by measures obtained from parent, teacher, peer, and child reports. Through statistical evaluation with different samples, Patterson found the connections between the constructs to be consistent with the model. Other models are included in Patterson's (1986) account to explain the impact of events such as stressors on the mother's discipline practices and characteristics of the child that sustain antisocial behavior.

The benefits of the models are the direct evaluation of specific influences that promote aggressive behavior in children. The models could be criticized

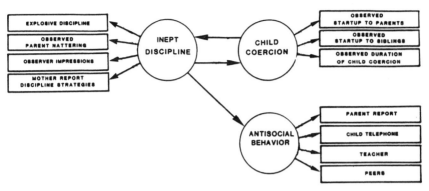

Figure 7.1. Model for training child antisocial behaviors based on the influence of discipline practices and child coercive behavior. (From: Patterson, G. R. (1986). Performance models for antisocial behavior. *Amercian Psychologist, 41*, 432–444.)

for what is omitted. Many influences likely to contribute to antisocial behavior (e.g., genetic) are excluded. Also, how antisocial behavior may be accelerated in the home (e.g., through marital discord or family violence) is incompletely analyzed. However, the model directly culls known influences from research on aggressive child behavior and integrates these into a sequential chain that suggests how aggressive behavior is shaped and sustained. Rather than a limitation, the restricted focus and limited set of variables are strengths of the approach. By identifying a subset of influences, the model can focus on identifiable processes and chart their influence. When clear building blocks are developed in this way, they can then be expanded to include other influences or qualifiers upon which generality of the model may depend.

A few points are critical about the use of such models generally and their role in accelerating advances on child psychopathology and treatment. The first is that the models can be tested directly. Correlational analyses can provide tests of the extent to which the directions of influence are plausible. The analyses do not demonstrate that one variable is a cause of another. Rather, they show if the data from a particular set of variables is consistent with the model. In the case of Patterson's work, the model has developed in several tests so that the specific influences and the direction of their impact have been empirically identified and replicated.[1]

For present purposes, the specific models are not critical for the analysis. The primary point is the need for further theory and research about

[1]The connections between various constructs can be quantified through alternative correlational statistics that support the plausibility of the model and direction of influence. The interested reader may wish to consult Patterson (1986), which includes data in direct support for the models highlighted here or further information on the methods of analyses (Bentler, 1980; Kenny, 1979; Li, 1975).

childhood problems. Theoretical work is an investment in the future of application, such as the development of treatment. Without thought about the processes accounting for clinical problems and direct tests of these processes, treatment research can flounder endlessly.

Problem Identification

There are many debates about the means of identifying and diagnosing childhood problems. The debates reflect different polarities including approaches to diagnosis (e.g., clinically derived vs. multivariate methods) and professional boundaries (e.g., psychiatry vs. psychology). There is no need for agreement on a single method of diagnosing childhood dysfunction. To be sure, adoption of a standardized method would be very beneficial in communicating about childhood dysfunction in a consistent way. Yet, advances in developing effective child treatment techniques do not necessarily depend on an illusive unanimity in the method of diagnosing childhood disorders. The two major methods of describing dysfunction include clinically derived psychiatric diagnoses or severity criteria from dimensional assessment. Of course, investigations that utilize both types of information to describe the sample make a special contribution. It is easier to interpret findings and to integrate them into a body of literature, when diagnostic and other assessment characteristics are explicit and the instruments to obtain the information are standardized.

Apart from diagnosis, more descriptive information about the nature of the clinical problem and characteristics of children and their families are needed in research. There is no need for agreement in the specific assessment battery that is adopted for all outcome studies. Laudatory efforts to standardize assessments in the area of adult psychotherapy research (Waskow & Parloff, 1975) have met with little success because of disputes about the adequacy of individual instruments and their relevance to different sorts of problems or approaches to treatment (Beutler & Crago, 1983; Kolotkin & Johnson, 1983). There might be agreement in principle among child researchers to conduct assessments that reflect child behavior at home and at school or different areas of performance, such as broad areas of deviant behavior and social functioning.

There has been no cohesive model or proposal for a broad-based evaluation that samples multiple domains of child functioning. As an exception, Achenbach (1985; Achenbach et al., 1987) has proposed a multiaxial assessment of children in which several specific domains are assessed. Impetus for the model has been the repeated demonstration that there is very low correspondence in the reports of children, parents, teachers, and mental health workers in their evaluations of child emotional and behavioral problems (Achenbach et al., 1987). The low correspondence could stem from the fact that a particular informant provides unreliable or invalid data. Yet research from several quarters suggests that data from different sources (child, parent, teacher, mental health worker) are internally consistent and have their own correlates with other criteria (Achenbach et al., 1987; Kazdin, in press b). The low correspondence appears to reflect the fact that child functioning varies across situations, settings, and informants.

The model that Achenbach has proposed includes five different assessment axes : I : Parent Reports; II : Teacher Reports; III : Cognitive Assessment; IV : Physical Assessment; and V: Direct Assessment of the Child. Table 7.1 reflects the different axes and possible measures for each of the axes. The different measures included in the table are illustrative. For present purposes, it is the overall model rather than these instruments that warrants consideration. The model provides a systematic way of identifying diverse domains that are likely to be important for childhood functioning and for evaluating treatment outcomes.

A clear benefit of the model is an effort to provide a comprehensive evaluation of child functioning. It is not difficult to conceive of areas or measures that are missing from the model and that might be of interest in the case of a particular clinical problem. However, the point of departure for evaluation of the model stems from current assessment approaches and child descriptions in clinical research. Typically, a narrow set of domains is sampled to describe child functioning. The proposed model identifies areas that might be adopted to improve upon current child treatment studies.

Treatments

Conceptualization of Treatment. Several issues need to be addressed regarding the treatments evaluated in contemporary outcome studies. The lack of conceptualization of the treatment is perhaps the most critical deficit. We are not at a loss for procedures and the techniques, but are quite deficient in conceptualizations that describe what components of treatment are needed and why and how these components interface with specific clinical dysfunctions. Conceptualizations often are at such a global level that they defy empirical evaluation. The safety of a technique is assured in the short run by hiding behind global interpretations and clinical experience. However, the techniques and their interpretations will wither with changing times and fads if not subjected to and bolstered by empirical research. The needed conceptualizations of treatment will propose ways of understanding what we do and why it is or should be helpful.

Stronger Tests of Treatment. Apart from conceptualization, stronger tests of treatment are needed more than current clinical trials of child treatments provide. Perhaps the most basic question of the field is what can we

Table 7.1. Examples of Multiaxial Assessment

Age Range	Axis I Parent Reports	Axis II Teacher Reports	Axis III Cognitive Assessment	Axis IV Physical Assessment	Axis V Direct Assessment of Child
0–2	Minnesota Child Development Inventory Developmental history Parent interview		Developmental testing e.g., Bayley Infant Scales	Height, weight Medical exam Neurological exam	Observations during developmental testing
2–5	Child Behavior Checklist (CBCL) Developmental history Parental interview	School Records Teacher interview	Intelligence tests, e.g., McCarthy Scales of Children's Ability Perceptual-motor tests Speech and language tests	Height, weight Medical exam Neurological exam	Observations during play interview Direct Observation Form (DOF)
6–11	CBCL Developmental history Parent interview	Teacher's Report Form (TRF) School records Teacher interview	Intelligence test e.g., WISC-R Achievement tests Perceptual-motor tests Speech and language tests	Height, weight Medical exam Neurological exam	DOF Semistructured Clinical Interview for Children (SCIC) SCIC–Observation Form SCIC–Self-Report Form
12–18	CBCL Developmental history Parent interview	TRF School records Teacher interview	Intelligence tests e.g., WISC-R, WAIS-R Achievement tests Speech and language tests	Height, weight Medical exam Neurological exam	Youth Self-Report (YSR) Clinical interview Self-concept measures Personality tests

From: Achenbach, T. M. (1985). *Assessment and taxonomy of child and adolescent psychopathology*. Beverly Hills, CA: Sage.

effectively treat? An inventory of what can and cannot be accomplished with psychosocial treatments would be very difficult to create with a reasonable amount of consensus. Rather than an inventory of what is known, writings often consider an inventory of alternative approaches to child treatment (e.g., family, behavioral, psychodynamic) or alternative techniques (e.g., play therapy, social skills training). This strategy would be more obviously amusing in another context, such as medical treatment where it would be of little interest to catalogue all the approaches or techniques that *might be used* to treat various diseases or afflictions (e.g., pneumonia, cancers, appendicitis) *without regard to their effectiveness.* The difficulty with psychosocial treatments for childhood disorders is the paucity of empirical tests of treatment.

It would valuable to subject the most promising treatments (based on conceptual, empirical, or clinical criteria) to systematic experimental tests and to provide truly strong versions of those treatments. There is certainly room to quibble about what the most promising treatments are and what the strongest feasible version would be. There is no need to use such deliberations as cause for delay. There need not be consensus. Strong tests of any plausible treatments would be quite valuable even if there are widely discrepant views about what treatments should be tested. In general, strong tests are needed for many different treatments currently assumed to be effective in clinical work.

We need to know the magnitude of change we can hope to accomplish for a given clinical problem. The goal is not to see what the limits are of treatment in a general sense, because what we can accomplish now is presumably less than what we will be able to accomplish in the future. But the absence of a clear idea of what we can accomplish now limits the vision we need to seek improvements.

Extratreatment Influences. Increased attention may need to focus on diverse factors that can influence treatment effectiveness. The general comment is not too helpful because the specific factors that are to be considered depend on the conceptualization of the nature of the clinical problem and the treatment. However, it is useful to consider the likelihood that the efficacy of treatment interacts with a host of other influences, some of which may be essential to harness to produce clinically significant changes.

There are obvious candidates for variables that interact with treatment to produce therapeutic change. In the adult therapy literature, patient, therapist, and relationship factors are primary candidates. Although these warrant study in the context of child treatment, the general point is made here to entertain different sorts of influences. Factors in the parents' lives may warrant special attention given their relation to deviant child behavior. For example, research has shown that the mother's positive social contacts outside of the home are related to the aversiveness of her interactions with her child and the level of her child's deviant behavior (Wahler, 1980). It is quite possible that treatment for the child may need to address features of the mother's life that extend beyond the child's specific problems and other facets of intrafamily life. This is not merely a restatement of the position that the child is an "identified patient" and reflects problems of the family. Rather, the suggestion is based on emerging evidence that specific aspects of the parents' lives outside of the home may have direct bearing on the child's functioning. What features of parent functioning affect what problems, and whether or how they need to be incorporated into treatment, remain uncharted. Yet, consideration of the full range of events that impinge on parents as individuals, on parents as a couple, and on families, need to be studied empirically as moderators of therapy effects.

Replication of Research

Replication refers to repetition of an investigation.[2] The objective of replication is to see if the results hold in a separate and independent test (Smith, 1970). Although a given investigator can replicate his or her own findings in a new investigation, the strength and persuasiveness of a replication are increased when the findings are duplicated by another investigator or investigative team in a different setting. The reason, of course, is to preclude the possibility that some unrecognized characteristic of the original setting (e.g., demographic characteristics of a sample or "something in the water") does not contribute to the results.

Because replication is a virtue to be sought in all investigative endeavors, it is unclear why this is mentioned here in the context of child psychotherapy research. In the child treatment literature, it is not clear what we know and what we can rely on as reasonably firm findings. Replication is essential to help establish the reliability of a finding. Stated somewhat differently, replication is an important basis for the faith that scientists place in a particular finding. In fact, without multiple replications, the scientist must rely solely on faith. This is faith that the finding has some generality beyond the very specific conditions of a single investigation and special circumstances. This kind of faith is not a sound basis to develop general principles or practices. The more separate or independent replications there are of a given finding, the less need there is for "faith" as a basis for believing

---

[2]There are many different types of replication. One of the more frequent distinctions is between direct and systematic replication. *Direct replication* refers to an attempt to repeat an investigation exactly as it was conducted originally. The conditions and procedures used in the replication experiment are as identical as possible to those of the original investigation. *Systematic replication* refers to an attempt to repeat the experiment by purposely allowing components of the study to vary. Some variation is introduced (e.g., in the characteristics of the sample or treatment) to see if the results are still evident.

in the relationship between treatment and therapeutic change. If two different techniques have been shown to produce therapeutic change for a given clinical problem, the technique that has effects replicated across more than one investigation is one that should be more readily endorsed.[3]

In child psychotherapy literature, we not only need investigations of the new questions before us, but also an inventory of what is reliable among the few established findings. In many ways, it is premature to lobby for replication. The vast majority of techniques have yet to be subjected to any empirical investigation. Certainly, outcome evidence is needed before credence or claims of efficacy are warranted. Once tested, replication becomes very important as the technique is moved through the stages of hoped-for- to demonstrated-benefits and then onto predictable and reliable benefits.

PLANNING, IMPLEMENTING, AND EVALUATING AN OUTCOME STUDY

The previous comments are directed to issues in the field and priorities of child therapy research in general. Although general strategies may accelerate advances, major methodological improvements are needed at the level of the individual investigation. The specific methodological practices that make research high quality are not universally agreed upon. There are general principles of research that yield wide agreement such as the types of validity that experiments need to satisfy (Cook & Campbell, 1979).[4] Yet, precisely

---

[3]Although replication is often praised in principle, there are often contingencies within the profession that compete with repetition of another investigation. For example, in the journal review process, investigators submit their manuscripts that are considered for publication in various professional journals. One of the criteria invoked by colleagues who review the manuscripts is that the investigation provide new information and make a unique contribution. If a study replicates previous work, it is often criticized as not being new. The danger of such a policy is that we often have little idea of what is "old" that we can rely on as veridical or robust findings.

[4]Cook and Campbell (1979) refer to four types of validity. *Statistical conclusion validity* refers to the extent to which conclusions about the impact of the experimental manipulation or independent variable (e.g., treatment) can be inferred based on the statistical evidence and adequacy of the experimental test. Once an effect is established, one can raise the question of *internal validity*. This refers to the extent to which the variable of interest to the investigator (e.g., treatment) rather than extraneous influences (e.g., maturation or repeated exposure to the assessment battery) accounts for the changes. *External validity* refers to the extent to which conclusions drawn from the experiment can be extended across populations, settings, time, and other domains of interest (e.g., clinical problems, cultures). Finally, *construct validity* refers to the extent to which the specific operations of the experiment that define the variable of interest can be viewed as reflecting the broader construct of interest. Construct validity reflects concerns about the basis for the relationship between the experimental manipulation and outcome.

how these principles are addressed in practice and in a given study is not at all straightforward. For example, in therapy research, what needs to be controlled for adequate methodology is constantly a matter of active discussion. What appears to be an artifact or possible confound to be controlled in one study, occasionally is viewed as a central treatment component in another study.

Although it is difficult to prescribe methodological practices that are universal for all clinical trials, there are guidelines that can be proffered that, if followed, are likely to improve the quality of outcome research. Rather than directives or practices with multiple exceptions, the guidelines are provided here in the form of questions that need to be raised by the investigator embarking on an outcome investigation. In order to ensure that the investigator is not "embarking up the wrong tree," he or she should ask several questions before the investigation is conducted and, of course, incorporate the answers into the design.[5] Presented in Table 7.2 are a set of some of the major questions that would be useful to address. These are discussed as follows.

Sample Characteristics

Investigations could be improved by specifying the criteria of clinical dysfunction that served as the basis for selection of the sample. Frequently, investigators allude to the fact that patients were referred for treatment. However, this is of little use in terms of understanding the problems the patients present. Progress can be enhanced by specifying the inclusion and exclusion criteria for patient selection. Use of a specific diagnostic system such as DSM III-R or scores on a dimensional scale to describe or to select patients would be helpful as well. It is unreasonable to expect that different investigators will adopt the same criteria for a given clinical problem. Yet, in any study it is reasonable to demand that the criteria be specified and operationalized.

Specification of the sample involves more than a clarification of the clinical dysfunction and criteria for selection. Subject and demographic variables, including of course child age, sex, socioeconomic status, and intelligence and achievement are prime candidates. These characteristics are often related to the nature of clinical dysfunction and may influence treatment efficacy. They need to be specified so that it is clear to others who exactly was treated. In the case of child treatment, it is often quite important to assess parent and family

---

[5]The questions that are raised here reflect particular weaknesses from the child therapy outcome literature. There are several basic questions that need to be addressed in any well designed investigation. No effort is made to encompass the full range of issues that apply across multiple areas of work. Thorough presentations of the issues that need to be addressed in any given investigation have been provided by Cook and Campbell (1979) and Krathwohl (1985).

Table 7.2
Selected Questions to Raise in Planning a Child Therapy Outcome Study

Sample Characteristics
1. By what criteria regarding dysfunction have the sample been chosen?
2. How were the criteria operationalized?
3. Can the selection procedure be replicated in principle and practice?
4. What are the subject and demographic characteristics of the children and families?
5. Why were these children selected or studied?
6. With regard to clinical dysfunction or subject and demographic characteristics, is this a relatively homogeneous or heterogeneous sample?

Therapists
1. Who is selected to serve as therapists and why?
2. Can the influence of the therapist be evaluated in the design either as a "factor" (as in a factorial design) or can therapist effects be evaluated within a condition?
3. Are the therapists adequately trained? By what criteria?
4. Can the quantity and quality of their training and implementation of treatment be measured?

Treatment
1. What characteristics of the clinical problem or of children, parents, or families make this particular treatment a reasonable approach?
2. Does the version of treatment represent the treatment as it is usually carried out?
3. Does the investigation provide a strong test of treatment? On what basis has one decided this is a strong test?
4. Has treatment been specified in manual form or have explicit guidelines been provided?
5. Has the treatment been carried out as intended? (Integrity is examined during but evaluated after the study is completed.)
6. Can the degree of adherence of therapists to the treatment manual be codified?
7. What defines a complete case (e.g., completion of so many sessions)?

Assessment
1. If specific processes in the child (parent, family, environment) are hypothesized to change with treatment, are these to be assessed?
2. If therapy is having the intended effect on these processes, how would performance be evident on the measure? How would groups differ on this measure?
3. Are there additional processes in therapy that are essential or facilitative to this treatment and are these being assessed?
4. Does the outcome assessment battery include a diverse range of measures to reflect different perspectives, methods, and domains of functioning?
5. Are treatment effects evident in measures of daily functioning (e.g., school attendance, participation in activities or clubs)?
6. Are outcomes being assessed at different points in time after treatment?

General
1. What is the status of contemporary research that makes this particular test worthwhile?
2. What is the likely effect size that will be found based on other treatment studies or meta-analyses?
3. Given the likely effect size, how large of a sample is needed to provide a strong (powerful) test of treatment (e.g., power of at least .80)?
4. What is the likely rate of attrition over the course of treatment and posttreatment and follow-up assessments?
5. With the anticipated loss of cases, is the test likely to be sufficiently powerful to demonstrate differences between groups?

variables as well. Prime candidates for assessment include parent psychopathology, marital status, and life events. These factors can readily impinge on the child. Of course, the range of factors that can influence the child is limitless. Hence, basic information and/or factors suggested as potentially significant as moderators of clinical dysfunction or treatment need to serve as guides. To be avoided is the cursory description of the children (e.g., "Children included third and fourth grade students in a lower to middle class school district.").

With respect to both the nature of the clinical dysfunction and subject and demographic variables, the investigator needs to consider whether relatively homogeneous or heterogeneous samples should be selected. A relatively *homogeneous sample* in this context refers to the fact that subjects are selected for their narrow range of variation with regard to the clinical problem and/or subject and demographic characteristics. A *heterogeneous sample* would include patients that varied more broadly with regard to the clinical problem and/or subject and demographic characteristics.

A homogeneous sample would be selected if the investigator believes that the treatment is likely to be effective with a very specific type of problem or set of patients, or wishes to minimize variance due to intersubject differences. On the other hand, the investigator may believe or wish to test that the treatment is more effective with some problems rather that others (e.g., anxiety rather than eating disorders) or some types of youths (e.g., boys vs. girls, children vs. adolescents). In such cases, a more heterogeneous sample would be selected.

Homogeneity versus heterogeneity is always a matter of degree. An investigator invariably imposes some restrictions on the sample. Thus, youths of all ages (e.g., 2–18 years) or with all presenting problems (e.g., anxiety disorders, psychoses, conduct disorder) are not likely to be entered into the study. However, the precise rationale for selecting patients and the characteristics that are or are not allowed to vary need to be carefully planned.

Therapists/Trainers

The therapist questions in Table 7.2 refer to characteristics of the therapists and the rationale for their selection. The reason(s) why a particular set of therapists or trainers was selected are rarely stated. It is possible that the therapists were selected because of convenience or their availability to work on a project or because of a special orientation. The selection for convenience (e.g., graduate student therapists) is not inherently undesirable. However, persons available to serve as therapists might have special skills, orientations, or status that could influence the generality of the results. It is important to specify the characteristics that might be unique to those who were selected to serve as therapists because selection usually cannot be assumed to reflect a representative or random sample from the population of persons who are therapists.

In general, it is valuable to specify characteristics of the therapists in a similar way to those that are identified for the patients. The relevant dimensions may vary, but presumably include experience and level of training, age, and sex. In some studies, given the clinical focus, population, or technique, race and ethnicity may be essential to specify as well (e.g., Costantino, Malgady, & Rogler, 1986). An especially critical feature of course is the level of training. Specific criteria to define competence of therapists to administer the techniques in the study (e.g., successfully completed a particular course or training experience) would be important to note. It is valuable to describe as much as can be said about the training experience therapists have received and, if possible, why this experience can be used to infer competence. In the usual study, therapists are described by referring to therapist experience, orientation, and professional degree. This is fine, but further information on competence in use of the technique(s) in the study would be very helpful. The likelihood of replicating the findings of the study may be influenced greatly by knowing the characteristics of the therapists and the details of their training.

The design of the study should permit an evaluation of the influence of therapists on outcome. If each therapist administers each of the conditions, then the effects can be examined in a factorial design. Statistical analyses at posttreatment will examine if therapists differed (main effect of therapist) or if some therapists were more (or less) effective with one or more of the treatments compared to other therapists (therapist $\times$ condition interaction).

It is often the case that different therapists administer the different treatment conditions. The reason is that each treatment may require special skills and one person has not been trained to conduct both. Thus, therapists A, B, and C administer treatment 1 and therapists D, E, F administer treatment 2. For a given treatment, the investigator should be able to evaluate the effects of therapists (A vs. B vs. C for treatment 1). An evaluation of therapists is important to present even when a factorial design does not isolate the effects independently (i.e., statistically) of treatments.

Treatment

Questions regarding the treatment pertain to conceptualization of the clinical problem. The treatment implicitly embraces a particular conceptual view about processes related to the specific clinical dysfunction and the way in which these are to be addressed in treatment. The connections between means, ends, and intervening processes of treatment and the connection of the clinical problem and this particular treatment need to be explicitly stated. It is quite likely that the investigator will not be able to trace fully the connections between conceptualization of the clinical problem, treatment techniques, intervening processes that produce change, and improvements on the outcome measures. The importance of the process of specifying the connections stems from revealing those areas that are not clear. The gaps in the conceptual process generate thoughts and hypotheses about what may be needed in treatment and can accelerate the development of techniques.

Several questions about the specific version of treatment are important to raise including whether the version represents the treatment the investigator wishes to study, whether the version is a strong test, and whether the treatment could be followed and replicated by others. The use of a treatment manual facilitates training of therapists, replication of treatment by others, and evaluation of treatment integrity.

Assessment

Questions of assessment in Table 7.2 include important issues related to treatment. It is very helpful to specify and then to assess processes within treatment that are assumed to mediate therapeutic change. Assessment of such processes as attributions and beliefs or self-esteem, if these are central to the technique of interest, can provide extremely valuable information. Apart from the evaluation of treatment outcome, the investigator can correlate changes in processes with changes in outcome. In effect, the study can become a test of the model of therapeutic change as well as a measure of outcome.

The processes through which treatment leads to change are critical to understand. Yet they may be relegated to a secondary importance in one sense. It is critical to demonstrate that the treatment produces reliable and clinically important changes. There are too few such treatments available with replicable results for problems of children and adolescents. Once an effective treatment is in hand, an analysis of the process(es) is especially important.

It is of course reasonable to state that understanding processes is important even prior to developing a treatment. Clearly, understanding the processes underlying the clinical problem is helpful to ensure that these are addressed in treatment. Once a treatment is developed, processes remain important. Yet, the clinical priority of developing an effective treatment needs to be the initial goal. This may need to be achieved before rather than after the study of process. It is difficult to defend an unvarying sequence in the study of processes and treatment outcomes. Programs of research involving various treatment techniques such as parent management training, functional family therapy, and problem-solving skills training, as discussed earlier (chapter 4), have been successful in part because of their investigation of processes and outcomes and integrating the findings from one of these areas to generate insights in the other. The study of process and outcome is intertwined.

Central assessment questions pertain to the outcome assessment battery and the administration of this battery over time. A great deal has been written about the assessment of therapeutic change (e.g., Lambert et al., 1983) which cannot be paraphrased or summarized here. Suffice it to say that multiple domains of functioning need to be selected that directly reflect the basis for clinical referral. Usually this refers to reductions of symptoms in specific areas of functioning. In addition, it is important to examine prosocial functioning. The ultimate adjustment of the child may not derive from the reduction of symptoms but rather, or in addition, the integration of the child in his or her everyday life.

The timing of assessment is important too. Whenever possible, the assessment battery should be administered prior to treatment. Initial pretest data increase the power of the statistical analyses to identify treatment differences. Posttreatment assessment obviously is provided to evaluate the change after treatment. Follow-up assessment permits examination of the extent to which treatment effects are stable and/or change in relation to other treatment and control conditions within the study. Studies of diverse techniques cited earlier have shown that the conclusions drawn about the effects of a treatment or relative effectiveness of alternative treatments may vary greatly over time. Different assessment occasions (e.g., posttreatment, 1-year and 2-year follow-up assessments) are difficult to obtain but very important to seek.

General Comments

There are additional questions listed in Table 7.2 that address general issues. These include the rationale for the particular study and where it fits in current theory, research, and practice. Careful evaluation of their contexts for the study are likely to influence concrete decisions (e.g., number and duration of sessions) of the study as well as more basic features such as selection of treatment and control conditions.

Other questions pertain to statistical power. The ability of the study to detect differences is obviously critical. The likely effects that a given treatment produces can be estimated in different ways. Meta-analyses that report effect sizes for different types of treatment, clinical problems, and measures provide one source of guidelines. From the information, the sample size needed to detect differences, if differences exist, between (or among) conditions can be easily extracted (see Cohen, 1977). Because there are relatively few tests of child treatment in clinical settings and the studies are time-consuming and costly, it is essential that they be designed to provide powerful tests.

Attention to these and the other questions in Table 7.2 will not yield uniform answers among clinical researchers. Different conceptualizations of treatments and research will yield variability in methodological approaches.

The advantage of the preceding questions is not in dictating answers, but rather in increasing the explicitness of the research process. Attention to the questions would not only improve the yield of individual investigations, but also facilitate replication in clinical practice and research.

PROFESSIONAL ISSUES

The discussions in previous chapters suggest that there has not been enough research, or not enough methodologically adequate or sophisticated research to make significant progress in developing effective treatments for children. The narrow range of models that guide research was also discussed. If these were the only or even primary problems of current child psychotherapy research, the solutions would be likely to emerge rather uneventfully. More and better research are likely to evolve in the normal course of things and need not depend on special conceptual, methodological, or technological breakthroughs. Yet, the central theses of this text have been that progress is quite slow and that very little high-caliber work has been completed to yield clear conclusions about child treatment. Perhaps that evolution by its very nature is likely to be slow and the answers will come with patience. Yet, some influences can be identified that may restrict progress and the placement of child psychotherapy on firm empirical grounds.

Myths, Half-truths, and Therapy Clichés

An assumption underlying this book is that research is critical and indeed central for obtaining answers to questions about psychosocial treatments for children and adolescents. There are beliefs held among many professionals about the nature and goals of treatment that discount the utility and relevance of research. It is important to consider some of these beliefs at least briefly. The beliefs constitute a number of myths, half-truths, and clichés about therapy. Their value stems from pinpointing professional issues that partially serve as obstacles to provide strong empirical grounding of therapy. The obstacles reflect in part the ambivalent professional views about clinical research. More importantly many of the issues reflect problems with the kind of research that has been completed and the need to design research to reflect clinical issues more directly.

"Therapy is Too Complex." The complexity of psychosocial treatments and the problems to which they are applied is raised as one reason why research is seen as potentially irrelevant to clinical work. Clinical dysfunctions consist of personal problems and involve dynamic interactions among multiple spheres of a person's life (e.g., family, friends, school, or work). Research attempts to operationalize, simplify, and define the range of influences to

permit their evaluation. But given the complexity of therapy, research may misrepresent and oversimplify the therapeutic experience. For these reasons, research is often seen as irrelevant and artificial.

This concern focuses on the fact that evaluating a treatment in the context of research introduces artificialities and conditions that are not inherent in clinical practice. Once facets of the clinical problem and treatment are defined for study, critical features are changed so that the phenomenon no longer seems like that seen in clinical work. Thus, it may be impossible to study psychosocial treatments, so the argument goes, in the context of research.

Clinical trials of specific interventions do alter (distort) the conditions of treatment from their practice. The alterations may make research depart from clinical work along several different dimensions including the nature of the clinical problems that are studied, the manner in which clients are recruited, the client's expectations for treatment, and characteristics of the therapists (Kazdin, 1978b).

As a concrete illustration, in treatment research, patients are usually selected because of a particular presenting problem or dysfunction. Treatment is then applied to that problem. In a treatment study, there is a need to adhere to the clinical focus and treatment procedures rather closely. Changes in either domain on the basis of demands of the individual patient may interfere with the evaluation of the treatment. Although this strategy is understandable for purposes of research, more than half of clinical patients (at least in the treatment of adults), may change the problems they identify as important during the course of treatment (Sorenson, Gorsuch, & Mintz, 1985). In clinical work as opposed to clinical research, fluctuations in what is identified as the primary problem or treatment focus is not problematic; it may even be expected. Treatment procedures and the focus readily change in response to emerging problems and patient changes. This is quite different from the usually fixed nature of the research project. The point to note is that the manner of handling presenting problems of the patient may vary more in clinical practice than in research. Consequently, research would not represent treatment as it is conducted in practice.

The specific techniques that are utilized in clinical practice are different from and probably more "complex" than those investigated in outcome research. In clinical practice with child cases, traditional forms of individual psychotherapy (e.g., psychodynamically oriented and relationship therapy) appear to be the dominant treatment (Koocher & Pedulla, 1977; Silver & Silver, 1983; Tuma & Pratt, 1982). Yet, these are rarely studied in treatment outcome studies (Casey & Berman, 1985; Weisz et al., 1987). Cognitive and behavioral interventions which are more readily operationalized and specifiable are overrepresented in outcome research relative to their use in practice.

"Research is Too Difficult to Conduct." Another belief is that research on alternative forms of therapy is too difficult to conduct and not really feasible as a strategy for developing a knowledge base. Many resources are required for such research; staff is needed to carry out treatment, to collect assessment information, to maintain contact with patients, and to gather follow-up data. These tasks are costly in both time and money. Grants from federal or private agencies usually serve as the sources of support for such research. Without extensive support (grants), treatment outcome research may be too difficult to conduct and simply not feasible.

Actually, there are a variety of research designs available for the evaluation of treatment techniques. The large-scale study involving groups of patients and requiring a special research effort with extensive funding is only one type of evaluation project. The overall objective of clinical research is to evaluate treatment systematically and to examine the factors that contribute to outcome. Many different types of evaluation strategies can achieve this goal. Most of these do *not* include large-scale group studies. Consider three alternatives: First, systematic collection and evaluation of information from clinical records (charts) can be used to shed light on the effects of alternative treatments (Garfield, 1980). Multiple cases can be evaluated to study the application of treatments for different types of problems and patients. Although the information is retrospective, systematic data can yield important information about treatment. Second, case studies in clinical practice can provide information about the effects of treatment for a given problem. This is not the usual anecdotal case report. By introducing assessment of patient functioning before, during, and after treatment, the inferences that can be drawn about treatment are substantially improved over the anecdotal case report (Kazdin, 1981). Finally, a set of experimental designs are available that can be used to evaluate treatments with the individual case (Barlow, Hayes, & Nelson, 1984; Kazdin, 1982). These designs permit rigorous evaluation of treatment as they are applied to cases in clinical practice.

The task of research is to rule out alternative rival explanations that can explain the results. Alternative assessment and control procedures central to research accomplish these goals in various ways (Cook & Campbell, 1979). A variety of options mentioned previously and only in passing, provide alternatives to large-scale group investigations that can be used in clinical research and practice (Kazdin, 1980b). The design options can yield systematic knowledge about the "ultimate" treatment question, that is, the effects of treatment under alternative conditions and applications.

"Therapy is an Art." A related belief is that therapy is an art rather than a technical skill or scientific practice. The skill of the therapist, the experience,

intuitive reactions, feelings, and good judgment are aspects of treatment administration that are beyond specification and scrutiny. Also, emergent processes in therapy such as the unique relationship between patient and therapist reflect something more like a creative process than an application of techniques.

There is some truth to the notion that therapy is an art. There are certainly special talents and creative processes over and above the skills that therapists are taught. It is not difficult to identify very creative and uncannily intuitive or otherwise difficult-to-evaluate skills of the therapist (Reik, 1948). Yet, this is different from saying that therapy is an entirely creative process with unspecified and unspecifiable attributes. The artistic qualities presumably are over and above those skill areas that can be specified, trained, and learned. Those skills that can be trained and learned may be very subtle and include different levels of complexity that make explicit and clear many features that without careful analysis, might appear entirely unspecificable or creative (Bugental, 1987).

It is important not to lean too heavily in implying that psychotherapy is a technology, or the mere application of procedures and techniques. The initial and primary task is to specify those skills, techniques, and therapist characteristics that are central to a given treatment and to evaluate their impact. The demystification of treatment is needed to make way for empirical evaluation. The focus on skills, techniques, and emergent processes does not gainsay the "art" of the individual therapists. There are no doubt some therapists who are unusually excellent in how or what they do in therapy. This is no different from noting that there are exceptional persons in any specialized area of work. Investigation of what such therapists may do is of keen interest and may reveal new dimensions of treatment. Yet, this is different from the view that all of treatment may be an "art" and should avoid the scrutiny that empirical specification and evaluation provide.

"Everyone is an Individual." Another issue often raised to argue against the relevance or utility of research is the individuality of each patient. These individual differences must be taken into account into treatment. Research often relies on standardized diagnostic labels and categories for patient selection. Seemingly rigid treatment regimens are then applied similarly across all persons in a study. Individual differences serve as the point of departure in clinical work and are usually ignored in the research applications of treatment.

Individual differences of patients and the problems and life situations they bring to treatment are always present and often marked. These facts do not gainsay the potential applicability of general principles, strategies, and procedures. The application of various medications and medical interventions (e.g., antibiotics, by-pass surgery) for alternative disorders (e.g., pneumonia, myocardial infarction) does not assume that all individuals have the identical disorder or are identical in how they respond to treatment. Alternative interventions, whether for medical or psychological problems, can be investigated and shown to help certain classes or types of people and problems. The search and successful identification of such treatments does not require denying individual differences. It could well be that the view that "everyone is an individual" is overly relied-upon as a rationale for not investigating treatments with different types of clinical problems.

Actually, the idea of individual differences enters systematically into treatment research but in ways that are disguised. The first way is by identifying different types of disorders, whether medical or psychological. This initial division of "all people" with diseases or problems into those with one condition versus another begins the grouping process. Over time, finer distinctions are made so that subtypes of the disorder are identified with evidence showing that treatments suitable for one subtype are less suitable or ineffective with another subtype. Eventually, further distinctions may be made in sub-subtypes to match classes of treatment with types of dysfunction. In this process, it is unclear and undemonstrated that identifying effective treatments requires considering each individual as an entirely unique entity.

General Comments. The preceding beliefs about therapy are very important to consider in the progress for the field. They reflect half-truths. The half-truth value is acknowledged here because the points are cogent. Perhaps the concerns can be encompassed by the notion that psychosocial treatments of childhood problems in clinical practice are complex and multifaceted. Acknowledgement of the complexity of treatment or individual differences in responses should not be used as the basis of avoiding to conduct or to utilize the findings from research. *Because* of the complexity of therapy, all facets of treatment need to be subjected to very careful scrutiny. If clinical problems, psychosocial treatments, and outcome effects were not so complex, we might be able to obtain the answers we seek without the intricacies of research.

The other side is important to note as well. Research has not invariably taken into account the complexities of treatment and individual differences that might contribute to outcome (Cohen, Sargent, & Sechrest, 1986). Some of the research strategies presented earlier such as ensuring that treatment is representative of the versions used in clinical work, identifying strong treatments, and selecting patients who vary in their likely amenability to treatment, are efforts to increase the quality of research in relation to the concerns about the complexity of treatment.

"Set" Toward Evaluation

The myths, half-truths, and cliches reflect a broader "set" or attitude in clinical work where evaluation and research are not uniformly valued. The findings from research are not seen as criteria on which decisions ought to be made. In fact, the major deterrent to progress in identifying effective treatments for children is not the paucity or quality of research conducted to date. These deficits are visible enemies that can be directly attacked. The larger issue is the set or general stance that empirical findings are not the relevant criteria and that evaluation by the clinician is sufficient to draw conclusions.

The set or general stance may be reflected in the focus of training. The techniques selected for inculcation of those persons undergoing training are largely drawn from an approach or philosophy of treatment, rather than evidence of what treatments look promising from current research. For example, many different treatments have been shown to lead to reliable improvements in various adult anxiety disorders (Rachman & Wilson, 1980). These techniques do not seem to be incorporated into programs that train psychiatric residents or clinical psychology interns who will eventually administer treatment for such problems.

Assume for a moment that individual studies or research in general is not seen as relevant by most professionals as the basis for selecting treatments for individual patients or for techniques to be trained among persons in training. This view may not merely reflect an unsympathetic set toward the importance or potential benefits of research. Rather, the research may be viewed as generally irrelevant because the research questions that are addressed and the way they are studied do not systematically address the issues or practices of clinical work (Cohen et al., 1986).

Training Issues

There may be important issues related to professional training that impede progress in developing effective and empirically based treatments for children. Consider first, characteristics of clinical training in alternative psychotherapy techniques. Typically, training includes course work and supervised practice during one's graduate career. Excluded from the training experiences are clear criteria of what needs to be mastered and evaluation to see if the objectives have been achieved (Kazdin, et al., 1986). For example, one survey revealed that less than 20% of psychology training clinics ever attempt to evaluate the acquisition of clinical skills in their trainees (Stephenson & Norcross, 1983). At the level of training, it is unclear what needs to be learned to perform treatment well, whether the experiences designed to provide the relevant skills actually do so, and how competence in delivering treatment ought to be measured.

The topic of clinical training is a weighty issue in its own right. It is mentioned here to draw attention to the fact that even in training, there is tacit acceptance that therapy is not to be evaluated and that the criteria for being a good therapist are judgmental and not systematically assessed. There are multiple problems at the level of training. One of the more obvious issues is that it is unclear what we are training, if the specific skills are not explicitly identified and measured. The failure to specify and to measure the skills of administering treatment also fosters the *"therapy is an art"* view that will continue to thwart empirical progress.

Consider parallel issues regarding research training. In the context of this discussion, research training refers to the training of investigators to conduct research on child therapy. The regimen for research training is rather clear; course work on experimental design and statistics are obviously critical. Emphasis is placed on the science requirements; theory and research training rather than clinical exposure or experience usually are provided.

The very nature of research training may also interfere with progress in developing or identifying effective treatments. In clinical psychology, as one example, it is likely that graduate students in training will receive an internship experience in a mental health facility or hospital where they will be exposed to various clinical problems. The 1-year exposure, often including "rotations" through several clinical services, cannot begin to provide the knowledge of clinical phenomena in any depth. Thus, direct knowledge of a clinical problem and direct experience with the specific treatments that are to be investigated are not likely to be common among persons beginning their program of clinical research. Without extensive clinical experience, the questions that are addressed and the manner in which they are addressed may foster the hiatus between clinical research and clinical practice and make the nature of the treatment trial quite far removed from clinical work.

The training issues raise broad professional concerns that have implications beyond the topic of research on child treatment. The issues are important to mention here because the training of clinicians and researchers includes practices that may be detrimental to the development of effective child treatments. The bifurcation of professional paths (clinicians vs. researchers) at worst could mean that most of the persons conducting treatment will not appreciate, see as relevant, or draw upon scientific findings on child treatment and that persons conducting research will not understand, represent, or evaluate genuine clinical problems and treatments as they may need to be applied in practice. These are serious and potentially chronic maladies the field has suffered.

CONCLUSIONS

Advances in child psychotherapy research will not derive from a single line of work or breakthrough. Progress can be greatly accelerated if a diversified strategy of research were adopted. More specifically, child psychotherapy research might make gains at a more detectable rate if there were:

- More research and model testing on the nature of child dysfunctions;
- Improved conceptualizations of treatment to interrelate treatment procedures to what is known about the dysfunction that is being treated;
- Broader based assessment that evaluated child functioning in several different domains;
- Stronger (i.e., statistically more powerful) tests of treatment;
- Tests of stronger or more intensive treatments;
- Integration, assessment, and evaluation of a wider range of child, parent, and family influences that may moderate treatment outcome;
- Improved methodology, as reflected in better specification of patient, therapist, and treatment characteristics, and the rationales underlying decision points within the design; and
- Replication efforts to help establish the reliability of findings for a given treatment.

Many specific issues can be identified which, if resolved, would definitely improve the yield of individual outcome studies. Yet, there are more global, less easily specified issues that may be as important to address as any concrete set of recommendations. There remains a mixed appreciation of the role of evaluation in the area of child psychotherapy. Anecdotal information, impressions, clinical experience and judgment, theoretical orientation, and untested assumptions continue to guide the decisions regarding treatment. Indeed, such judgments are central to deciding what interventions are taught to interns and residents in training, the basis for selecting interventions for a given patient or clinical problem, and the criteria for evaluating treatment with an individual patient.

There is still a strong commitment to approaches (e.g., psychodynamic, behavioral, eclecticism) rather than to evidence. To be sure, there is a much greater security in remaining faithful to an approach. There is particular safety in the generic eclecticism in which one can claim to use all the good ("I use what works") and to reject the bad among the different treatments. In contrast, appeal to evidence as a criterion is less peaceful. Evidence is always mixed, invariably reinterpreted, occasionally reanalyzed, and remarkably difficult to decipher. Yet, the most humane, sensitive, and clinically responsible approach would be one in which we identify empirically what treatments work with what kinds of children and under what circumstances. A first step is acknowledging what is and is not known and to begin to identify what information we need. Recognition of the initial areas of ignorance and some agreement on how to attain the answers are essential steps that could greatly accelerate the process of identifying effective treatments for children and adolescents.

References

Abramowitz, C. V (1976). The effectiveness of group psychotherapy with children. *Archives of General Psychiatry, 33,* 320-326.

Achenbach, T.M. (1985). *Assessment and taxonomy of child and adolescent psychopathology.* Beverly Hills, CA: Sage.

Achenbach, T.M., & Edelbrock, C.S. (1981). Behavioral problems and competencies reported by parents of normal and disturbed children aged 4 through 16. *Monographs of the Society for Research in Child Development, 46* (Serial No. 188).

Achenbach, T. M., & Edelbrock, C. S. (1983). *Manual for the Child Behavior Checklist and Revised Child Behavior Profile.* Burlington, VT: University Associates in Psychiatry.

Achenbach, T. M., McConaughy, S.H., & Howell, C. T. (1987). Child/adolescent behaviors and emotional problems: Implications of cross-informant correlations for situational specificity. *Psychological Bulletin, 101,* 213-232.

Adams, S. (1970). The PICO Project. In N. Johnston, L. Savitz, & M. E. Wolfgang (Eds.), *The sociology of punishment and correction* (pp. 548-561). New York: John Wiley & Sons.

Adelman, H. S., Kaser-Boyd, N., & Taylor, L. (1984). Children's participation in consent for psychotherapy and their subsequent response to treatment. *Journal of Clinical Child Psychology, 13,* 170-178.

Alexander, J. F. (1973). Defensive and supportive communications in normal and deviant families. *Journal of Consulting and Clinical Psychology, 40,* 223-231.

Alexander, J. F., Barton, C., Schiavo, R. S., & Parsons, B. V. (1976). Systems-behavioral intervention with families of delinquents: Therapist characteristics, family behavior, and outcome. *Journal of Consulting and Clinical Psychology, 44,* 656-664.

Alexander, J. F., & Parsons, B. V. (1973). Short-term behavioral intervention with delinquent families: Impact on family process and recidivism. *Journal of Abnormal Psychology, 81,* 219-225.

Alexander, J. F., & Parsons, B. V. (1982). *Functional family therapy.* Monterey, CA: Brooks/Cole.

American Psychiatric Association. (1952). *Diagnostic and statistical manual of mental disorders.* Washington, DC: Author.

American Psychiatric Association. (1968). *Diagnostic and statistical manual of mental disorders* (2nd ed.). Washington, DC: Author.

American Psychiatric Association. (1980). *Diagnostic and statistical manual of mental disorders* (3rd ed.). Washington, DC: Author.

American Psychiatric Association. (1987). *Diagnostic and statistical manual of mental disorders-Revised.* Washington, DC: Author.

American Psychologist. (1986). Psychotherapy research, [Special issue], *41* (2).

131

Andrews, G., & Harvey, R. (1981). Does psychotherapy benefit neurotic patients? *Archives of General Psychiatry, 38*, 1203-1208.

Arbuthnot, J., & Gordon, D. A. (1986). Behavioral and cognitive effects of a moral reasoning development intervention for high-risk behavior-disordered adolescents. *Journal of Consulting and Clinical Psychology, 54*, 208-216.

Axline, V. M. (1947). *Play therapy*. Boston: Houghton Mifflin.

Azrin, N. H., & Foxx, R. M. (1971). A rapid method of toilet training the institutionalized retarded. *Journal of Applied Behavior Analysis, 4*, 89-99.

Azrin, N. H., & Foxx, R. M. (1974). *Toilet training in less than a day*. New York: Simon & Schuster.

Bachman, J. G., Johnston, L. D., & O'Malley, P. M. (1978). Delinquent behavior linked to educational attainment and post-high school experiences. In L. Otten (Ed.), *Colloquium on the correlates of crime and the determinants of criminal behavior* (pp. 1-43). Arlington, VA: The Mitre Corp.

Baenen, R. S., Stephens, M. A. P., & Glenwick, D. S. (1986). Outcome in psychoeducational day school programs: A review. *American Journal of Orthopsychiatry, 56*, 263-270.

Barlow, D. H., Hayes, S. C., & Nelson, R. O. (1984). *The scientist-professional: Research and accountability in clinical and research settings*. New York: Pergamon.

Barrett, C. L., Hampe, I. E., & Miller, L. C. (1978). Research on child psychotherapy. In S. L. Garfield & A. E. Bergin (Eds.), *Handbook of psychotherapy and behavior change: An empirical analysis* (2nd ed., pp. 411-435). New York: John Wiley & Sons.

Barton, C., & Alexander, J. F. (1981). Functional family therapy. In A. S. Gurman & D. P. Kniskern (Eds.), *Handbook of family therapy* (pp. 403-443). New York: Brunner/Mazel.

Baum, C. G., & Forehand, R. (1981). Long-term follow-up assessment of parent training by use of multiple outcome measures. *Behavior Therapy, 12*, 643-652.

Bellack, A. S., & Hersen, M. (Eds.). (1985). *Dictionary of behavior therapy techniques*. New York: Pergamon.

Bentler, P. M. (1980). Multivariate analysis with latent variables: Causal modeling. *Annual Review of Psychology, 31*, 419-455.

Bergin, A. E., & Lambert, M. J. (1978). The evaluation of therapeutic outcomes. In S. L. Garfield & A. E. Bergin (Eds.), *Handbook of psychotherapy and behavior change: An empirical analysis* (2nd. ed., pp. 139-189). New York: John Wiley & Sons.

Beutler, L. E., & Crago, M. (1983). Self-report measures of psychotherapy outcome. In M. J. Lambert, E. R. Christensen, & S. S. De Julio (Eds.), *The assessment of psychotherapy outcome* (pp. 453-497). New York: John Wiley & Sons.

Beutler, L. E., Crago, M., & Arizmendi, T. G. (1986). Therapist variables in psychotherapy process and outcome. In S. L. Garfield & A. E. Bergin (Eds.), *Handbook of psychotherapy and behavior change* (3rd ed., pp. 257-310). New York: John Wiley & Sons.

Bien, N. Z. & Bry, B. H. (1980). An experimentally designed comparison of four intensities of school-based prevention programs for adolescents with adjustment problems. *Journal of Community Psychology, 8*, 110-116.

Bornstein, P. H., & Kazdin, A. E. (Eds.). (1985). *Handbook of clinical behavior therapy with children*. Homewood, IL: Dorsey.

Boy, A. V. (1971). A critique by Angelo V. Boy. In A. O. DiLoreto (Ed.), *Comparative psychotherapy: An experimental analysis* (pp. 233-245). Chicago: Aldine-Atherton.

Brown, J. (1987). A review of meta-analyses conducted on psychotherapy outcome research. *Clinical Psychology Review, 7*, 1-23.

Bry, B. H. (1982). Reducing the incidence of adolescent problems through preventive intervention: One- and five-year follow-up. *American Journal of Community Psychology, 10*, 265-276.

Bry B. H., & George, F. E. (1980). The preventive effects of early intervention on the attendance and grades of urban adolescents. *Professional Psychology, 11*, 252-260.

Bugental, J. F. T. (1987). *The art of the psychotherapist.* New York: W. W. Norton.

Buss, A. H. (1966). *Psychopathology.* New York: John Wiley & Sons.

Camp, B. W., & Bash, M. A. S. (1985). *Think aloud: Increasing social and cognitive skills — A problem solving program for children.* Champaign, IL: Research Press.

Cantwell, D. P., & Carlson, G. A. (Eds.). (1983). *Affective disorders in childhood and adolescence: An update.* New York: Spectrum.

Casey, R. J., & Berman, J. S. (1985). The outcome of psychotherapy with children. *Psychological Bulletin, 98*, 388-400.

Chambers, W. J., Puig-Antich, J., Hirsch, M., Paez, P., Ambrosini, P. J., Tabrizi, M. A., & Davies, M. (1985). The assessment of affective disorders in children and adolescents by semistructured interview. *Archives of General Psychiatry, 42*, 696-702.

Clarizio, H. F., & McCoy, G. F. (1983). *Behavior disorders in children* (3rd ed.). New York: Harper & Row.

Cohen, J. (1962). The statistical power of abnormal-social psychological research: A review. *Journal of Abnormal and Social Psychology, 65*, 145-153.

Cohen, J. (1977). *Statistical power analysis for the behavioral sciences* (2nd ed.). New York: Academic Press.

Cohen, L. H., Sargent, M. M., & Sechrest, L. B. (1986). Use of psychotherapy research by professional psychologists. *American Psychologist, 41*, 198-206.

Cole, P. M., & Kazdin, A. E. (1980). Critical issues in self-instruction training with children. *Child Behavior Therapy, 2*, 1-23.

Compas, B. E., Friedland-Bandes, R., Bastien, R., & Adelman, H. S. (1981). Parent and causal attributions related to the child's clinical picture. *Journal of Abnormal Child Psychology, 9*, 389-397.

Cook, T. D., & Campbell, D. T. (Eds). (1979). *Quasi-experimentation: Design and analysis issues for field settings.* Chicago: Rand McNally .

Corsini, R. J. (Ed.), (1981). *Handbook of innovative psychotherapies.* New York: John Wiley & Sons.

Costantino, G., Malgady, R. G., & Rogler, L. H. (1986). Cuento therapy: A culturally sensitive modality for Puerto Rican children. *Journal of Consulting and Clinical Psychology, 54*, 639-645.

Craighead, L. W., Stunkard, A. J., & O'Brien, R. (1981). Behavior therapy and pharmacotherapy for obesity. *Archives of General Psychiatry, 38*, 763-768.

Cross, D. G., Sheehan, P. W., & Khan, J. A. (1982). Short- and long-term follow-up of clients receiving insight-oriented therapy and behavior therapy. *Journal of Consulting and Clinical Psychology, 50*, 103-112.

Dadds, M. R., Schwartz, S., & Sanders, M. R. (1987). Marital discord and treatment outcome in behavioral treatment of child conduct disorders. *Journal of Consulting and Clinical Psychology, 55*, 396-403.

Davidson, W. S., Gottschalk, R., Gensheimer, L., & Mayer, J. (in press). Interventions with juvenile delinquents: A meta-analysis of treatment efficacy. In C. Hampton (Ed.), *Current approaches to troubled youth.* Washington, DC: U.S. Government Printing Office.

Deffenbacher, J. L., & Shelton, J. L. (1978). Comparison of anxiety management training and desensitization in reducing test and other anxieties. *Journal of Counseling Psychology, 25*, 277-282.

DeRubeis, R. J., Hollon, S. E., Evans, M. D., & Bemis, K. M. (1982). Can psychotherapies for depression be discriminated? A systematic investigation of cognitive therapy and interpersonal therapy. *Journal of Consulting and Clinical Psychology, 50*, 744-756.

DeWitt, K. N. (1978). The effectiveness of family therapy: A review of outcome measures. *Archives of General Psychiatry, 35*, 549-561.

DeWitt, K. N. (1980). The effectiveness of family therapy: A review of outcome research. In J. G. Howells (Ed.), *Advances in family psychiatry* (Vol. 2, pp. 437-465). New York: International Universities Press.

DiLoreto, A. O. (1971). *Comparative psychotherapy: An experimental analysis.* Chicago: Aldine-Atherton.

Dodds, J. B. (1985). *A child psychotherapy primer: Suggestions for the beginning therapist.* New York: Human Sciences Press.

Dodge, K. A. (1985). Attributional bias in aggressive children. In P. C. Kendall (Ed.), *Advances in cognitive-behavioral research and therapy* (Vol. 4, pp. 73-110). Orlando, FL: Academic Press.

Dollinger, S. J., Thelen, M. H., & Walsh, M. L. (1980). Children's conceptions of psychologic problems. *Journal of Clinical Child Psychology, 9*, 191-194

Dreger, R. M. (1981). The classification of children and their emotional problems. *Clinical Psychology Review, 1*, 415-430.

Dumas, J. E., & Wahler, R. G. (1983). Predictors of treatment outcome in parent training: Mother insularity and socioeconomic disadvantage. *Behavioral Assessment, 5*, 301-313.

Dush, D. M., Hirt, M.L., & Schroeder, H. (1983). Self-statement modification with adults: A meta-analysis. *Psychological Bulletin, 94*, 408-422.

Edelbrock, C. S. (1983). *The antecedents of antisocial behavior: A cross-sectional analysis.* Unpublished manuscript, University of Pittsburgh School of Medicine.

Edelbrock, C. S., Costello, A. J., Dulcan, M. K., Conover, N. C., & Kalas, R. (1986). Parent–child agreement on child psychiatric symptoms assessed via structured interview. *Journal of Child Psychology and Psychiatry, 27*, 181-190.

Edwards, A. L., & Cronbach, L. J. (1952). Experimental design for research in psychotherapy. *Journal of Clinical Psychology, 8*, 51-59.

Eisenberg, L., & Gruenberg, E. M. (1961). The current status of secondary prevention in child psychiatry. *American Journal of Orthopsychiatry, 31*, 355-367.

Ellis, A. (1971). A critique by Albert Ellis. In A. O. DiLoreto (Ed.), *Comparative psychotherapy: An experimental analysis* (pp. 213-221). Chicago: Aldine-Atherton.

Ellis, P. L. (1982). Empathy: A factor in antisocial behavior. *Journal of Abnormal Child Psychology, 10*, 123-134.

Endicott, J., & Spitzer, R. L. (1978). A diagnostic interview: The Schedule of Affective Disorders and Schizophrenia. *Archives of General Psychiatry, 35*, 837-844.

Eyberg, S. M., & Johnson, S. M. (1974). Multiple assessment of behavior modification with families: Effects on contingency contracting and order of treated problems. *Journal of Consulting and Clinical Psychology, 42*, 594-606.

Eysenck, H. J. (1952). The effects of psychotherapy: An evaluation. *Journal of Consulting Psychology, 16*, 319-324.

Eysenck, H. J. (1966). *The effects of psychotherapy.* New York: International Science Press.

Feighner, J. P., Robins, E., Guze, S. B., Woodruff, R. A., Winokur, G., & Munoz, R. (1972). Diagnostic criteria for use in psychiatric research. *Archives of General Psychiatry, 26*, 57-63.

Feldman, R. A., Caplinger, T. E., & Wodarski, J. S. (1983). *The St. Louis conundrum: The effective treatment of antisocial youths.* Englewood Cliffs, NJ: Prentice-Hall.

Fleischman, M. J. (1981). A replication of Patterson's intervention for boys with conduct problems. *Journal of Consulting and Clinical Psychology, 49*, 342-351.

Fleischman, M. J. (1982). Social learning interventions for aggressive children: From the laboratory to the real world. *The Behavior Therapist, 5*, 55-58.

Fleischman, M. J., & Szykula, S. A. (1981). A community setting replication of a social learning treatment for aggressive children. *The Behavior Therapist, 12*, 115-122.

Fo, W. S. O., & O'Donnell, C. R. (1975). The buddy system: Effect of community intervention on delinquent offenses. *Behavior Therapy, 6*, 522-524.

Forehand, R., Lautenschlager, G. J., Faust, J., & Graziano, W. G. (1986). Parent perceptions and parent–child interactions in clinic-referred children: A preliminary investigation of the effects of maternal depressive moods. *Behaviour Research and Therapy, 24*, 73-75.

Forehand, R., & Long, N. (in press). Outpatient treatment of the acting-out child: Procedures, long-term follow-up data, and clinical problems. *Journal of Child and Adolescent Psychotherapy*.

Forehand, R., & McMahon, R. J. (1981). *Helping the noncompliant child: A clinician's guide to parent training*. New York: Guilford.

Forman, S. G. (1980). A comparison of cognitive training and response cost procedures of modifying aggressive behavior of elementary school children. *Behavior Therapy, 11*, 594-600.

Freud, A. (1946). *The psychoanalytic treatment of children*. New York: International Universities Press.

Gard, G. C., & Berry, K. K. (1986). Oppositional children: Taming tyrants. *Journal of Clinical Child Psychology, 15*, 148-158.

Garfield, S. L. (1980). *Psychotherapy: An eclectic approach*. New York: John Wiley & Sons.

Garfield, S. L. (1982). Eclecticism and integration in psychotherapy. *Behavior Therapy, 13*, 610-623.

Garfield, S. L. (1983). Effectiveness of psychotherapy: The perennial controversy. *Professional Psychology, 14*, 35-43.

Garfield, S. L., & Bergin, A. E. (Eds.). (1978). *Handbook of psychotherapy and behavior change: An empirical analysis* (2nd ed.). New York: John Wiley & Sons.

Garfield, S. L., & Bergin, A. E. (Eds.). (1986). *Handbook of psychotherapy and behavior change: An empirical analysis* (3rd. ed.). New York: John Wiley & Sons.

Garrison, W. T., & Earls, F. (1987). *Temperament and childhood psychopathology*. Newbury Park, CA: Sage.

Gelfand, D. M., & Peterson, L. (1985). *Child development and psychopathology*. Beverly Hills, CA: Sage.

Gilbert, G.M. (1957). A survey of "referral problems" in metropolitan child guidance centers. *Journal of Clinical Psychology, 13*, 37-42.

Glass, G. V., McGaw, B., & Smith, M. L. (1981). *Meta-analysis in social research*. Beverly Hills, CA: Sage.

Glick, S. J. (1972). Identification of predelinquents among children with school behavior problems as basis for multiservice treatment program. In S. Glueck & E. Glueck (Eds.), *Identification of predelinquents* (pp. 84-90). New York: Intercontinental Medical Book Corp.

Gould, M. S., Wunsch-Hitzig, R., & Dohrenwend, B. P. (1980). Formulation of hypotheses about the prevalence, treatment, and prognostic significance of psychiatric disorders in children in the United States. In B. P. Dohrenwend, B. S. Dohrenwend, M. S. Gould, B. Link, R. Neugebauer, & R. Wunsch-Hitzig (Eds), *Mental illness in the United States: Epidemiological estimates* (pp. 9-44). New York: Praeger.

Graham, P. J. (Ed.). (1977). *Epidemiological approaches in child psychiatry*. New York: Academic Press.

Gresham, F. M. (1985). Utility of cognitive–behavioral procedures for social skills training with children: A critical review. *Journal of Abnormal Child Psychology, 13*, 411-423.

Griest, D. L., Forehand, R., Rogers, T., Breiner, J., Furey, W., & Williams, C. A. (1982). Effects of parent enhancement therapy on the treatment outcome and generalization of a parent training program. *Behaviour Research and Therapy, 20*, 429-436.

Gumaer, J. (1984). *Counseling and therapy for children*. New York: Free Press.

Gurman, A. S., & Kniskern, D. P. (1981). Family therapy outcome research: Knowns and unknowns. In A. S. Gurman & D. P. Kniskern (Eds.), *Handbook of family therapy* (pp. 742-775). New York: Brunner/Mazel.

Gurman, A. S., Kniskern, D. P., & Pinsof, W. M. (1986). Research on the process and outcome of marital and family therapy. In S. L. Garfield & A. E. Bergin (Eds.), *Handbook of psychotherapy and behavior change* (3rd ed., pp. 565-624). New York: John Wiley & Sons.

Gurman, A. S., & Razin, A. M. (Eds.). (1977). *Effective psychotherapy: A handbook of research.* New York: Pergamon.

Hackler, J. C., & Hagan, J. L. (1975). Work and teaching machines as delinquency prevention tools: A four-year follow-up. *Social Science Review, 49,* 92-106.

Harrison, S. E. (Ed.). (1979). *Basic handbook of child psychiatry: Therapeutic interventions* (Vol. 3). New York: Basic Books.

Hartmann, D. P., Roper, B. L., & Gelfand, D. M. (1977). An evaluation of alternative modes of child psychotherapy. In B. B. Lahey & A. E. Kazdin (Eds.), *Advances in clinical child psychology* (Vol. 1, pp. 1-46). New York: Plenum.

Heimberg, R. G., & Becker, R. E. (1984). Comparative outcome research. In M. Hersen, L. Michelson, & A. S. Bellack (Eds.), *Issues in psychotherapy research* (pp. 251-283). New York: Plenum.

Heinicke, C. M. (1969). Frequency of psychotherapeutic session as a factor affecting outcome: Analysis of clinical ratings and test results. *Journal of Abnormal Psychology, 74,* 553-560.

Heinicke, C. M., & Goldman, A. (1960). Research on psychotherapy with children: A review and suggestions for further study. *American Journal of Orthopsychiatry, 30,* 483-494.

Heinicke, C. M., & Ramsey-Klee, D. M. (1986). Outcome of child psychotherapy as a function of frequency of session. *Journal of the American Academy of Child Psychiatry, 25,* 247-253.

Heinicke, C. M., & Strassman, L. H. (1975). Toward more effective research on child psychotherapy. *Journal of the American Academy of Child Psychiatry, 3,* 561-588.

Herink, R. (Ed.). (1980). *The psychotherapy handbook.* New York: New American Library.

Herjanic, B., & Reich, W. (1982). Development of a structured psychiatric interview for children: Agreement between child and parent on individual symptoms. *Journal of Abnormal Child Psychology, 10,* 307-324.

Hobbs, N. (1982). *The troubled and troubling child.* San Francisco: Jossey-Bass.

Hobbs, S. A., & Lahey, B. B. (1983). Behavioral treatment. In T. H. Ollendick & M. Hersen (Eds.), *Handbook of child psychopathology* (pp. 427-460). New York: Plenum.

Hood-Williams, J. (1960). The results of psychotherapy with children: A reevaluation. *Journal of Consulting Psychology, 24,* 84-88.

Howard, K. I., Kopta, S. M., Krause, M. S., & Orlinsky, D. E. (1986). The dose–effect relationship in psychotherapy. *American Psychologist, 41,* 159-164.

Howard, K. I., Krause, M. S., & Orlinsky, D. E. (1986). The attrition dilemma: Toward a new strategy for psychotherapy research. *Journal of Consulting and Clinical Psychology, 54,* 106-110.

Hugdahl, K., & Ost, L. (1981). On the difference between statistical and clinical significance. *Behavioral Assessment, 3,* 289-295.

Jacobson, N. S. (1984). A component analysis of behavioral marital therapy: The relative effectiveness of behavior exchange and communication/problem-solving training. *Journal of Consulting and Clinical Psychology, 52,* 295-305.

Jacobson, N. S., Follette, W. C., & Revenstorf, D. (1984). Psychotherapy outcome research: Methods for reporting variability and evaluating clinical significance. *Behavior Therapy, 15,* 336-352.

Jesness, C. F. (1971). The role of verbal mediation in mental development. *Journal of Genetic Psychology, 118,* 39-70.

Johnson, J. H. (1986). *Life events as stressors in childhood and adolescence.* Newbury Park, CA: Sage.

Johnson, J. H., Rasbury, W. C., & Siegel, L. J. (1986). *Approaches to child treatment: Introduction to theory, research, and practice.* New York: Pergamon.

Joint Commission of Mental Health of Children. (1969). *Crisis in child mental health: Challenge for the 1970s.* New York: Harper & Row.

Journal of Consulting and Clinical Psychology. (1986). Psychotherapy research, *54,* [Special issue].

Kadushin, A. (1974). *Child welfare services* (2nd ed.). New York: Macmillan.

Karasu, T. B. (1985). Personal communication, March 1, 1985.

Kazdin, A. E. (1978a). *History of behavior modification: Experimental foundations of contemporary research.* Baltimore: University Park Press.

Kazdin, A. E. (1978b). Evaluating the generality of findings in analogue therapy research. *Journal of Consulting and Clinical Psychology, 46,* 673-686.

Kazdin, A. E. (1980a). Acceptability of time out from reinforcement procedures for disruptive child behavior. *Behavior Therapy, 11,* 329-344.

Kazdin, A. E. (1980b) *Research design in clinical psychology.* New York: Harper & Row.

Kazdin, A. E. (1981). Drawing valid inferences from case studies. *Journal of Consulting and Clinical Psychology, 49,* 183-192.

Kazdin, A. E. (1982). *Single-case research designs: Methods for clinical and applied settings.* New York: Oxford University Press.

Kazdin, A. E. (1983). Psychiatric diagnosis, dimensions of dysfunction, and child behavior therapy. *Behavior Therapy, 14,* 73-99.

Kazdin, A. E. (1985). *Treatment of antisocial behavior in children and adolescents.* Homewood, IL: Dorsey Press.

Kazdin, A. E. (1986a). Comparative outcome studies of psychotherapy: Methodological issues and strategies. *Journal of Consulting and Clinical Psychology, 54,* 95-105.

Kazdin, A. E. (1986b). The evaluation of psychotherapy: Research design and methodology. In S. L. Garfield & A. E. Bergin (Eds.), *Handbook of psychotherapy and behavior change* (3rd ed., pp. 23-68). New York: John Wiley & Sons.

Kazdin, A. E. (1987a). *Conduct disorder in childhood and adolescence.* Newbury Park, CA; Sage.

Kazdin, A. E. (1987b). Children's Depression Scale: Validation with child psychiatric inpatients. *Journal of Child Psychology and Psychiatry, 28,* 29-41.

Kazdin, A. E. (1987c). Treatment of antisocial behavior in children: Current status and future directions. *Psychological Bulletin, 102,* 187-203.

Kazdin, A. E. (in press a). Hospitalization of antisocial children: Clinical course, follow-up status, and predictors of outcome. *Journal of Child and Adolescent Psychotherapy.*

Kazdin, A. E. (in press b). Assessment of childhood depression: Current issues and strategies. *Behavioral Assessment.*

Kazdin, A. E., Esveldt-Dawson, K., French, N. H., & Unis, A. S. (1987). Problem-solving skills training and relationship therapy in the treatment of antisocial child behavior. *Journal of Consulting and Clinical Psychology, 55,* 76-85.

Kazdin, A. E., Esveldt-Dawson, K., Unis, A. S., & Rancurello, M. D. (1983). Child and parent evaluations of depression and aggression in psychiatric inpatient children. *Journal of Abnormal Child Psychology, 11,* 401-413.

Kazdin, A. E., Kratochwill, T. M., & VandenBos, G. R. (1986). Beyond clinical trials: Generalizing from research to practice. *Professional Psychology: Research and Practice, 17,* 391-398.

Kazdin, A. E., & Wilson, G. T. (1978a). Criteria for evaluating psychotherapy. *Archives of General Psychiatry, 35,* 407-416.

Kazdin, A. E., & Wilson, G. T. (1978b). *Evaluation of behavior therapy: Evidence, and research strategies.* Cambridge, MA: Ballinger.

Kendall, P. C. & Braswell, L. (1982). Cognitive–behavioral self-control therapy for children: A components analysis. *Journal of Consulting and Clinical Psychology, 50,* 672-689.

Kendall, P. C., & Braswell, L. (1985). *Cognitive–behavioral therapy for impulsive children.*

New York: Guilford.

Kendall, P. C., & Norton-Ford, J. D. (1982). Therapy outcome research methods. In P. C. Kendall & J. N. Butcher (Eds.), *Handbook of research methods in clinical psychology* (pp. 429-460). New York: John Wiley & Sons.

Kenny, D. A. (1979). *Correlation and causality.* New York: John Wiley & Sons.

Kent, R. N., & O'Leary, K. D. (1976). A controlled evaluation of behavior modification with conduct problem children. *Journal of Consulting and Clinical Psychology, 44,* 586-596.

Kiesler, D. J. (1971). Experimental designs in psychotherapy research. In A. E. Bergin & S. L. Garfield (Eds.), *Handbook of psychotherapy and behavior change: An empirical analysis* (pp. 36-74). New York: John Wiley & Sons.

Kingsley, R. G., & Wilson, G. T. (1977). Behavior therapy for obesity: A comparative investigation of long-term efficacy. *Journal of Consulting and Clinical Psychology, 45,* 288-298.

Kirigin, K. A., Braukmann, C. J., Atwater, J. D., & Wolf, M. M. (1982). An evaluation of teaching-family (Achievement Place) group homes for juvenile offenders. *Journal of Applied Behavior Analysis, 15,* 1-16.

Klein, N. C., Alexander, J. F., & Parsons, B. V. (1977). Impact of family systems intervention on recidivism and sibling delinquency: A model of primary prevention and program evaluation. *Journal of Consulting and Clinical Psychology, 45,* 469-474.

Klerman, G. L., & Schechter, G. (1982). Drugs and psychotherapy. In E. S. Paykel (Ed.), *Handbook of affective disorders* (pp. 329-337). New York: Guilford.

Knitzer, J. (1982). *Unclaimed children: The failure of public responsibility to children and adolescents in need of mental health services.* Washington, DC: Children's Defense Fund.

Kolotkin, R. L., & Johnson, M. (1983). Crisis intervention and measurement of treatment outcome. In M. J. Lambert, E. R. Christensen, & S. S. DeJulio (Eds.), *The assessment of psychotherapy outcome* (pp. 453-497). New York: John Wiley & Sons.

Kolvin, I., Garside, R. F., Nicol, A. R., MacMillan, A., Wolstenholme, F., & Leitch, I. M. (1981). *Help starts here: The maladjusted child in the ordinary school.* London: Tavistock.

Koocher, G. P., & Pedulla, B. M. (1977). Current practices in child psychotherapy. *Professional Psychology, 8,* 275-287.

Kovacs, M., & Paulauskas, S. (1986). The traditional psychotherapies. In H. C. Quay & J. S. Werry (Eds.), *Psychopathological disorders of childhood* (3rd ed., pp. 496-522). New York: John Wiley & Sons.

Kraepelin, E. (1883). *Compendium der psychiatrie.* Leipzig: Abel.

Krathwohl, D. R. (1985). *Social and behavioral science research: A new framework for conceptualizing, implementing, and evaluating research studies.* San Francisco, CA: Jossey-Bass.

Lambert, M. J. (1979). *The effects of psychotherapy* (Vol. 2). New York: Human Sciences Press.

Lambert, M. J., Christensen, E. R., & DeJulio, S. S. (Eds.). (1983). *The assessment of psychotherapy outcome.* New York: John Wiley & Sons.

Landman, J. T., & Dawes, R. M. (1982). Psychotherapy outcome: Smith and Glass' conclusions stand up under scrutiny. *American Psychologist, 37,* 504-516.

Langner, T. S., Gersten, J C., & Eisenberg, J. G. (1974). Approaches to measurement and definition in the epidemiology of behavior disorders: Ethnic background and child behavior. *International Journal of Health Services, 4,* 483-501.

Lapouse, R., & Monk, M. A. (1958). An epidemiologic study of behavior characteristics in children. *American Journal of Public Health, 48,* 1134-1144.

Last, C. G., Francis, G., Hersen, M., Kazdin, A. E., & Strauss, C. C. (1987). Separation anxiety and school phobia: A comparison using DSM-III criteria. *American Journal of Psychiatry, 144,* 653-657.

Lerner, J. A., Inui, T. S., Trupin, E. W., & Douglas, E. (1985). Preschool behavior can predict future psychiatric disorders. *Journal of the American Academy of Child Psychiatry, 24*, 42-48.

Levitt, E. E. (1957). The results of psychotherapy with children: An evaluation. *Journal of Consulting Psychology, 21*, 189-196.

Levitt, E. E. (1963). Psychotherapy with children: A further evaluation. *Behaviour Research and Therapy, 60*, 326-329.

Levitt, E. E. (1971). Research on psychotherapy with children. In S. L. Garfield & A.E. Bergin (Eds.), *Handbook of psychotherapy and behavior change: An empirical analysis* (pp. 474-494). New York: John Wiley & Sons.

Li, C. C. (1975). *Path analysis: A primer*. Pacific Grove, CA: Boxwood Press.

Liberman, R. P., & Eckman, T. (1981). Behavior therapy vs. insight-oriented therapy for repeated suicide attempters. *Archives of General Psychiatry, 38*, 1126-1130.

Lochman, J. E. (1985). Effects of different treatment lengths in cognitive behavioral interventions with aggressive boys. *Child Psychiatry and Human Development, 16*, 45-56.

Lochman, J. E., Burch, P. R., Curry, J. F., & Lampron, L. B. (1984). Treatment and generalization effects of cognitive-behavioral and goal-setting interventions with aggressive boys. *Journal of Consulting and Clinical Psychology, 52*, 915-916.

Lord, J. P. (1985). *A guide to individual psychotherapy with school-age children and adolescents*. Springfield, IL: Charles C Thomas.

Lovaas, O. I. (1987). Behavioral treatment and normal educational/intellectual functioning in young autistic children. *Journal of Consulting and Clinical Psychology, 55*, 3-9.

Luborsky, L., & DeRubeis, R. J. (1984). The use of psychotherapy treatment manuals: A small revolution in psychotherapy research style. *Clinical Psychology Review, 4*, 5-14.

Luborsky, L., Singer, B., & Luborsky, L. (1975). Comparative studies of psychotherapies: Is it true that "everyone has won and all must have prizes"? *Archives of General Psychiatry, 32*, 995-1008.

MacFarlane, J. W., Allen, L., & Honzik, M. P. (1954). *A developmental study of the behavior problems of normal children between 21 months and 14 years*. Berkeley: University of California Press.

Mahler, M. (1961). On sadness and grief in infancy and childhood. *Psychoanalytic Study of the Child, 16*, 332.

Mash, E. J., & Johnson, C. (1983). Parental perceptions of child behavior problems, parenting self-esteem, and mothers' reported stress in younger and older hyperactive and normal children. *Journal of Consulting and Clinical Psychology, 51*, 86-99.

Massimo, J. L., & Shore, M. F. (1963). The effectiveness of a comprehensive vocationally oriented psychotherapeutic program for adolescent delinquent boys. *American Journal of Orthopsychiatry, 33*, 634-642.

Massimo, J. L., & Shore, M. F. (1967). Comprehensive vocationally oriented psychotherapy: A new treatment technique for lower-class adolescent delinquent boys. *Psychiatry, 30*, 229-236.

Masten, A. S. (1979). Family therapy as a treatment for children: A critical review of outcome research. *Family Process, 18*, 323-335.

Matson, J. L., Rotatori, A. F., & Helsel, W. J. (1983). Development of a rating scale to measure social skills in children: The Matson Evaluation of Social Skills with Youngsters (MESSY). *Behaviour Research and Therapy, 21*, 335-340.

McCord, J. (1978). A thirty-year follow-up of treatment effects. *American Psychologist, 33*, 284-289.

McMahon, R. J., Forehand, R., & Griest, D. L. (1981). Effects of knowledge of social learning principles on enhancing treatment outcome and generalization in a parent training program. *Journal of Consulting and Clinical Psychology, 49*, 526-532.

Meador, A. E., & Ollendick, T. H. (1984). Cognitive behavior therapy with children: An evaluation of its efficacy and clinical utility. *Child and Family Behavior Therapy, 6*, 25-44.

Michelson, L. (1985). Editorial: Introduction and commentary. *Clinical Psychology Review, 5*, 1-2.

Michelson, L., Sugai, D. P., Wood, R. P., & Kazdin, A. E. (1983). *Social skills assessment and training with children.* New York: Plenum.

Miller, L. C. (1977). *School Behavior Checklist manual.* Los Angeles: Western Psychological Services.

Miller, L. C., Barrett, C. L., Hampe, E., & Noble, H. (1972). Comparison of reciprocal inhibition, psychotherapy, and waiting list control for phobic children. *Journal of Abnormal Psychology, 79,* 269-279.

Miller, L. C., & Berman, J. S. (1983). The efficacy of cognitive behavior therapies: A quantitative review of the research evidence. *Psychological Bulletin, 94,* 39-53.

Moreland, J. R., Schwebel, A. I., Beck, S., & Wells, R. (1982). Parents as therapists: A review of the behavior therapy parent training literature—1975 to 1981. *Behavior Modification, 6,* 250-276.

Morris, R. J., & Kratochwill, T. R. (Eds.). (1983) *The practice of child therapy.* New York: Pergamon.

Morris, S. B., Alexander, J. F., & Waldron, H. (in press). Functional family therapy: Issues in clinical practice. In I. R. H. Falloon (Ed.), *Handbook of behavior therapy.* New York: Guilford.

National Institute of Mental Health. (1975). *Research in the service of mental health.* DHEW Publication No. (ADM) 75-236. Rockville, MD.

Newman, F. L., & Howard, K. I. (1986). Therapeutic effort, treatment outcome, and national health policy. *American Psychologist, 41,* 181-187.

Nicholson, R. A., & Berman, J. S. (1983). Is follow-up necessary in evaluating psychotherapy? *Psychological Bulletin, 93,* 555-565.

O'Donnell, C. R., Lydgate, T., & Fo., W. S. O. (1979). The buddy system: Review and follow-up. *Child Behavior Therapy, 1,* 161-169.

Ollendick, T. H., & Cerny, J. A. (1981). *Clinical behavior therapy with children.* New York: Plenum.

Orvaschel, H., Puig-Antich, J., Chambers, W., Tabrizi, M. A., & Johnson, R. (1982). Retrospective assessment of prepubertal major depression with the Kiddie-SADS-E. *Journal of the American Academy of Child Psychiatry, 21,* 392-397.

Parker, J. G., & Asher, S. R. (in press). Peer relations and later personal adjustment: Are low-accepted children "at risk"? *Psychological Bulletin.*

Parloff, M. B. (1982). Psychotherapy research evidence and reimbursement decisions: Bambi meets Godzilla. *American Journal of Psychiatry, 139,* 718-727.

Parloff, M. B. (1984). Psychotherapy research and its incredible credibility crisis. *Clinical Psychology Review, 4,* 95-109.

Parloff, M. B. (1986). Placebo controls in psychotherapy research: A sine qua non or a placebo for research problems? *Journal of Consulting and Clinical Psychology, 54,* 79-87.

Parsons, B. V., & Alexander, J. F. (1973). Short-term family intervention: A therapy outcome study. *Journal of Consulting and Clinical Psychology, 41,* 195-201.

Patterson, G. R. (1974). Interventions for boys with conduct problems: Multiple settings, treatments, and criteria. *Journal of Consulting and Clinical Psychology, 42,* 471-481.

Patterson, G. R. (1982). *Coercive family process.* Eugene, OR: Castalia.

Patterson, G. R. (1986). Performance models for antisocial boys. *American Psychologist, 41,* 432-444.

Patterson, G. R., Chamberlain, P., & Reid, J. B. (1982). A comparative evaluation of a parent-training program. *Behavior Therapy, 13,* 638-650.

Patterson, G. R., & Fleischman, M. J. (1979). Maintenance of treatment effects: Some considerations concerning family systems and follow-up data. *Behavior Therapy, 10,* 168-185.

Patterson, V., Levene, H., & Breger, L. (1977). A one-year follow-up of two forms of brief psychotherapy. *American Journal of Psychotherapy, 31,* 76-82.

Paul, G. L. (1966). *Insight versus desensitization in psychotherapy: An experiment in anxiety reduction.* Stanford, CA; Stanford University Press.

Paul, G. L. (1967). Outcome research in psychotherapy. *Journal of Consulting Psychology, 31,* 109-118.

Powers, E., & Witmer, H. (1951). *An experiment in the prevention of delinquency: The Cambridge-Sommerville Youth Study.* New York: Columbia University Press.

President's Commission on Mental Health Task Panel Reports, Vols. I-II. (1978). Washington, DC: U.S. Government Printing Office.

Prioleau, L., Murdock, M., & Brody, N. (1983). An analysis of psychotherapy versus placebo studies. *The Behavioral and Brain Sciences, 6,* 275-310.

Prout, H. T., & Brown, D. T. (Eds.). (1985). *Counseling and psychotherapy with children and adolescents: Theory and practice for school and clinic settings.* Bradon, VT: Clinical Psychology Publishing Company.

Puig-Antich, J., Lukens, E., Davies, M., Goetz, D., Brennan-Quattrock, J., & Todak, G. (1985a). Psychosocial functioning in prepubertal major depressive disorders. I. Interpersonal relationships during the depressive episode. *Archives of General Psychiatry, 42,* 500-507.

Puig-Antich, J., Lukens, E., Davies, M., Goetz, D., Brennan-Quattrock, J., & Todak, G. (1985b). Psychosocial functioning in prepubertal major depressive disorders. II. Interpersonal relationships after sustained recovery from affective episode. *Archives of General Psychiatry, 42,* 511-517.

Quay, H. C. (1977). The three faces of evaluation: What can be expected to work. *Criminal Justice and Behavior, 4,* 341-354.

Quay, H. C. (1986). A critical analysis of DSM-III as a taxonomy of psychopathology in childhood and adolescence. In T. Millon & G. Klerman (Eds.), *Contemporary issues in psychopathology* (pp. 151-165) New York: Guilford Press.

Rachman, S., & Hodgson, R. I. (1974). Synchrony and desynchrony in fear and avoidance. *Behaviour Research and Therapy, 12,* 311-318.

Rachman, S. J., & Wilson, G. T. (1980). *The effects of psychological therapy* (2nd ed.). Oxford: Pergamon.

Reik, T. (1948). *Listening with the third ear.* New York: Farrrar, Straus.

Reynolds, W. M. (1985). Depression in childhood and adolescence: Diagnosis, assessment, intervention strategies, and research. In T. R. Kratochwill (Ed.), *Advances in school psychology* (Vol. 4, pp. 133-189). Hillsdale, NJ: Lawrence Erlbaum.

Rie, H. E. (1966). Depression in childhood: A survey of some pertinent contributions. *Journal of the American Academy of Child Psychiatry, 5,* 653-685.

Roback, H. B. (1971). The comparative influence of insight and non-insight psychotherapies on therapeutic outcome: A review of experimental literature. *Psychotherapy: Theory, Research and Practice, 8,* 23-25.

Robins, L. N. (1973). Evaluation of psychiatric services for children in the United States. In J. K. Wing & H. Hafner (Eds.), *Roots of evaluation: The epidemiological basis for planning psychiatric services* (pp. 101-129). London: Oxford University Press.

Rosen, B. M., Bahn, A. K., & Kramer, M. (1964). Demographic and diagnostic characteristics of psychiatric clinic outpatients in the USA, 1961. *American Journal of Orthopsychiatry, 34,* 455-468.

Rossi, J. S., Rossi. S. R., & Cottrill, S. D. (1984, April). *Statistical power of research in social and abnormal psychology: What have we gained in 20 years?* Paper presented at the meeting of the Eastern Psychological Association, Baltimore, Maryland.

Rush, A. J., Beck, A. T., Kovacs, M., & Hollon, S. (1977). Comparative efficacy of cognitive therapy and pharmacotherapy in the treatment of depressed outpatients. *Cognitive Therapy and Research, 1,* 17-38.

Rutter, M. (1982). Psychological therapies in child psychiatry: Issues and prospects.

Psychological Medicine, 12, 723-740.

Rutter, M., Cox, A., Tupling, C., Berger, M., & Yule, W. (1975). Attainment and adjustment in two geographical areas. I. The prevalence of psychiatric disorder. *British Journal of Psychiatry, 126*, 493-509.

Rutter, M., & Giller, H. (1983). *Juvenile delinquency: Trends and perspectives.* New York: Penguin Books.

Rutter, M., Tizard, J., & Whitmore, K. (Eds.). (1970). *Education, health and behaviour.* London: Longmans.

Schaefer, C. E. (1979). *The therapeutic use of child's play* (2nd ed). New York: Jason Aronson.

Schaefer, C. E., Briesmeister, J. M., & Fitton, M. E. (1984). *Family therapy techniques for problem behaviors of children and teenagers.* San Francisco: Jossey-Bass.

Schaefer, C. E., Johnson, L., & Wherry, J. N. (1982). *Group therapies for children and youth: Principles and practices for group treatment.* San Francisco: Jossey-Bass.

Schaefer, C. E., & Millman, H. L. (1977). *Therapies for children.* San Francisco: Jossey-Bass.

Schaefer, C. E., Millman, H. L., Sichel, S. M., & Zwilling, J. R. (1986). *Advances in therapies for children.* San Francisco, CA: Jossey-Bass.

Sechrest, L., West, S. G., Phillips, M. A., Redner, R., & Yeaton, W. (1979). Some neglected problems in evaluation research: Strength and integrity of treatments. In L. Sechrest, S. G. West, M. A. Phillips, R. Redner, & W. Yeaton (Eds.), *Evaluation studies: Review annual* (Vol. 4, pp. 15-35). Beverly Hills: Sage.

Sechrest, L., White, S. O., & Brown, E. D. (Eds.). (1979). *The rehabilitation of criminal offenders: Problems and prospects.* Washington, DC: National Academy of Sciences.

Shapiro, D. A., & Shapiro, D. (1982). Meta-analysis of comparative therapy outcome studies: A replication and refinement. *Psychological Bulletin, 92*, 581-604.

Shure, M. B., & Spivack, G. (1978). *Problem-solving techniques in child-rearing.* San Francisco: Jossey-Bass.

Shure, M. B., & Spivack, G. (1982). Interpersonal problem-solving in young children: A cognitive approach to prevention. *American Journal of Community Psychology, 10*, 341-356.

Silver, L. B., & Silver, B. J. (1983). Clinical practice of child psychiatry: A survey. *Journal of the American Academy of Child Psychiatry, 22*, 573-579.

Sloane, R. B., Staples, F. R., Cristol, A. H., Yorkston, N. J., & Whipple, K. (1975). *Psychotherapy versus behavior therapy.* Cambridge, MA: Harvard University Press.

Smith, M. L., & Glass, G. V. (1977). Meta-analysis of psychotherapy outcome studies. *American Psychologist, 32*, 752-760.

Smith, M. L., Glass, G. V., & Miller, T. I. (1980). *The benefits of psychotherapy.* Baltimore, MD: Johns Hopkins University Press.

Smith, N. C., Jr. (1970). Replication studies: A neglected aspect of psychological research. *American Psychologist, 25*, 970-975.

Sorenson, R. L., Gorsuch, R. L., & Mintz, J. (1985). Moving targets: Patients' changing complaints during psychotherapy. *Journal of Consulting and Clinical Psychology, 53*, 49-54.

Sowder, B. J. (1975). *Assessment of child mental health needs* (Vols. I-VIII). McLean, VA: General Research Corp.

Sowder, B. J., & Burt, M. R. (1980). *Utilization of psychiatric facilities by children and youth.* Bethesda, MD: Burt Associates.

Spitzer, R. L., Endicott, J., & Robins, E. (1975). Research Diagnostic Criteria. *Psychopharmacology Bulletin, 11*, 22-25.

Spivack, G., & Shure, M. B. (1982) The cognition of social adjustment: Interpersonal cognitive problem solving thinking. In B. B. Lahey & A. E. Kazdin (Eds.), *Advances in clinical child psychology* (Vol. 5, pp. 323-372). New York: Plenum.

Spivack, G., Platt, J. J., & Shure, M. B. (1976). *The problem-solving approach to adjustment.* San Francisco: Jossey-Bass.

Steinbrueck, S. M., Maxwell, S. E., & Howard, G. S. (1983). A meta-analysis of psychotherapy and drug therapy in the treatment of unipolar depression with adults. *Journal of Consulting and Clinical Psychology, 51*, 856-863.

Stephenson, J. F., & Norcross, J.C. (1983). *Evaluation activity of psychology training clinics: National survey findings.* Unpublished manuscript, University of Rhode Island.

Strain, P. S., Young, C. C., & Horowitz, J. (1981). Generalized behavior change during oppositional child training: An examination on child and family demographic variables. *Behavior Modification, 5*, 15-26.

Straw, R. B. (1983). Deinstitutionalization in mental health: A meta-analysis. In R. J. Light (Ed.), *Evaluation studies: Review annual.* (Vol. 8, pp. 253-278). Beverly Hills, CA: Sage.

Strober, M., & Carlson, G. (1982). Bipolar illness in adolescents with major depression: Clinical, genetic, and psychopharmacologic predictors in a three-to-four-year prospective follow-up investigation. *Archives of General Psychiatry, 39*, 549-555.

Strupp, H. H., & Hadley, S. W. (1977). A tripartite model of mental health and therapeutic outcomes. *American Psychologist, 32*, 187-196.

Tramontana, M. G. (1980). Critical review of research on psychotherapy outcome with adolescents: 1967—1977. *Psychological Bulletin, 88*, 429-450.

Tuma, J. M., & Pratt, J. M. (1982). Clinical child psychology practice and training: A survey. *Journal of Clinical Child Psychology, 11*, 27-34.

Tuma, J. M., & Sobotka, K. R. (1983). Traditional therapies with children. In T. H. Ollendick & M. Hersen (Eds.), *Handbook of child psychopathology* (pp. 391-426). New York: Plenum.

United States Congress, Office of Technology Assessment. (1986). *Children's mental health: Problems and services—A background paper.* Washington, DC: United States Government Printing Office.

Viale-Val, G., Rosenthal, R. H., Curtiss, G., & Marohn, R. C. (1984). Dropout from adolescent psychotherapy: A preliminary study. *Journal of the American Academy of Child Psychiatry, 23*, 562-568.

Wahler, R. G. (1980). The insular mother: Her problems in parent–child treatment. *Journal of Applied Behavior Analysis, 13*, 207-219.

Wahler, R. G., Berland, R. M., & Coe, T. D. (1979). Generalization processes in child behavior change. In B. B. Lahey and A. E. Kazdin (Eds.), *Advances in clinical child psychology* (Vol. 2, pp. 35-69). New York: Plenum.

Wahler, R. G., & Fox, J. J. (1980). Solitary toy play and time out: A family treatment package for children with aggressive and oppositional behavior. *Journal of Applied Behavior Analysis, 13*, 23-39.

Walter, H. I., & Gilmore, S. K. (1973). Placebo versus social learning effects in parent training procedures designed to alter the behavior of aggressive boys. *Behavior Therapy, 4*, 361-377.

Waskow, I. E., & Parloff, M. B. (Eds.). (1975). *Psychotherapy change measures.* Washington, DC: Department of Health, Education and Welfare.

Weisz, J. R., Weiss, B., Alicke, M. D., & Klotz, M. L. (1987). Effectiveness of psychotherapy with children and adolescents: A meta-analysis for clinicians. *Journal of Consulting and Clinical Psychology, 55*, 542-549.

Wells, K. C., Forehand, R., & Griest, D. L. (1980). Generality of treatment effects from treated to untreated behaviors resulting from a parent training program. *Journal of Clinical Child Psychology, 9*, 217-219.

Wells, R. A., & Dezen, A. E. (1978). The results of family therapy revisited: The nonbehavioral methods. *Family Process, 17*, 251-274.

Wells, R. A., Dilkes, T. C., & Burckhardt, N. T. (1976). The results of family therapy: A critical review of the literature. In D. H. L. Olson (Ed.), *Treating relationships* (pp. 499-516). Lake Mills, IA: Graphic Publishing.

Werry, J. S., & Quay, H.C. (1971). The prevalence of behavior symptoms in younger elementary school children. *American Journal of Orthopsychiatry, 41,* 136-143.

Williams, J.B. W., & Spitzer, R. L. (Eds.). (1983). *Psychotherapy research: Where are we and where should we go?* New York: Guilford.

Wiltz, N. A., & Patterson, G. R. (1974). An evaluation of parent training procedures designed to alter inappropriate aggressive behavior of boys. *Behavior Therapy, 5,* 215-221.

Wing, J. K., Cooper, J. E., & Sartorius, N. (1974). *Description and classification of psychiatric symptoms.* Cambridge, England: Cambridge University Press.

World Health Organization. (1978). *Mental disorders: Glossary and guide to their classification in accordance with the 9th revision of the International Classification of Diseases.* Geneva: Author.

Wright, D. M., Moelis, I., & Pollack, L. J. (1976). The outcome of individual child psychotherapy: Increments at follow-up. *Journal of Child Psychology and Psychiatry, 17,* 275-285.

Yeaton, W. H., & Sechrest, L. (1981). Critical dimensions in the choice and maintenance of successful treatments: Strength, integrity, and effectiveness. *Journal of Consulting and Clinical Psychology, 49,* 156-167.

Yu, P., Harris, G. E., Solovitz, B. L., & Franklin, J. L. (1986). A social problem-solving intervention for children at high risk for later psychopathology. *Journal of Clinical Child Psychology, 15,* 30-40.

Author Index

Abramowitz, C. V., 39
Achenbach, T. M., 15, 18, 66, 67, 75, 76, 84, 110, 111, 112
Adams, S., 97
Adelman, H. S., 23
Alexander, J. F., 57, 58, 59, 91
Alicke, M. D., 31
Allen, L., 7, 20
American Psychiatric Association, 4, 5, 13, 15, 17
American Psychologist, 8
Andrews, G., 33fn
Arbuthnot, J., 60
Arizmendi, T. G., 74
Asher, S. R., 77
Atwater, J. D., 104
Axline, V. M., 26
Azrin, N. H., 22

Bachman, J. G., 100
Baenen, R. S., 100
Bahn, A. K., 14
Barlow, D. H., 124
Barrett, C. L., 21, 31, 67
Barton, C., 57, 58
Bash, M. A. S., 59, 61, 70
Bastien, R., 23
Baum, C. G., 55
Beck, A. T., 82
Beck, S., 53
Becker, R. E., 69
Bellack, A. S., 29fn, 44fn
Bemis, K. M., 71

Bentler, P. M., 109
Berger, M., 6
Bergin, A. E., 3, 8, 30
Berland, R. M., 55
Berman, J. S., 31, 33fn, 34, 35, 36, 37, 38, 41, 52fn, 62, 70, 79, 83, 93, 123
Berry, K. K., 39
Beutler, L. E., 74, 110
Bien, N. Z., 90
Bornstein, P. H., 39
Boy, A. V., 69
Braswell, L., 59, 60, 61, 70
Braukmann, C. J., 104
Breger, L., 78
Briesmeister, J. M., 9
Brody, N., 33fn
Brown, D. T., 9
Brown, E. D., 70
Brown, J., 33
Bry, B. H., 90
Bugental, J. F. T., 125
Burch, P. R., 61
Burckhardt, N. T., 39
Burt, M. R., 7
Buss, A. H., 103

Camp, B. W., 59, 61, 70
Campbell, D. T., 115, 116, 124
Cantwell, D. P., 23
Caplinger, T. E., 49
Carlson, G. A., 23, 98
Casey, R. J., 31, 34, 35, 36, 37, 38, 41, 52fn, 62, 70, 83, 93, 123

Cerny, J. A., 56, 70
Chamberlain, P., 54
Chambers, W. J., 17, 75
Christensen, E. R., 4
Clarizio, H. F., 100
Coe, T. D., 55
Cohen, J., 81, 82, 83, 121, 126, 127
Cole, P. N., 61
Compas, B. E., 23
Conover, N. C., 75
Cook, T. D., 115, 116, 124
Cooper, J. E., 17
Corsini, R. J., 29fn, 44fn
Costantino, G., 119
Costello, A. J., 75
Cottrill, S. D., 81
Cox, A., 6
Crago, M., 74, 110
Craighead, L. W., 78
Cristol, A. H., 69
Cronbach, L. J., 3
Cross, D. G., 82
Curry, J. F., 61
Curtiss, G., 82

Daads, M. R., 55, 68
Davidson, W. S., 33fn
Dawes, R. M., 33fn
Deffenbacher, J. L., 78
DeJulio, S. S., 4
DeRubeis, R. J., 70, 71
DeWitt, K. N., 39, 40
Dezen, A. E., 39, 40
Dilkes, T. C., 39
DiLoreto, A. O., 69, 82
Dodds, J. B., 9
Dodge, K. A., 59, 101
Dohrewend, B. P., 5
Dollinger, S. J., 23
Douglas, E., 8
Dreger, R. M., 13
Dulcan, M. K., 75
Dumas, J. E., 55, 74
Dush, D. M., 33fn

Earls, F., 98
Eckman, T., 82

Edelbrock, C. S., 22, 67, 75, 76, 84
Edwards, A. L., 3
Eisenberg, J. G., 6
Eisenberg, L., 31
Ellis, A., 69
Ellis, P. L., 59
Endicott, J., 12, 17
Esveldt-Dawson, K., 60, 75, 86
Evans, M. D., 71
Eyberg, S. M., 54
Eysenck, H. J., 5fn, 30

Faust, J., 24
Feighner, J. P., 12
Feldman, R. A., 49, 82
Fitton, M. E., 9
Fleischman, M. J., 54, 55, 82
Fo, W. S. O., 26
Follette, W. C., 83
Forehand, R., 24, 54, 55, 84
Forman, S. G., 82
Fox, J. J., 26, 55
Foxx, R. M., 22
Francis, G., 98
Franklin, J. L., 82
French, N. H., 60, 86
Freud, A., 26
Friedland-Bandes, R., 23

Gard, G. C., 39
Garfield, S. L., 1, 4, 8, 30, 37, 124
Garrison, W. T., 98
Gelfand, D. M., 13, 79
Gensheimer, L., 33fn
George, F. E., 90
Gersten, J. C., 6
Gilbert, G. M., 99
Giller, H., 65
Gilmore, S., K., 54
Glass, G. V., 31, 33, 34
Glenwick, D. S., 100
Glick, S. J., 101
Goldman, A., 31
Gordon, D. A., 60
Gorsuch, R. L., 123
Gottschalk, R., 33fn
Gould, M. S., 5, 6, 62, 67, 70

Graham, P. J., 6, 67
Graziano, W. G., 24
Gresham, F. M., 60
Griest, D. L., 54, 55, 68
Gruenberg, E. M., 31
Gumaer, J., 9, 29fn, 44fn
Gurman, A. S., 5fn, 39, 40

Hackler, J. C., 26
Hadley, S. W., 75
Hagan, J. L., 26
Hampe, E., 21, 67
Harris, G. E., 82
Harrison, S. E., 9, 39fn
Hartmann, D. P., 79
Harvey, R., 33fn
Hayes, S. C., 124
Heimberg, R. G., 69
Heinicke, C. M., 31, 38, 78, 79, 90, 91
Helsel, W. J., 77
Herink, R., 4, 17, 29fn, 44fn
Herjanic, B., 17
Hersen, M., 29fn, 44fn, 98
Hirt, M. L., 33fn
Hobbs, N., 100
Hobbs, S. A., 39
Hodgson, R. I., 79
Hollon, S. E., 71, 82
Honzik, M. P., 7, 20
Hood-Williams, J., 31
Horowitz, J., 55
Howard, G. S., 33fn
Howard, K. I., 12, 93, 94
Howell, C. T., 75
Hugdahl, K., 83

Inui, T. S., 8

Jacobson, N. S., 78, 83, 85
Jesness, C. F., 66
Johnson, J. H., 9, 29fn, 44fn, 98
Johnson, L., 9
Johnson, M., 110
Johnson, R., 75
Johnson, S. M., 54
Johnston, C., 24
Johnston, L. D., 100

Joint Commission of Mental Health of Children, 6
Journal of Consulting and Clinical Psychology, 8

Kadushin, A., 32
Kalas, R., 75
Karasu, T. B., 4
Kaser-Boyd, N., 23
Kazdin, A. E., 5, 12, 15, 23, 30, 33, 39, 48, 53, 60, 68, 70, 75, 81, 86, 89, 91, 97, 98, 101, 103, 111, 123
Kendall, P. C., 59, 60, 61, 70, 83
Kenny, D. A., 109
Kent, R. N., 80
Khan, J. A., 82
Kiesler, D. J., 66
Kingsley, R. G., 78
Kirigin, K. A., 104
Klein, N. C., 58
Klerman, G. L., 101
Klotz, M. L., 31
Kniskern, D. P., 39
Knitzer, J., 7
Kolotkin, R. L., 110
Kolvin, I., 7, 38, 46, 49, 66, 68, 74, 78, 79, 91
Koocher, G. P., 25, 62, 70, 123
Kopta, S. M., 93, 94
Kovacs, M., 26, 39, 82
Kraepelin, E., 13
Kramer, M., 14
Krathwohl, D. R., 116
Kratochwill, T. R., 29fn, 39, 44fn, 71
Krause, M. S., 12, 93, 94

Lahey, B. B., 39
Lambert, M. J., 3, 4, 5fn, 75, 121
Lampron, L. B., 61
Landman, J. T., 33fn
Langner, T. S., 6
Lapouse, R., 7, 19
Last, C. G., 98
Lautenschlager, G. J., 24
Lerner, J. A., 8
Levene, H., 78
Levitt, E. E., 7, 12, 21, 30, 31, 89

Li, C. C., 109
Liberman, R. P., 82
Lochman, J. E., 61
Long, N., 55, 84
Lord, J. P., 9
Lovaas, O. I., 95
Luborsky, L., 70, 91
Lydgate, T., 26

MacFarlane, J. W., 7, 19, 20, 67
Mahler, M., 22
Malgady, R. G., 119
Marohn, R. C., 82
Mash, E. J., 24
Massimo, J. L., 101
Masten, A. S., 39, 40
Matson, J. L., 77
Maxwell, S. E., 33fn
Mayer, J., 33fn
McConaughy, S. H., 75
McCord, J., 26
McCoy, G. F., 100
McGaw, B., 33
McMahon, R. J., 55
Meador, A. E., 39
Michelson, L., 37, 60
Miller, L. C., 21, 33fn, 67, 77
Miller, T. I., 5fn
Millman, H. L., 9, 29fn, 39fn, 44fn, 106
Mintz, J., 123
Moelis, I., 78
Monk, M. A., 7, 19
Moreland, J. R., 53, 55
Morris, R. J., 29fn, 39, 44fn
Morris, S. B., 57
Murdock, M., 33fn

National Institute of Mental Health, 4
Nelson, R. O., 124
Newman, F. L., 93
Nicholson, R. A., 79
Noble, H., 67
Norcross, J. C., 127
Norton-Ford, J. D., 83

O'Brien, R., 78
O'Donnell, C. R., 26

O'Leary, K. D., 80
O'Malley, P. M., 100
Ollendick, T. H., 39, 56, 70
Orlinsky, D. E., 12, 93, 94
Orvaschel, H., 75
Ost, L., 83

Parker, J. G., 77
Parloff, M. B., 5, 12, 69, 110
Parsons, B. V., 57, 58, 59, 91
Patterson, G. R., 22, 53, 54, 55, 56, 82,
    84, 108, 109
Patterson, V., 78
Paul, G. L., 3, 69
Paulauskas, S., 26, 39
Pedulla, B. M., 25, 62, 70, 123
Peterson, L., 13
Phillips, M. A., 69
Pinsof, W. M., 39
Platt, J. J., 59
Pollack, L. J., 78
Powers, E., 102
Pratt, J. M., 61, 62, 70, 123
President's Commission on Mental
    Health Task Panel Reports, 6
Prioleau, L., 33fn, 37
Prout, H. T., 9
Puig-Antich, J., 75, 100

Quay, H. C., 7, 18, 19, 70

Rachman, S., 5fn, 30, 38, 69, 79, 127
Ramsey-Klee, D. M., 38, 78, 79, 91
Rancurello, M. D., 75
Rasbury, W. C., 9
Razin, A. M., 5fn
Redner, R., 69
Reich, W., 17
Reid, J. B., 54
Reik, T., 125
Revenstorf, D., 83
Reynolds, W. M., 39
Rie, H. E., 22
Roback, H. B., 69
Robins, E., 12
Robins, L. N., 32, 79
Rogler, L. H., 119

Roper, B. L., 79
Rosen, B. M., 14
Rosenthal, R. H., 82
Rossi, J. S., 81, 82
Rossi, S. R., 81
Rotatori, A. F., 77
Rush, A. J., 82
Rutter, M., 6, 7, 32, 65

Sanders, M. R., 55
Sargent, M. M., 126
Sartorius, N., 17
Schaefer, C. E., 9, 29fn, 39fn, 44fn, 106
Schechter, G., 101
Schiavo, R. S., 58
Schroeder, H., 33fn
Schwartz, S., 55
Schwebel, A. I., 53
Sechrest, L., 69, 70, 83, 126
Shapiro, D., 33fn, 35
Shapiro, D. A., 33fn, 35
Sheehan, P. W., 82
Shelton, J. L., 78
Shore, M. F., 102
Shure, M. B., 59, 60, 61
Sichel, S. M., 9
Siegel, L. J., 9
Silver, B. J., 123
Silver, L. B., 123
Singer, B., 91
Sloane, R. B., 69, 82
Smith, M. L., 5fn, 30, 31, 32, 33, 34
Smith, N. C., Jr., 114
Sobotka, K. R., 39
Solovitz, B. L., 82
Sorenson, R. L., 123
Sowder, B. J., 7
Spitzer, R. L., 8, 2, 17
Spivack, G., 59, 60, 61, 77, 101
Staples, F. R., 69
Steinbrueck, S. M., 33fn
Stephens, M. A. P., 100
Stephenson, J. F., 127
Strain, P. S., 55
Strassman, L. H., 31
Strauss, C. C., 98
Straw, R. B., 33fn

Strober, M., 98
Strupp, H. H., 75
Stunkard, A. J., 78
Sugai, D. P., 70
Szykula, S. A., 54

Tabrizi, M. A., 75
Taylor, L., 23
Thelen, M. H., 23
Tizard, J., 7
Tramontana, M. G., 32, 41
Trupin, E. W., 8
Tuma, J. M., 39, 61, 62, 70, 123
Tupling, C., 6

Unis, A. S., 60, 75, 86
United States Congress, Office of
    Technology Assessment, 5, 6, 24

VandenBos, G. R., 71
Viale-Val, G., 82

Wahler, R. G., 25, 55, 74, 114
Waldron, H., 57
Walsh, M. L., 23
Walter, H. I., 54
Waskow, I. W., 110
Weiss, B., 31
Weisz, J. R., 31, 36, 38, 41, 52fn, 62,
    70, 83, 123
Wells, K. C., 54
Wells, R. A., 39, 40, 53
Werry, J. S., 7, 19
West, S. G., 69
Wherry, J. N., 9
Whipple, K., 69
White, S. O., 70
Whitmore, K., 7
Williams, J. B. W., 8
Wilson, G. T., 5fn, 30, 38, 69, 75, 77,
    83, 91, 127
Wiltz, N. A., 54
Wing, J. K., 17
Witmer, H., 102
Wodarski, J. S., 49
Wolf, M. M., 104
Wood, R. P., 70
World Health Organization, 13

Wright, D. M., 78, 79   Young, C. C., 55
Wunsch-Hitzig, R., 5   Yu, P., 82
                                         Yule, W., 6
Yeaton, W. H., 69, 70, 83
Yorkston, N. J., 69   Zwilling, J. R., 9

Subject Index

Academic Performance, 90-91, 99-100
Administration of Treatment *see*
 Treatment Integrity
Age, 13, 19-23, 67
 course of behavior, 13, 19-22
 treatment effects and, 67
Amenability-to-Treatment Model, 96-
 98, 105
 description of, 96-97
 illustration of, 97-98
Anorexia Nervosa, 16
Antisocial Behavior, 49-51, 53-54, 84,
 97, 104, 108-109
Arithmetic Disorder, 17
Articulation Disorder, 16
Assessment, 3, 4, 21-22, 75-80, 110-111,
 116-117, 120-121, 124
 client reactions to treatment, 77
 correspondence among measures, 3,
 4, 110-111
 diagnostic, 17
 multiaxial, 110-112
 parent report, 24, 75
 self-report, 75, 110-111
 timing of, 38, 78-80, 121
 treatment outcome, 4, 75-77, 111
Attention Deficit-Hyperactivity
 Disorder, 15, 17
Attrition, 77, 82-83, 96
Autistic Disorder, 15, 95
 high-strength treatment of, 95-96

Behavior Modification *see* Behavior
 Therapy
Behavior Therapy, 34-37, 46, 47, 49-51,
 123
Broad-Based Intervention Model, 98-
 103, 105
 description of, 98-100
 illustration of, 100-101
Bulimia Nervosa, 16

Case Reports, 106, 124
Child Behavior Checklist, 77, 84-86,
 112
Childhood Depression *see* Depression
Child Development, 7, 13, 19-23, 24,
 27, 46, 61, 66-67
 age, 19, 27, 46, 67
 stages, 13, 27, 66-67, 80
Child Psychotherapy, 8-10, 34-37
 limited progress in, 8-9
 obstacles to research in, 12-27
 see also Psychotherapy
Childhood Disorders, 5-6, 13-15, 18,
 35, 107-110
 major types defined, 15-17
 neglect of, 12-13
 prevalence of, 5-6
Children, 5fn, 25
 mental health needs of, 5-6
 protection of rights, 26
 services for, 6-7
Chronic Disease Model of Treatment,
 103-104, 105-106

Chronic Motor or Vocal Tic Disorder, 16
Client and Therapist Variation Strategy, 91-92, 97
Client-Centered Therapy, 26, 34, 35, 37, 46, 58, 59, 70, 91
Client Reactions to Treatment, 77-78
Clinical Practice, 62, 69, 70, 123
Clinical Problems, 5-6, 8, 20-21, 24-25, 39, 64, 66, 110-111
  child development and, 7, 21-23, 24
  diversity of, 15-17, 24
  prevalence of, 5-6
  referral for, 23-24
Clinical Significance, 83
  versus statistical significance, 83-85
Cluttering, 16
Coercion, 53
Cognitive Problem-Solving Skills Training, 59-62, 84
  background and rationale, 59
  characteristics of, 59-60
  evaluation of, 61-62
  outcome evidence for, 60-61
Cognitive Processes, 57, 59-60, 61-62
  overt behavior and, 59
Community-Based Treatment, 49-52
Comparative Outcome Research, 69, 91, 92
Comparative Treatment Strategy, 91
Conceptualization of Treatment, 69-70, 87, 93, 111, 129
Conduct Disorder, 15, 18, 46-49, 104
Construct Validity, 115fn
Constructive Treatment Strategy, 89-90
Control Groups, 30-31, 40, 48, 80-81, 89
Conventional Model of Treatment Outcome Research, 88-92, 96, 104, 105
  description of, 88
  treatment strategies of the, 89-92
Coordination Disorder, 17

Depression, 22-23, 24, 100-101
Developmental Considerations see Child Development

Diagnosis of Childhood Disorders, 4-6, 12-14, 27, 31, 66, 110, 116
  identification of dysfunction, 116
  multivariate approaches, 17-18, 110
Diagnostic and Statistical Manual of Mental Disorders (DSM), 4, 13-18
DSM I, 4, 13
DSM II, 4, 14
DSM III, 4, 14
DSM III-R, 15-17, 100fn, 116
Dismantling Treatment Strategy, 89, 96
Disorders First Evident in Infancy, Childhood or Adolescence, 14, 15-17
Duration of Treatment, 48, 55, 61, 93-94

Effect Size, 33, 35-37, 83
Effectiveness of Psychotherapy, 3-5, 29-41
Elective Mutism, 16
Evaluating Psychotherapy, 1-5
  issues and obstacles, 122-127
Expressive Language Disorder, 16
Expressive Writing Disorder, 17
External Validity, 115fn
Externalizing Behavior, 35fn, 46, 52, 61
Extratreatment Influences, 24-25, 55, 65-66

Family Therapy, 7, 25-26, 39-40, 54, 56-59, 62, 70, 91
  functional family therapy, 56-59, 62, 91
  reviews of, 39-40
Follow-up, 38, 78-80, 82, 87, 121
  problems with timing of, 38, 78-80, 121
Functional Encopresis, 16
Functional Enuresis, 16
Functional Family Therapy, 56-59, 62, 91
  background and rationale, 56-57
  characteristics of, 57-58
  evaluation of, 58-59
  outcome evidence for, 58

Gender Identity Disorder of Childhood, 16

Group for the Advancement of Psychiatry, 14
Group Therapy, 7, 36, 46-47

High-Strength Intervention Model, 92-96, 105
  description of, 92-93
  illustration of, 94-96
  therapeutic effort, 93-94
Hyperactivity *see* Attention Deficit-Hyperactivity Disorder

Identification of Clinical Dysfunction, 64-65
  referral of children, 23-24
  research issues in, 64-65
Insight-oriented Therapy, 62
Internal Validity, 89, 115fn
International Classification of Diseases, 13fn
Internalizing Behavior, 35fn, 46-49
Interpersonal Cognitive Problem-Solving Skills, 59-61
  see also Cognitive Problem-solving Skills Training
Intrapsychic Process, 48

Juvenile Delinquents, 57-58, 66, 97-98, 102

Maturation, 19-23
  behavioral problems and, 7, 19-23
  treatment evaluation and, 21
Medical Models, 103
Medication, 2, 7, 26, 100-101, 125
Mental Retardation, 15
Meta-Analysis, 29-30, 32-38, 45, 52, 62, 83, 121
  child psychotherapy effects, 34-37
  conclusions from, 33-34, 35, 37
  defined, 33
  effect size, 33, 35-37, 83
  limitations of, 37-38
Methodology of Outcome Studies, 32, 63, 64-87, 129
  assessment issues, 75-80
  patient issues, 64-68
  questions to address, 116-122

sampling issues, 116-118
  therapist issues, 72-74, 118-119
  treatment issues, 68-72
Models of Treatment Outcome Research, 88-105
  amenability to treatment, 96-98, 105
  broad based, 98-103, 105
  chronic disease, 103-106
  conventional treatment, 88-92, 96, 104, 105
  high strength, 92-96, 105
Multivariate Approaches to Diagnosis, 17-18, 110
  consistent patterns from, 17-18
Multiaxial Assessment, 110-112
Myths and Half-Truths about Therapy, 122-127
  everyone is an individual, 125-126
  research is too difficult to conduct, 124
  therapy is an art, 124-125, 128
  therapy is too complex, 122-123

Narrative Reviews of Psychotherapy, 29-32, 45, 62
  historically significant, 30-31
  narrowly focused, 38
Nontranssexual Cross Gender Disorder, 15-16

Overactivity, 18
  see also Attention Deficit-Hyperactivity Disorder
Oppositional-Defiant Disorder, 15
Outcome, 75, 111, 121
  assessment, 75-77
  follow-up, 38, 78-80, 82, 87, 121
  selection of measures, 75
Overanxious Disorder, 15

Parametric Treatment Strategy, 90-91, 96
Paraprofessionals, 25, 74
Parent-Child Interaction, 53, 56-58, 100
Parent Management Training, 53-56, 62, 68, 74, 101
  background and rationale, 53-54

characteristics of, 54
evaluation of, 56
factors that influence outcome, 55
outcome evidence for, 54-55
Parents, 24, 65, 75, 89, 113-114
    psychopathology, 24, 55, 56, 98
    ratings by, 24
    treatment and, 25
Pica, 15
Power of the Test, 48, 80-83, 87, 121, 129
Prevalence of Behavioral Problems, 5-6
Prevention, 8
Processes of Change see Treatment Processes
Professional Issues, 122-128
    myths, half-truths, and therapy clichés, 122-126
    research versus practice, 123, 126-127, 128
    "set" toward evaluation, 127
    training, 127-128
Promising Approaches to Treatment, 45-62
Prosocial Functioning, 75-76
    assessment of, 75-77
    relation to symptoms, 76
Psychoanalytic Therapy, 26, 90-91
Psychodynamic Therapy, 123
Psychotherapy, 1, 8-9
    defined, 1-2
    goals vs. means, 2
    research, 9
    techniques, 3-4
    see also Treatment Techniques
Psychosocial Interventions, 2, 26, 29

Qualitative Reviews see Narrative Reviews of Psychotherapy
Quantitative Reviews see Meta-Analysis

Reactive Attachment Disorder of Infancy and Early Childhood, 16
Reading Disorder, 16
Receptive Language Disorder, 16
Recommendations for Research, 107, 128-129
    basic research on child dysfunction, 107-110, 129
    constructing "mini-theories", 108-109
    describing clinical dysfunction, 110
    extratreatment influences, 113-114
    replication, 114-115, 129
    stronger tests of treatment, 111-112, 129
Referral of Children for Treatment, 23-24, 39
Reinforcement Trap, 53
Relationship Therapy, 62, 84, 123
Replication, 114-115, 129
Representativeness of Treatment, 68-69, 87
Residential Treatment, 76, 101
Reviews of Treatment Research, 29
    focused reviews, 38
    meta-analysis, 29-30, 32-38, 45
    narrative reviews, 29-32, 45
Rumination Disorder of Infancy, 15

Sample Characteristics, 5-6, 34-35, 65, 83, 116-118
School Behavior Checklist, 84-86
Self-Report, 75
    discrepancies from other reports, 75, 110-111
Separation Anxiety Disorder, 15
Sex Differences, 67-68
Sleeper Effects, 78-79
Social Work, 49
Specification of Treatment, 69-70, 129
Spontaneous Remission, 30-31, 89
Statistical Conclusion Validity, 115fn
Stereotypy/Habit Disorder, 16
St. Louis Experiment, 49-52
Strength of Treatment, 93, 111, 113, 129
    dose, 93-94
    therapeutic effort, 93-94
Stuttering, 16
Symptoms, 3, 4, 75-76, 121
    prosocial behavior and, 76-77
    reduction, 75-76, 121
    substitution, 21

Systems Approach, 57

Therapeutic Effort, 93-94
Therapeutic Relationship, 1, 58
Therapist Characteristics, 36, 72-74
  and treatment evaluation, 72-73
Therapist, 72-74, 117
  experience, 50-51, 73
  evaluating the impact of, 119
  training, 47, 55, 71, 72, 83, 118-119
Timing of Follow-Up Assessment, 38,
  78-80, 121
Tourette's Disorder, 16
Training, 71, 72, 119, 127-128
  issues, 72, 127-128
Transient Tic Disorder, 16
Transsexualism, 15
Treatment, 117, 119, 123
  approaches, 129
  conceptualization of, 69-70, 93, 111,
    129
  focus of, 25-26, 48
  integrity, 51, 70-72, 83, 102
  issues in evaluating, 12-27, 30-31
  list of available treatments, 41-44
  moderating variables of, 31, 65-68,
    97-98, 113-114, 119, 129
  representativnees of, 68-69, 87
  research designs to evaluate, 124
  specification of, 69-70
  strong tests of, 92-96, 111-112, 129
  untoward side effects of, 26, 77

Treatment Integrity, 70-72, 83, 102
  breakdown of, 51, 70-71
  procedural specification and, 70-71
Treatment Manuals, 56, 61, 69, 50, 120
Treatment Package Strategy, 89
Treatment Processes, 58-59, 62, 120-121
  assessment of, 77
Treatment Techniques, 36, 38-39, 41-
    44, 46-47
  behavior therapy, 34, 35, 36-37, 46,
    47, 49-51, 123
  client-centered therapy, 26, 34, 35,
    37, 46, 58, 59, 70, 91
  cognitively based, 37, 123
  community-based, 49-52
  family therapy, 7, 25-26, 39-40, 54,
    56-59, 62, 70, 91
  group, 7, 36, 46-47
  insight-oriented therapy, 62
  number of, 3-4, 9, 29
  parent management training, 53-56
  problem-solving skills, 59-62, 84-85
  psychoanalytic therapy, 26, 90-91
  psychodynamic therapy, 34, 35, 37,
    58, 59, 70, 91, 123
  relationship therapy, 62, 84, 123
  school-based, 46-49, 90

"Ultimate Question" of Psychotherapy,
  3-5, 64, 124
Uniformity Myth, 66

About the Author

Alan E. Kazdin is Professor of Child Psychiatry and Psychology at the University of Pittsburgh School of Medicine, and Research Director of the Child Psychiatric Treatment Service of Western Psychiatric Institute and Clinic. He received his PhD from Northwestern University and taught at The Pennsylvania State University before accepting his present position at the University of Pittsburgh. He has been a Fellow at the Center for Advanced Study in the Behavioral Sciences at Stanford, President of the Association for Advancement of Behavior Therapy, and Editor of the journal *Behavior Therapy*.

Currently, he is a Fellow of the American Psychological Association, Editor of the *Journal of Consulting and Clinical Psychology*, and Editor of the Sage Book Series on Developmental Clinical Psychology and Psychiatry. His other books include: *Treatment of Antisocial Behavior in Children and Adolescents, Research Design in Clinical Psychology, Conduct Disorder in Childhood and Adolescence, Behavior Modification in Applied Settings, Single-Case Research Designs, History of Behavior Modification,* and *The Token Economy.* In addition, he co-edits (with Benjamin Lahey) the annual series *Advances in Clinical Child Psychology.*

Pergamon General Psychology Series

Editors: **Arnold P. Goldstein,** Syracuse University; **Leonard Krasner,** Stanford University & SUNY at Stony Brook

Vol. 1. WOLPE – The Practice of Behavior Therapy, Third Edition
Vol. 2. MAGOON et al. – Mental Health Counselors at Work*
Vol. 3. McDANIEL – Physical Disability and Human Behavior, Second Edition*
Vol. 4. KAPLAN et al. – The Structural Approach in Psychological Testing
Vol. 5. LaFAUCI & RICHTER – Team Teaching at the College Level*
Vol. 6. PEPINSKY et al. – People and Information*
Vol. 7. SIEGMAN & POPE – Studies in Dyadic Communication
Vol. 8. JOHNSON – Existential Man: The Challenge of Psychotherapy
Vol. 9. TAYLOR – Climate for Creativity
Vol. 10. RICKARD – Behavioral Intervention in Human Problems*
Vol. 14. GOLDSTEIN – Psychotherapeutic Attraction
Vol. 15. HALPERN – Survival: Black/White
Vol. 16. SALZINGER & FELDMAN – Studies in Verbal Behavior: An Empirical Approach
Vol. 19. LIBERMAN – A Guide to Behavioral Analysis and Therapy
Vol. 22. PEPINSKY & PATTON – The Psychological Experiment: A Practical Accomplishment*
Vol. 23. YOUNG – New Sources of Self
Vol. 24. WATSON – Child Behavior Modification: A Manual for Teachers, Nurses and Parents
Vol. 25. NEWBOLD – The Psychiatric Programming of People: Neo-Behavioral Orthomolecular Psychiatry
Vol. 26. ROSSI – Dreams and the Growth of Personality: Expanding Awareness in Psychotherapy*
Vol. 27. O'LEARY & O'LEARY – Classroom Management: The Successful Use of Behavior Modification, Second Edition
Vol. 28. FELDMAN– College and Student: Selected Readings in the Social Psychology of Higher Education
Vol. 29. ASHEM & POSER – Adaptive Learning: Behavior Modification with Children
Vol. 30. BURCK et al. – Counseling and Accountability: Methods and Critique*
Vol. 31. FREDERIKSEN et al. – Prediction of Organizational Behavior
Vol. 32. CATTELL – A New Morality from Science: Beyondism
Vol. 33. WEINER –Personality: The Human Potential

157

158   Pergamon General Psychology Series

Vol. 34.   LIEBERT, SPRAFKIN & DAVIDSON – The Early Window: Effects of Television on Children and Youth, Third Edition

Vol. 35.   COHEN et al. – Psych City: A Simulated Community

Vol. 36.   GRAZIANO – Child Without Tomorrow

Vol. 37.   MORRIS – Perspectives in Abnormal Behavior

Vol. 38.   BALLER – Bed Wetting: Origins and Treatment*

Vol. 40.   KAHN, CAMERON & GIFFEN – Methods and Evaluation in Clinical and Counseling Psychology

Vol. 41.   SEGALL – Human Behavior and Public Policy: A Political Psychology

Vol. 42.   FAIRWEATHER et al. – Creating Change in Mental Health Organizations

Vol. 43.   KATZ & ZLUTNICK – Behavior Therapy and Health Care: Principles and Applications

Vol. 44.   EVANS & CLAIBORN – Mental Health Issues and the Urban Poor

Vol. 46.   BARBER, SPANOS & CHAVES – Hypnosis, Imagination and Human Potentialities

Vol. 47.   POPE – The Mental Health Interview: Research and Application

Vol. 48.   PELTON – The Psychology of Nonviolence*

Vol. 49.   COLBY –Artificial Paranoia – A Computer Simulation of Paranoid Processes

Vol. 50.   GELFAND & HARTMAN – Child Behavior Analysis and Therapy, Second Edition

Vol. 51.   WOLPE – Theme and Variations: A Behavior Therapy Casebook

Vol. 52.   KANFER & GOLDSTEIN – Helping People Change: A Textbook of Methods, Third Edition

Vol. 53.   DANZIGER – Interpersonal Communication

Vol. 55.   GOLDSTEIN & STEIN – Prescriptive Psychotherapies

Vol. 56.   BARLOW & HERSEN – Single-Case Experimental Designs: Strategies for Studying Behavior Changes, Second Edition

Vol. 57.   MONAHAN – Community Mental Health and the Criminal Justice System

Vol. 58.   WAHLER, HOUSE & STAMBAUGH – Ecological Assessment of Child Problem Behavior: A Clinical Package for Home, School and Institutional Settings

Vol. 59.   MAGARO – The Construction of Madness: Emerging Conceptions and Interventions into the Psychotic Process

Vol. 60.   MILLER – Behavioral Treatment of Alcoholism*

Vol. 61.   FOREYT – Behavioral Treatments of Obesity

Vol. 62.   WANDERSMAN, POPPEN & RICKS – Humanism and Behaviorism: Dialogue and Growth

Vol. 63.   NIETZEL, WINETT, MACDONALD & DAVIDSON – Behavioral Approaches to Community Psychology

Vol. 64.   FISHER & GOCHROS – Handbook of Behavior Therapy With Sexual Problems. Vol. I: General Procedures. Vol. II: Approaches to Specific Problems

Vol. 65.   HERSEN & BELLACK – Behavioral Assessment: A Practical Handbook, Third Edition

Vol. 66.   LEFKOWITZ, ERON, WALDER & HUESMANN – Growing Up to Be Violent: A Longitudinal Study of the Development of Aggression

Vol. 67.   BARBER – Pitfalls in Human Research: Ten Pivotal Points

Vol. 68.   SILVERMAN – The Human Subject in the Psychological Laboratory

Vol. 69.   FAIRWEATHER & TORNATZKY – Experimental Methods for Social Policy Research*

Vol. 70.   GURMAN & RAZIN – Effective Psychotherapy: A Handbook of Research*

Vol. 71.   MOSES & BYHAM – Applying the Assessment Center Method

Vol. 72.   GOLDSTEIN – Prescriptions for Child Mental Health and Education

Vol. 73.   KEAT – Multimodal Therapy with Children

Vol. 74.   SHERMAN – Personality: Inquiry & Application

Vol. 75. GATCHEL & PRICE – Clinical Applications of Biofeedback: Appraisal and Status

Vol. 76. CATALANO – Health, Behavior and the Community: An Ecological Perspective

Vol. 77. NIETZEL – Crime and Its Modification: A Social Learning Perspective

Vol. 78. GOLDSTEIN, HOYER & MONTI – Police and the Elderly

Vol. 79. MIRON & GOLDSTEIN – Hostage

Vol. 80. GOLDSTEIN et al. – Police Crisis Intervention

Vol. 81. UPPER & CAUTELA – Covert Conditioning

Vol. 82. MORELL – Program Evaluation in Social Research

Vol. 83. TEGER – Too Much Invested to Quit

Vol. 84. MONJAN & GASSNER – Critical Issues in Competency-Based Education

Vol. 85. KRASNER – Environmental Design and Human Behavior: A Psychology of the Individual in Society

Vol. 86. TAMIR – Communication and the Aging Process: Interaction Throughout the Life Cycle

Vol. 87. WEBSTER, KONSTANTAREAS, OXMAN & MACK – Autism: New Directions in Research and Education

Vol. 89. CARTLEDGE & MILBURN – Teaching Social Skills to Children: Innovative Approaches, Second Edition

Vol. 90. SARBIN & MANCUSO – Schizophrenia – Medical Diagnosis or Moral Verdict?*

Vol. 91. RATHJEN & FOREYT – Social Competence: Interventions for Children and Adults

Vol. 92. VAN DE RIET, KORB & GORRELL – Gestalt Therapy: An Introduction

Vol. 93. MARSELLA & PEDERSEN – Cross-Cultural Counseling and Psychotherapy

Vol. 94. BRISLIN – Cross-Cultural Encounters: Face-to-Face Interaction

Vol. 95. SCHWARTZ & JOHNSON – Psychopathology of Childhood: A Clinical-Experimental Approach, Second Edition

Vol. 96. HEILBRUN – Human Sex-Role Behavior

Vol. 97. DAVIDSON, KOCH, LEWIS, WRESINSKI – Evaluation Strategies in Criminal Justice

Vol. 98. GOLDSTEIN, CARR, DAVIDSON, WEHR – In Response to Aggression: Methods of Control and Prosocial Alternatives

Vol. 99. GOLDSTEIN –Psychological Skill Training: The Structured Learning Technique

Vol. 100. WALKER – Clinical Practice of Psychology: A Guide for Mental Health Professionals

Vol. 101. ANCHIN & KIESLER – Handbook of Interpersonal Psychotherapy

Vol. 102. GELLER, WINNETT, EVERETT – Preserving the Environment: New Strategies for Behavior Change

Vol. 103. JENKINS – The Psychology of the Afro-American: A Humanistic Aproach

Vol. 104. APTER – Troubled Children/Troubled Systems

Vol. 105. BRENNER – The Effective Psychotherapist: Conclusions from Practice and Research

Vol. 106. KAROLY & KANFER – Self-Management and Behavior Change: From Theory to Practice

Vol. 107. O'BRIEN, DICKINSON, ROSOW – Industrial Behavior Modification: A Management Handbook

Vol. 108. AMABILE & STUBBS – Psychological Research in the Classroom: Issues for Educators and Researchers*

Vol. 110. DiMATTEO & DiNICOLA – Achieving Patient Compliance: The Psychology of the Medical Practitioner's Role

Vol. 111. CONOLEY & CONOLEY – School Consultation: A Guide to Practice and Training

Vol. 112. PAPAJOHN – Intensive Behavior Therapy: The Behavioral Treatment of Complex Emotional Disorders

Vol. 113.   KAROLY, STEFFEN, O'GRADY – Child Health Psychology: Concepts and Issues
Vol. 114.   MORRIS & KRATOCHWILL – Treating Children's Fears and Phobias: A Behavioral Approach
Vol. 115.   GOLDSTEIN & SEGALL – Aggression in Global Perspective
Vol. 116.   LANDIS & BRISLIN – Handbook of Intercultural Training
Vol. 117.   FARBER – Stress and Burnout in the Human Service Professions
Vol. 118.   BEUTLER – Eclectic Psychotherapy: A Systematic Approach
Vol. 119.   HARRIS – Families of the Developmentally Disabled: A Guide to Behavioral Intervention
Vol. 120.   HERSEN, KAZDIN, BELLACK – The Clinical Psychology Handbook
Vol. 121.   MATSON & MULICK – Handbook of Mental Retardation
Vol. 122.   FELNER, JASON, MORITSUGU, FARBER – Preventive Psychology: Theory, Research and Practice
Vol. 123.   CENTER FOR RESEARCH ON AGGRESSION – Prevention and Control of Aggression
Vol. 124.   MORRIS & KRATOCHWILL – The Practice of Child Therapy
Vol. 125.   VARNI – Clinical Behavioral Pediatrics: An Interdisciplinary Biobehavioral Approach
Vol. 126.   RAMIREZ – Psychology of the Americas: Mestizo Perspectives on Personality and Mental Health
Vol. 127.   LEWINSOHN & TERI – Clinical Geropsychology: New Directions in Assessment and Treatment
Vol. 128.   BARLOW, HAYES, NELSON – The Scientist Practitioner: Research and Accountability in Clinical and Educational Settings
Vol. 129.   OLLENDICK & HERSEN – Child Behavioral Assessment: Principles and Procedures
Vol. 130.   BELLACK & HERSEN – Research Methods in Clinical Psychology
Vol. 131.   GOLDSTEIN & HERSEN – Handbook of Psychological Assessment
Vol. 132.   BELLACK & HERSEN – Dictionary of Behavior Therapy Techniques
Vol. 133.   COOK – Psychological Androgyny
Vol. 134.   DREW & HARDMAN – Designing and Conducting Behavioral Research
Vol. 135.   APTER & GOLDSTEIN – Youth Violence: Programs and Prospects
Vol. 136.   HOLZMAN & TURK – Pain Management: A Handbook of Psychological Treatment Approaches
Vol. 137.   MORRIS & BLATT – Special Education: Research and Trends
Vol. 138.   JOHNSON, RASBURY, SIEGEL – Approaches to Child Treatment: Introduction to Theory, Research and Practice
Vol. 139.   RYBASH, HOYER & ROODIN – Adult Cognition and Aging: Developmental Changes in Processing, Knowing and Thinking
Vol. 140.   WIELKIEWICZ – Behavior Management in the Schools: Principles and Procedures
Vol. 141.   PLAS – Systems Psychology in the Schools
Vol. 142.   VAN HASSELT & HERSEN – Handbook of Adolescent Psychology
Vol. 143.   BRASSARD, GERMAIN & HART – Psychological Maltreatment of Children and Youth
Vol. 144.   HERSHENSON & POWER – Mental Health Counseling: Theory and Practice
Vol. 145.   GOLDSTEIN & KRASNER – Modern Applied Psychology
Vol. 146.   CARSTENSEN & EDELSTEIN – Handbook of Clinical Gerontology
Vol. 147.   HERSEN & BELLACK – Dictionary of Behavioral Assessment Techniques
Vol. 148.   VAN HASSELT, STRAIN & HERSEN – Handbook of Developmental and Physical Disabilities
Vol. 149.   BLECHMAN & BROWNELL – Handbook of Behavioral Medicine for Women

Vol. 150.   MAHER & ZINS – Psychoeducational Interventions in Schools: Methods and
            Procedures for Enhancing Student Competence
Vol. 151.   LAST & HERSEN – Handbook of Anxiety Disorders
Vol. 152.   KAZDIN – Child Psychotherapy: Developing and Identifying Effective Treatments
Vol. 153.   RUSSELL – Stress Management for Chronic Disease
Vol. 154.   HIGGINBOTHAM, WEST & FORSYTH – Psychotherapy and Behavior Change:
            Social, Cultural and Methodological Perspectives
Vol. 155.   HUGHES – Cognitive Behavior Therapy with Children in Schools

* Out of print in original format. Available in custom reprint edition.